Tony Scott

ALSO BY LARRY TAYLOR

John McTiernan: The Rise and Fall of an Action Movie Icon (McFarland, 2018)

Tony Scott
A Filmmaker on Fire

Larry Taylor

McFarland & Company, Inc., Publishers
Jefferson, North Carolina

LIBRARY OF CONGRESS CATALOGUING-IN-PUBLICATION DATA

Names: Taylor, Larry, 1981– author.
Title: Tony Scott : a filmmaker on fire / Larry Taylor.
Description: Jefferson, North Carolina : McFarland & Company, Inc., Publishers, 2019. | Includes bibliographical references and index.
Identifiers: LCCN 2018054291 | ISBN 9781476675664 (paperback : acid free paper) ∞
Subjects: LCSH: Scott, Tony, 1944–2012. | Motion picture producers and directors—Great Britain—Biography.
Classification: LCC PN1998.3.S3933 T39 2019 | DDC 791.4302/3092 [B] —dc23
LC record available at https://lccn.loc.gov/2018054291

BRITISH LIBRARY CATALOGUING DATA ARE AVAILABLE

ISBN (print) 978-1-4766-7566-4
ISBN (ebook) 978-1-4766-3549-1

© 2019 Larry Taylor. All rights reserved

No part of this book may be reproduced or transmitted in any form or by any means, electronic or mechanical, including photocopying or recording, or by any information storage and retrieval system, without permission in writing from the publisher.

Front cover: Director Tony Scott on the set of the 1996 film *The Fan* (TriStar Pictures/Photofest)

Printed in the United States of America

McFarland & Company, Inc., Publishers
 Box 611, Jefferson, North Carolina 28640
  www.mcfarlandpub.com

For Brandy, my Alabama.

Acknowledgments

Thank you to my mother, my father, my family and my friends. And a special thank you to Stephen Goldblatt, Bruce McGill, Dariusz Wolski, and Phoef Sutton for taking the time to contribute to this book on one of the more beloved filmmakers of a generation of action fans.

Table of Contents

Acknowledgments   vi

Preface   1

Introduction   3

Part I: Painting Vampires

1. The Artist   11
2. Vampires Out of Time   18

Part II: Into the Stratosphere

3. Top Guns   25
4. The Three Corners of *Top Gun* Analysis   37
5. Beverly Hills   41
6. Scott and Leary   46

Part III: Embracing the Edge

7. Sex, Violence and Revenge   51
8. Thunder Roadblock   56
9. Tony Scott and Shane Black, in Over Their Heads   62
10. A Marriage of Style and Sound   71
11. Scott, Tarantino and the Birth of the '90s Crime Aesthetic   83

Part IV: High-Tech Decade

12. Tension Under the Sea	91
13. The Simpson Tragedy	100
14. *The Fan* and Subverting Hero Worship	103
15. *Enemy of the State*	112
16. Spies and Sports Cars	118

Part V: The Denzel Years

17. Mexico City Bloodletting	127
18. Tony Scott's Signature Masterpiece	136
19. The Model and the Bounty Hunter	140
20. A Film Built Around Tragedies	148
21. Going Underground	155
22. *Unstoppable*	165

Part VI: Into the Wind

23. A Full Slate	175
24. August 2012	180
25. The Rock and Roll Alchemist	185

Filmography	191
Chapter Notes	193
Bibliography	197
Index	203

Preface

Tony Scott has always been a part of my cinematic life, and a part of the lives of an entire generation of action-movie fans. His movies were bold and bombastic, but they were never boring, no matter the warts. His life is fascinating, and his death confounding and tragic; it ripped a hole in Hollywood.

With extensive research, including news reports, biographies, interview archives, audio commentaries, documentaries, and one-on-one interviews with actors, writers, and crewmembers who worked alongside Tony Scott at different points in his career, I was able to paint a complete picture of a life lived to its fullest.

From the gray skies of northern England to the sunny shores of Southern California, I trace the tumultuous career of Tony Scott. It's about passion and love, about success and failure, about the importance of determination and focus in the face of adversity, and it's about a dark end nobody could have predicted.

Introduction

The 1970s in Hollywood were a time of great discovery, a fertile ground of creativity that helped free the industry from stifling studio productions that had grown stale in recent years. As Dennis Hopper, Peter Fonda, and a young, unknown actor with a grin a mile wide named Jack Nicholson rode across the big screen in 1969's counterculture touchstone *Easy Rider*, they effectively stoked the fire of creativity that would lay waste to the Hollywood studio system for the better part of a decade.

William Friedkin, Francis Ford Coppola, Martin Scorsese, Bob Fosse, Hal Ashby, Steven Spielberg, and a cavalcade of independent artists and filmmakers all helped change the landscape of cinema during the '70s. It was an exciting time of invention and innovation, unofficially kick started a second time with Friedkin's documentary-style police thriller *The French Connection* dominating the Academy Awards; likewise over the next few years with Coppola's two *Godfather* films, both of which won Best Picture and changed the tone and depth of the gangster genre forever. Martin Scorsese brought cinema to the criminal underbelly of New York City, to the world he knew the city to be, with *Mean Streets* and *Taxi Driver*. Steven Spielberg's *Jaws* proved to be ground zero for the summer movie season and helped usher in George Lucas and a science-fiction adventure called *Star Wars*.

And then, it all came crashing down.

Michael Cimino, upon winning Best Director and Best Picture in 1978 for his searing, epic Vietnam melodrama *The Deer Hunter*, would take his newfound creative clout and subsequently send an entire studio to the brink of bankruptcy. *Heaven's Gate*, Cimino's lugubrious western set against the backdrop of the Johnson County War in Wyoming, would give way to conflict and creative madness as Cimino drove the budget, and the cast and crew and producers, through the roof; when the dust settled, Cimino showed executives at United Artists a five-hour, twenty-five-minute melodrama, the very definition of creative excess run amok. While he was forced to cut it down,

Cimino's eventual three-hour, thirty-nine-minute version was still a mess, and did very little in the way of quelling concerns. United Artists was in the hole, Cimino had been an unbearable collaborator, and other studios noticed the trouble and steadily backed away from giving filmmakers carte blanche with their projects.

Heaven's Gate was not solely to blame for the decline in unbridled independent cinema. The world—more specifically, the United States—was changing, slowly coming out of its hangover from two decades of conflict in Vietnam. Government distrust and general cynicism, which had played a major role in so many films of the 1970s, was disappearing into the background, overwhelmed by the hedonistic America First attitude of the country's new commander in chief, a former actor named Ronald Reagan. No longer was paranoia and distrust the collective mood of the country—times were changing, getting "brighter" in America, and studios were back in charge of their budgets.

In 1981, Sir Richard Attenborough's biopic *Gandhi* would win Best Picture; *Amadeus*, one of the greatest films of the 1980s, a bold, epic production from Miloš Forman, won Best Picture in 1984. The next year, the Oscar went to Sidney Pollack's historical melodrama *Out of Africa* starring Robert Redford and Meryl Streep. Nineteen eighty-seven belonged to *The Last Emperor*, and Hollywood was humming along with prestigious pictures from the blue-blood studios.

On the other side of the coin, blockbuster films were getting bigger and bolder, and they began steering almost exclusively towards the franchise model, while genre filmmaking fractured into dozens of new avenues on the independent circuit. Spielberg's *Indiana Jones* films were a smash hit, as were Robert Zemeckis' *Back to the Future* trilogy, and the two *Star Wars* sequels in the early 1980s remain the second and third highest-grossing pictures of the decade. New technology was making the impossible possible—at least on the screen.

It turned out to be the perfect fertile ground for someone as lavish and colorful and daring as Tony Scott.

It is difficult to picture Tony Scott sitting at an easel, because it is difficult to picture Tony Scott sitting at all. Born into a working-class British family, under the ashen skies of a heavily industrial Northern England, to a soldier and dock-worker father and a mother who ran the home with a loving iron fist, Tony Scott followed in his middle brother's footsteps and gravitated towards creative disciplines, never stopping for a moment to take a breath. He wanted to be an artist, a painter, to escape the doldrums of Northern England, and he tried for years to make it happen. But the overwhelming allure of a steady income and the promise of fast cars and Southern California chateaus soon convinced Scott to alter his course.

Over the next few decades, and with a little help from his friends, Tony Scott began his journey to becoming an icon. Scott was a man who always seemed to be moving forward at a breakneck pace, in work and in life; he lived with the throttle pressed to the floor, and his thirst-fueled motor helped him create some of the more eclectic and experimental action films of an era when the genre was coming into its own. He loved the life as much as the art he was making, and he lived his life to the absolute, ultimate potential every day.

While that painting career he so desperately wanted never materialized, Tony Scott finally found his path as a director in 1983. After stumbling out of the gate, Scott forged a bond with a pair of producers and rebounded into the stratosphere. For 27 years, Scott took action filmmaking to untold heights; he unearthed darkness in his characters wherever possible, he painted his canvas blood-red with violence, and he expelled his demons through cathartic, visual therapy. While the 1980s may have been the perfect place to birth Tony Scott the director, his true passions as a creative were darker, more threatening. Occasionally, however, Scott was able to show his compassion on screen, amid all the chaos, and this unique empathy may have narratively rescued at least two of his films.

As varying as Tony Scott's oeuvre may have been from one film to the next, he still managed to stamp each frame with his distinct visual language. Scott's use of contrast, of light and shadow, of color and set design, proved to be one of his more recognizable cinematic signatures. In an era when special effects and marketing were beginning to cut into the creative pie of filmmaking and distribution in Hollywood, Tony Scott held fast to the idea that character supersedes all else. It may not have always come together for him, but directors who followed in his footsteps often tossed those invaluable aspects of character aside in order to make the spectacle the selling point.

Calling a director a "stylist" can sometimes be shorthand for saying he has no ability to handle actors or narrative, that the story and the emotion are vapid, and the film is beautiful and captivating strictly on a visual level. As a matter of fact, Tony's prolific and Oscar-winning older brother, Ridley Scott, has often been accused of valuing style—world building and set design are never better than they are in a Ridley Scott picture—over substantial characters and human storytelling. That is a shortsighted approach to a great deal of Ridley's work, but it may align with his personal history as a filmmaker more aptly than the work of his younger brother.

Tony Scott was a hedonist, but he was also a humanist, even in the face of the violence and brutality in his films. A tireless worker, Scott paid special attention to emotion every morning while he pored over storyboards, all the while burning through cigars and sucking down espressos. And much like famed painters over time, Tony Scott's work had movements, and eras, and "periods" of creative congruity in a career that spanned three decades. He went big, he went personal, he succeeded and he failed on spectacular levels, but he persisted and eventually built a body of work that is one of the more fascinating and energetic catalogues of any modern filmmaker.

Many of Scott's films did not connect when they were first released, for a number of reasons. Sometimes, the finished product could be messy and unfocused, like its creator tended to be from time to time. On other occasions, Tony Scott's films were ahead of their time, too idiosyncratic or esoteric to capture a wide enough cross section of the movie-going crowd to make them a success in the present. Regardless of his films' initial reception, or their overall quality, a piece of Tony Scott's soul was visible in every frame. He lived to entertain, to create wonderful pop art, critical praise and awards be damned.

And, over the years, as the cyclical nature of pop culture has begun to spin back around and re-evaluate nearly every bit of creative work from our collective past, some of Tony Scott's failures are finding the proper reappraisal. What may have once been seen as a cynical, violent piece of B-grade cinema has found its niche in the ever-expanding and evolving editorial spaces—pop culture websites and podcasts, specifically—where genre appreciation recalibrates legacies.

As the world of film becomes more fractured and content driven, propelled through the capitalist lens of franchise filmmaking and shared universes, many of the types of films Tony Scott made throughout his career have been squeezed out of cinemas, with only a few action filmmakers struggling to carry the torch. Much like the classical painters and famed artists Tony Scott admired, the director's own masterpieces began to shine after his passing.

Tony Scott's personal life often mirrored his filmography, a series of highs and lows and uphill battles and tumultuous relationships. Nevertheless, he had a lust for life and an unmatched determination to get what he wanted out of his films. The cigar-chomping thrill-seeker, often clad in short shorts, a tactical vest, and what became his signature pink baseball cap, approached his work with a wild-eyed zeal; he had a vision, and he pushed to get it across on the screen, sometimes even putting himself in harm's way to achieve his goals.

Scott rose before the sun, beating it to the day fully prepared with storyboards, cigars, and a fear of failure he would never shake. His drive as a filmmaker is not to say he didn't have some fun. Whether it was classic cars, Harley Davidsons, Beverly Hills mansions, or infamous friends of the counterculture movement in Southern California, Tony Scott lived life to the absolute fullest.

But Scott was never a tyrant, or a problem, at least not by any firsthand accounts. In an era of unchecked male dominance and predatory sexual aggression permeating Hollywood from the 1980s all the way to the late 2010s, Tony Scott was never accused of being abusive or hateful to his cast and crew—at least not without their creative consent. By all accounts, Scott was tough but focused, both rough and gentle, and lacking the sort of poisonous ego that would mutate into toxic working conditions. He worked hard, but at the end of the day he left the ego and the gruffness behind. In fact, Scott was driven at least partially by a fear of mediocrity, an insidious notion than he was going to fail, which certainly kept his ego in check. It kept him humble, even as he dangled from helicopters to capture a shot or scaled mountain facings in his downtime.

Once an actor or a crewmember became friends with Tony Scott, that friendship would endure even as careers began branching off in new directions. He made friends on every set, and often times he would bring many of the same people with him from set to set, a clear indication that though he was outwardly shy, Scott rarely met a stranger in his life. He was also in control of his sets (except maybe one), and he moved with fluidity and vigor that became infectious to everyone, but he commanded his sets with an overwhelming optimism and a "can do" mentality. He was beloved by just about everyone, and he is still missed to this day.

Scott recognized the importance of darkness in his characters. Even in his more bombastic, crowd-friendly tent pole features, Scott told the story of heroes wearing masks of valor to hide a bleary-eyed subconscious, action stars with skeletons in their closet, and protagonists filled with fear. Character was always first, no matter what the critics may have seen in his work.

That fear and anxiety he so carefully attributed to his characters must have haunted his personal life in ways nobody realized; it eventually got the better of him one morning in Los Angeles, in August of 2012. Scott's death was a shock to everyone inside and outside his circle of family and friends; it shook the industry, which lost not only a brilliant action filmmaker but also a beloved member of the Hollywood community.

The loss of Tony Scott also came at a strange time for Hollywood, when the mid-budgeted thrillers aimed at adult audiences were being leveraged out of the industry. Once Scott died, a niche in the culture seemed to die alongside him. There was a gap in the culture, one that is yet to be filled; without the pink-capped Scott on board, the films he would normally have directed disappeared, felled by an inability to secure funding or interest in a changing landscape. It was the tragic end of a charmed life, and the melancholy end of a cinematic era.

It was an incredible ride for Tony Scott, who shared the spotlight with his prolific, iconic director sibling, and crafted an eclectic catalogue of blockbusters, thrillers, adventures, and dizzying, frenetic action spectacles. The scope of Scott's filmography, all the way from moribund vampires to runaway locomotives, is filled with fascinating films made with blood, sweat, and tears of a family all charging to the finish line behind their leader. There will never be another Tony Scott to come through Hollywood, and the history of cinema has been made richer for his contributions.

PART I

Painting Vampires

1

The Artist

Colonel Francis Percy Scott was a faithful patriot to his beloved Great Britain as a member of the Army Corps of Royal Engineers, and he was a man dedicated to his family. When he was not serving his country in the military, Francis Scott worked the docks. His wife, Elizabeth, was a strong woman who applied herself to the task of being the best possible homemaker while her husband served. And Elizabeth would run a tight ship at home, the strong matronly balance of tough love that was necessary to control their children's rabble-rousing upbringing, given the circumstances just around the corner, where a world at war would require so many fathers to be absent on behalf of Queen and Country.

In 1935, the Colonel and Elizabeth welcomed their first son, Frank. Two years later, as Hitler's influence was growing stronger in Eastern Europe, and the second great war was beginning to reach the English shores, the couple had their second son, Ridley. It was not long after that when Francis Scott was called away to battle the encroaching Nazi forces, and this meant Elizabeth and the two boys would repeatedly relocate to different areas of England, depending on where Colonel Scott was stationed during the height of the war.

During these nomadic years the Scotts spent some time living in Ealing, a modest London suburb, where they were subject to the threat of bombing raids that ripped the city apart for several years. They survived, and England would survive. As the war pushed forth to its eventual end, Percy Scott returned home to his family, having served his time. He relocated the four of them to North Shields, outside the city of Tynemouth; shortly thereafter, on June 21, 1944, sixteen days after American troops stormed the beaches of Normandy, Anthony David Leighton Scott was born.

Like his older brother Ridley, Tony took an interest in the arts during his adolescent years. Both brothers dreamed of escaping the oppressively monochromatic, industrial world of Shields, a skyline of smokestacks and coughing chimneys. They were rough-and-tumble fish knabbers knocking around the neighborhood, never too far from one another; they shared a deep bond in art that they would never lose.[1]

Despite the allied victory in World War II, North Shields and several towns and cities across Great Britain were shuffling through the rubble left behind from air raid attacks. The dour ecosystem of Shields may have very well sparked the eccentric, vibrant careers of these two competitive brothers who were searching for something as far away as possible.

The desire for something different confused their father, and understandably so, given the fact that the oldest son, Frank, followed in Francis' footsteps and enlisted in the British merchant navy as a young man. The enlistment meant Frank would be shipped to ports all across the globe while Ridley and Tony grew up with their mother's discipline guiding the way. Elizabeth was firm, but fair and loving, a hard worker who kept the family afloat during more than a few lean financial times. Ridley and Tony's propensity for the arts may have been an unforeseen side effect of their childhood, at least to Francis and Elizabeth, but the work ethic and determination with which both brothers approached art could be traced directly to the strong

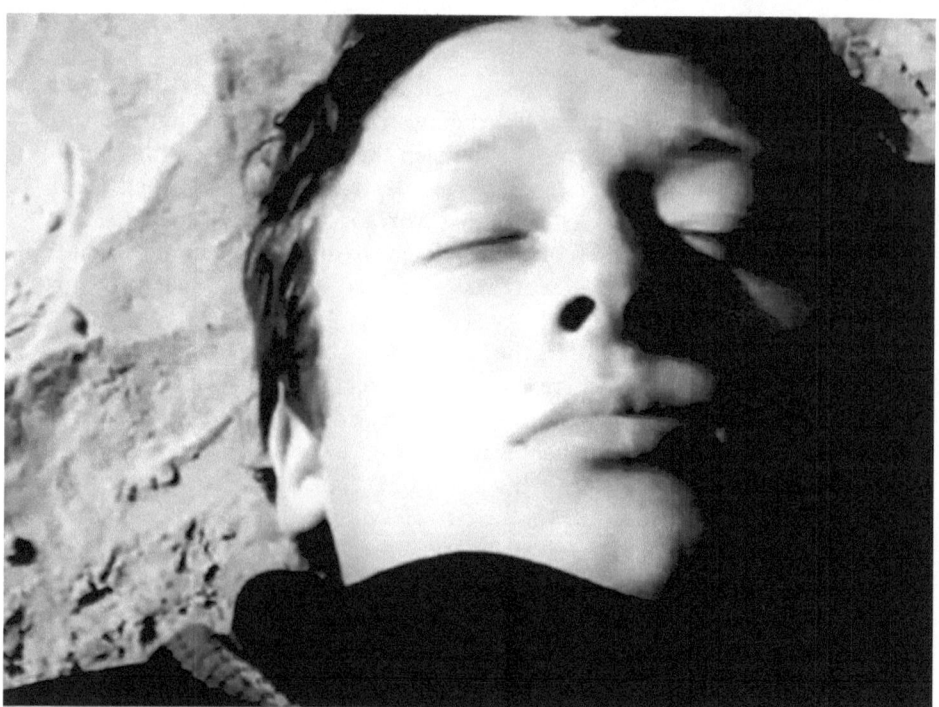

A young Tony Scott taking in the sunshine in Ridley Scott's student film *Boy and Bicycle* (1965).

foundation built by their mother and father. And despite not quite understanding the artistic leanings of their younger sons, Francis and Elizabeth supported the boys in whatever direction they would eventually choose.

Tony was perpetually competing with his older brother, trying to find his own footing in a sibling rivalry that skewed against him, which is at least part of the reason the early cinematic education of the two brothers shares so many commonalities. Both Ridley and Tony attended the Grangefield School as kids, then the Cleveland College of Art & Design in West Hartlepool, England. Neither brother was keen on formal education, barely scraping by but earning their diplomas nonetheless. After Tony graduated from the Cleveland College, their overlapping education trajectories unexpectedly split.

When he was sixteen, Tony had his first taste of filmmaking. Ridley, who had been attending the Royal College of Art in London for a few semesters, immediately took an interest in directing and cast Tony as the lead in his short film *Boy and Bicycle*. The film, shot in eight-millimeter black-and-white stock, is a quiet, contemplative story about a young boy spending the day riding his bike around northern England, smoking cigarettes and putting his own world into perspective with inner monologue. Ridley Scott is playing with the medium, testing his eye for light and shadow; he is also commenting on the steep economic class disparity in England at the time, as Tony meanders past a sweet shop, lamenting the fact that "nice people shop here."

In *Boy and Bicycle*, Ridley is already showing an attention for the environment surrounding his characters, something that would carry over into a filmmaking career chock full of tales told in fully realized, fictional worlds. Tony voices dreams, aspirations, hang-ups, and frustration as he rides around the city on his bicycle. It would serve as the beginning and the end of his acting career.

Tony was initially denied admission to London's Royal College of Art, the school from where Ridley had just graduated after submitting *Boy and Bicycle*. Ridley was working on getting a new commercial production company off the ground when Tony got the news he had been denied admission. He remained diligent, however (a trait he would carry with him into perpetuity), and continued to study art and art history nearby at the Sunderland University Art School. Like Ridley before him, and despite the fact painting was his major, Tony decided to dabble in the process of making movies to find a new avenue for his creativity.

One of the Missing is an Ambrose Bierce short story about Union soldiers during the American Civil War, and Scott put together a 26-minute film based on Bierce's prose. Since Ridley had given him a role in *Boy and Bicycle*, Tony reciprocated by hiring Ridley for a part in *One of the Missing*. Unlike Ridley's film, however, Tony's story was one of fear and death and madness, a story about a soldier so consumed by the prospect of his own death in battle that it eventually drives him mad. While there is very little sound, Scott plays with editing techniques and camera angles to create an unnerving portrait of fear in less than half an hour. *One of the Missing* was completed in 1969 and it was enough to get Scott into the Royal College on his second attempt.

He had dipped his toes into the filmmaking waters, but still, Tony graduated from the Royal College of Art in 1972 with a strict focus on becoming a painter. Painting was his first love, but like so many artists he found the monetary success of such an endeavor practically nonexistent. Making a living as a painter proved to be a near impossible task for Tony, and understandably so. A painter who is able to build a career and generate steady income from canvas work is one of the most incredibly rare individuals on the planet.

As Tony struggled to find his footing as an artist, his brother's commercial production company, Ridley Scott Associates, had begun to pick up steam. Ridley had spent the years right after his graduation working his way up the chain of television production before finally branching off and beginning his own company. RSA employed aspiring young filmmakers Alan Parker, Hugh Hudson, and Adrian Lyne in these early years, and began churning out memorable advertisements and gaining significant notoriety in the advertising industry for their fresh new approach to commercial directing. Scott and his peers utilized high contrast film stock and charged their advertisements with raw energy and mystery.

Although his fledgling painting career was steadily withering, Tony still fended off Ridley's pleas that he join RSA. For a moment, Tony flirted with the idea of documentary filmmaking with the British Broadcasting Company (BBC). But Ridley knew there was about as much potential income for Tony in publicly funded documentary filmmaking as there had been in painting. He convinced Tony to join him at RSA and start making money. Very little convincing was needed as Tony's bills were starting to pile up in the corner of his meager flat. On top of trying to find a foothold in an almost impossible career, Scott had married his girlfriend, Geraldine Boldy, in 1967.

Both Tony and Gerry had been students at Sunderland; both had loved art and painting, and both had found more potential for success in television and film. Gerry found her footing at the BBC as a production designer, which is why Tony first considered the BBC for documentaries. Whatever the direction, it was clear Tony needed to start making a little money on his own to try to carry his own weight in the marriage. Ridley's offer to join RSA directing commercials was not necessarily what Tony had in mind after immersing himself in the arts, but pragmatism took priority over artistic freedom, and Tony joined his brother.

The artistic freedom he so desired would come a few years later.

RSA turned out to be a terrific place for Ridley and Tony to begin honing their filmmaking craft. There were always things to shoot, and the prolific nature of commercial directing allowed the brothers to try one unique approach after another. In a sense, it was like painting, and Tony embraced every aspect of contrast, color, and light and shade.

Tony spent the 1970s churning out commercials, trying to break into feature directing. In 1971, he got the opportunity to direct a one-hour film for the British Film Institute called *Loving Memory*, a dark drama about elderly siblings who accidentally run over and kill a cyclist. Rather than call the authorities, they bring the boy's body to their house where they dress him in their dead brother's military garb. Tony also wrote the story, which became an early indication as to the sort of darkness that attracted him to filmmaking in the first place.

In 1976, Tony directed one episode of a television series based on the works of author Henry James. His episode was on "The Author of Belltrafio," a story about an American writer witnessing familial strife upon visiting a famous author at his home in the English countryside. The episode did not turn any heads Tony's way, but he remained persistent, directing eye-catching commercials and digging around for possible film projects. Meanwhile, his brother and some of the other commercial directors at RSA were beginning to get their own shots at feature filmmaking.

Alan Parker had found some success directing World War II films for the BBC in the early '70s, but in 1976 he was finally given a chance to direct his first movie, *Bugsy Malone*, based on a screenplay he had written himself. The breezy gangster comedy starred Jodie Foster and Scott Baio, and was a breath of fresh air at the Cannes Film Festival. The Cannes lineup in 1976 was weighed down with dour, violent pictures, like Martin Scorsese's first masterpiece, *Taxi Driver* (also starring Foster), and Roman Polanski's psychological horror film *The Tenant*. *Bugsy Malone* energized the crowd, and it set Parker ahead of his peers at RSA, much to the chagrin of the competitive Ridley Scott.

Two years later, Parker would direct the Turkish prison drama *Midnight Express*. The film starred Brad Davis, John Hurt, Randy Quaid, and was written by a young scribe shuffling around Hollywood named Oliver Stone. *Midnight Express* would nab six Academy Award nominations in 1979, including Best Picture and a Best Director nomination for Parker. It won two, including a Best Adapted Screenplay Oscar for the screenwriter, Oliver Stone. The overwhelming success of Parker's second feature announced his arrival as one of the fresh new faces of cinema; ten years later, he would get his second Best Director nomination, this time for the racially-charged historical drama *Mississippi Burning*.

Hugh Hudson, meanwhile, was building a successful documentary filmmaking career during his time at RSA. In 1981 he used that documentary style to direct *Chariots of Fire*, a story of British track stars during the 1924 Olympic Games that would go on to win four Academy Awards, including Best Picture. It cemented Hudson's place in the annals of film history, even if the rest of his career was a manic series of minor successes and forgettable failures.

In 1977, Ridley Scott released his first feature, *The Duellists*, a story about two French officers in the Napoleonic era who feud with each other for over a decade. Keith Carradine and Harvey Keitel starred, but it did not make any seismic waves in the industry—1977 was a year dominated by George Lucas and *Star Wars*. The domination was so prevalent across the industry that it played a hand in changing Ridley's filmmaking trajectory. He scrapped his planned adaptation of *Tristan and Iseult*, another period drama, and decided instead to take on a science-fiction horror film called *Alien*, written by a young new screenwriter named Dan O'Bannon. The motivation, at least early on in the process, was to try to capitalize on the new science-fiction craze in the wake of George Lucas' game-changing blockbuster.

The rest, for Ridley Scott, was history. *Alien* was a critical and commercial success, not to mention an absolute masterpiece that belongs in the highest echelon of science-fiction cinema. It took in $78.9 million at the box office, a mammoth number in 1979. Beyond that, it spawned a franchise that would follow Ridley Scott throughout his career, until he would come full circle in 2012 with his *Alien* prequel, *Prometheus*, and that film's 2017 sequel, *Alien: Covenant*. In between his *Alien* pictures, Ridley became one of the most prolific filmmakers of a new generation, dipping his toes in any number of genres, and building a robust catalogue of blockbusters and prestigious epics.

In 1980, Adrian Lyne directed his first feature, *Foxes*, a teenage coming-of-age drama starring, once again, Jodie Foster. It was enough to put him on the map. A pair of burgeoning producers named Jerry Bruckheimer and Don Simpson knew Adrian Lyne would be perfect for their new film, a drama called *Flashdance*, about a young woman working as a welder and exotic dancer, and driven by dreams of a prestigious ballet school. *Flashdance* was a massive hit, and Adrian Lyne would soon corner the market on sexually-charged yuppie thrillers and melodramas with films like *9 1/2 Weeks* and *Fatal Attraction*, the latter of which would become the second-highest-grossing film of 1987, behind the farcical New York comedy *Three Men and a Baby*.

In a span of four years, from 1976 to 1980, every young filmmaker at RSA had gotten their chance at feature directing, and each of them had found substantial success right off the bat. Everyone, that is, except Tony Scott, who was still toiling away directing commercials. He and Gerry Boldy had ended their marriage back in 1974, and he tried to stay busy while still fighting to break into filmmaking, even though nothing was falling into place. That is not to say he wasn't enjoying his time as a commercial director, a job that paid him to fly to exotic locations and direct beautiful women; he may have also had relationships with a few of the women in the years after his divorce from Boldy. Scott took advantage of his youth, but even in the face of success and jet setting and torrid affairs with beautiful women, Scott was still burning with the desire to become a feature filmmaker.[2] He was driven by the competition he had always stirred up with his equally competitive older brother, and he knew he had something bubbling up inside he was eager to throw at the world. The pictures were there in his mind, and he had a canvas, he just needed someone to supply him the paints.

In 1976, Tony read and fell in love with Anne Rice's new horror novel *Interview with the Vampire*, and tried time and time again to adapt it for the big screen. Nobody was particularly interested in that vampire tale, but there was another, similar screenplay floating around Hollywood that would find its way to him.

Before that, everything was put into perspective for Ridley and Tony, and the Scott family, in 1980. Frank Scott, the oldest son, the one who followed closely in his father's footsteps, died from skin cancer. He was 45. It was a devastating loss for the Scott family, who knew no other way than to keep moving, keep working, and keep climbing the mountain.

2

Vampires Out of Time

Richard Shepherd was only 34 years old when he produced *Breakfast at Tiffany's*, Blake Edwards' iconic 1961 film adaptation of the Truman Capote novel, the film that made Audrey Hepburn not only a star, but an icon of early pop-culture style. Prior to this, Shepherd had produced only two films, one of which was *The Fugitive Kind*, one of the earlier features from legendary filmmaker Sidney Lumet. *Breakfast at Tiffany's* would cement Shepherd's reputation in the industry; it was a hit, a critical darling, and it won two of five possible Academy Awards.

In 1970, Shepherd stepped into the role of head of production at Warner Bros., where he would run the show for six years. The Warner Bros. duties kept him away from the producer's chair for the most part; he only produced two films in the decade, *Robin and Marian* and *Alex & the Gypsy*. Shortly after producing these, both in 1976, Shepherd took the same head of production position at rival MGM Studios, and would stay in that position another six years before stepping down. It was 1982, and Shepherd suddenly had his sights set on an unlikely subject: vampires. The bloodsuckers had been out of the public consciousness for some time in the early '80s, as films like *American Werewolf in London*, *The Howling*, and *Wolfen* were pushing werewolves into the forefront. Vampires were old hat, but Shepherd thought it might be time for them to make a comeback.

Before Whitley Strieber's leering vampire drama *The Hunger* hit bookshelves, Richard Shepherd had purchased the rights and was setting up the film adaptation at MGM. He hired two young writers, Ivan Davis and Michael Thomas, to reconfigure Strieber's dense prose into a workable screenplay. Shepherd sought the employ of Alan Parker, still a hot commodity after the success of *Midnight Express* and his subsequent smash hit, 1980's *Fame*, to direct. Parker was too caught up directing Pink Floyd's film adaptation of their seminal album *The Wall*, so reluctantly passed on the opportunity. He did, however, have an idea of who might be a good fit.

Parker brought up the name of Tony Scott, who at the time was merely "Ridley Scott's younger brother," a commercial director who had been struggling to take the next step in his career. On Parker's suggestion—and a rumored influence from Ridley, who allegedly turned down the project as well—Shepherd brought Tony Scott on board to make his feature film debut. Besides, Scott had been trying to get *Interview with the Vampire* green lit for years, so he certainly had the proper mindset for this tale.[1]

The Hunger was going to be moody, detached, soaked to the brim in style and significantly leaner when it came to the plot. Scott and Shepherd worked together to try to find the right people to fill out the three central roles: two centuries-old bloodsuckers and an innocent young doctor who is seduced by the female vampire.

Miriam Blaylock was the name of the female vampire, hundreds of years old, but with a youthful exuberance. Scott and Shepherd both saw Miriam in legendary French actress Catherine Deneuve, 39 at the time, a sultry blonde who had built a career on provocative films like *Belle de Jour* and *Repulsion*. To play John, Miriam's lover who begins to waste away in the early scenes, the director and producer found what they wanted in the stony elegance of David Bowie.

For the last fifteen years, David Bowie had been crafting his image as an icon of eclectic, dreamy rock and roll. By the mid–1980s Bowie was selling out stadiums and more than once he had reshaped his image to coincide with new cutting-edge albums and tours. His acting career, however, was merely a whisper at this point. In 1976, he starred as an alien pretending to be human in Nicolas Roeg's sci-fi opus *The Man Who Fell to Earth*, which left most critics and potential audience members confused; these days, the languid sci-fi picture has found its pocket of supporters.

Bowie also starred in two obscure German pictures: *Just a Gigolo* and *Christiane F.* Neither of them received American distribution. The rock star agreed to be in *The Hunger*, perhaps sensing that this film would help him take a new path in is acting career; maybe this would be the breakthrough that would make Bowie a true double threat. His angular features and heterochromatic gaze would only appear in roughly the first twenty minutes in the film, however, as John begins rapidly aging before he is tucked away in a coffin to make way for the relationship between Miriam and the latest object of her affections, a young doctor named Sarah Roberts.

Shepherd and the production team did not have the funds to send Scott and his entire crew over to Manhattan—the film's setting—forcing Scott to use London as a stand in. The men did agree, however, that they needed a popular, young, American female to play Sarah Roberts. Her character would be central above the other two, and in order to sell in the United States, Scott and Shepherd both knew a familiar face would go a long way. Not only did

Susan Sarandon (seated) and Catherine Deneuve on the set of *The Hunger* (Warner Bros., 1983).

Susan Sarandon fit this profile, her unique eyes and open gaze was a perfect juxtaposition to the sharp European elegance of Catherine Deneuve.

After playing the lead role opposite Peter Boyle in John G. Avildsen's 1970 revenge thriller *Joe*, Susan Sarandon steadily built an incredibly prolific acting career throughout the decade, appearing on several television series and in a handful of feature films. She found cult fame status for her role as Janet Weiss in *The Rocky Horror Picture Show*, and in the spring of 1981 she enjoyed her first Academy Award nomination for her role as Sally in *Atlantic City*. Sarandon's arrow was pointing upward; the wide-eyed young redhead was ready to be a star, and Scott and Shepherd were banking on her bringing American audiences into the multiplexes. Little did Sarandon know, when she agreed to star in the film, that one particular scene in the film would stir up controversy and prove to be a headache for her and her family.

Tony Scott requested the talents of his friend from the Royal College of Art film school, Stephen Goldblatt, as director of photography, knowing they could find common ground on the sort of high-contrast imagery and set design for the film. Goldblatt had recently shot the rock musical *Breaking Glass* in 1980, and the science-fiction action film *Outland* in 1981; the combination of these two films felt like precisely what Scott wanted.

"The aesthetic was not new to what we were doing in London," Goldblatt said of the style he and Scott agreed on for *The Hunger*. "It was in there. Both of us, he as director and I as a cinematographer, were coming up in an unconventional way."

Like Scott, Goldblatt shot commercials quickly, and in rapid succession. They came from the same school of thought, and even though their style was outside the traditional Hollywood look of the time, they had no idea they were shooting outside the box. "The common thread here," he said, "is that we didn't know what we were doing in terms of the traditional way of doing stuff. Because we didn't know what we were doing, it was just much better than how people traditionally were using lighting and smoke and diffusion."

Near the beginning of the third act, Catherine Deneuve and Susan Sarandon's characters have an explicit lesbian encounter before Sarandon's Sarah is bitten and transformed into a vampire. Some factions found the encounter disagreeable and stirred up some tabloid controversy at the time. Sarandon never interpreted the scene as explicitly as some eventually would—it was a moment of transfusion, a utilitarian sequence more than anything else, albeit in an erotically charged situation. And Sarandon, Deneuve, and Scott would eventually handle the scene as such, with a focus on details and choreography, handling the sensual interaction with a wickedly antiseptic visual approach. The eroticism was unavoidable.

Tony Scott was beyond eager to direct his first feature film. His brother and all of his colleagues at RSA had already found substantial success as filmmakers, and Scott felt left behind. His eagerness did not help him feel any less intimidated when he stepped on set with the likes of a French acting legend in Catherine Deneuve, rock-and-roll icon David Bowie, and young Hollywood starlet Susan Sarandon. It wasn't long, however, before the minutiae of directing a feature film took over, and Scott found a calming groove.[2]

Scott pushed hard for a dark aesthetic on *The Hunger*, sometimes too dark for Goldblatt's comfort, but Goldblatt found a clever way to outsmart the director on set. "I would always put up two more lights than we needed," he said, "because he always had a habit of saying 'switch that off, switch something off.' So if I put something extra in, I'd just switch those off and we'd be just about right."

Scott also had a specific musical idea in mind when he began planning out the opening club scene of *The Hunger*. He had recently seen a European rock band named Bauhaus in a London nightclub, and their macabre style and gothic energy was precisely what Scott wanted. Bauhaus' music would help set the tone for the film, which would lean heavily into Scott's high-contrast commercial style.

Aside from the specific stark color palette and high contrast, Scott wanted *The Hunger* to feel like a surreal gothic opera, a move that might have eventually drowned the film in an oversaturation of style. Shepherd was not keen on the idea at first, but when he began seeing dailies of Scott's work, he eventually came around on what the rookie director was trying to show.

Working around financial constraints was the only true complication. There was not enough money in the $10 million budget to build Miriam and John's home, where a majority of the action would take place. They lucked out and found a proper home in Central London that fit what Scott had wanted as well as any existing structure could. One of the key elements of the home's design were the floor-to-ceiling windows, where Scott could attach blowing draperies to intensify the mood for which he was aiming.

Aside from maneuvering around a tight budget, the shoot proved to be surprisingly pleasant given Scott's inexperience.[3] "Tony was always very charming," Goldblatt said of the filmmaker's command of the set. "A good guy. And very attractive ... [but] a real pain in the ass," he said, laughing. "He would never make his mind up, he had to explore twelve or thirteen blind alleys before settling on the fourteenth."

The Hunger proved to be too alienating for audiences, and too hollow for many film critics when it opened on April 29, 1983. Some critics took issue with what they deemed to be blatant misogyny of the lesbian romance. Dave Kehr of *The Chicago Reader* said, "The obsessive conjunction of lesbian sex and flowing blood suggests a deep-seated misogyny, but neither this nor any other theme is registered with enough clarity to offend."[4] Roger Ebert was more flatly dismissive of Scott's film, calling it "an agonizingly bad vampire movie, circling around an exquisitely effective sex scene."[5]

Perhaps the film, which for critics had amounted to nothing more than an extended car or cologne commercial with vampires, was about six months away from a proper October release date. The substance may have resonated more for audiences thirsty for horror-related fare in the autumn, with Halloween in the air.

Nevertheless, *The Hunger* opened with just over $2.5 million, followed by $1.4 million the following weekend, followed by a quick and meek exit from multiplexes. Tony Scott's directing career was off to an inauspicious start, and the failures of the film were unsettling for him, for a while anyway. Unlike his collaborators at RSA, Tony had not found success right off the starting blocks; it would not be long, however, before his commercial career would catch the right set of eyes and change the course of his career and his life.

Part II

Into the Stratosphere

3

Top Guns

It was 1979 when Don Simpson met Jerry Bruckheimer, and they had no idea their eventual partnership would change the way movies were made forever.

Simpson was the president of production at Paramount Studios in 1979. Born in Alaska and raised by deeply religious parents, Simpson eventually broke free and made his way to Hollywood, where he would spend the better part of the 1970s climbing up various ladders. He began his career at Warner Bros. before bouncing over to Paramount Pictures, where he co-wrote the screenplay for the race-across-the-country film *Cannonball!* in 1976. Shortly thereafter, Simpson became president of production at the studio, and he had his eye on an envelope-pushing erotic thriller from *Taxi Driver* scribe Paul Schrader. It was called *American Gigolo*.

To produce the film, a murder mystery involving a male prostitute that Schrader was going to direct and a smoldering young actor named Richard Gere would star, Simpson brought in a then-unknown Jerry Bruckheimer, born and raised in Detroit, Michigan. In the early 1970s, around the time Simpson was first beginning to ascent in the Hollywood hierarchy, Bruckheimer was walking away from his steady advertising job as a commercial producer to create feature films. From 1972 to 1977, Bruckheimer had been associate producer or producer for four films—*The Culpepper Cattle Co.*, *Rafferty and the Gold Dust Twins*, *Farewell, My Lovely*, and *March or Die*—with a director named Dick Richards. After *March or Die*, Don Simpson knocked on his door and changed his life.

Though they found common ground in their working-class upbringings in Alaska and Detroit, Don Simpson and Jerry Bruckheimer could not have been more opposed personalities. Where Bruckheimer was generally calm and reserved, Don Simpson was fully invested in the hard-partying lifestyle of Hollywood and the booze and cocaine-addled cloud hanging over Southern California in the late 1970s and most of the 1980s. Simpson was a stereotypical Hollywood party animal, always the center of attention, using his storytelling chops, his ceaseless energy, and a big personality to make his moves in the industry. He indulged in cocaine, alcohol, and prostitutes regularly, and he moved through life as fast and reckless as the action movie ideas and characters that spilled out of his busy brain. Eventually, this lifestyle would catch up with Simpson, but before that he and Jerry Bruckheimer had some seismic shifts in store for Hollywood.

American Gigolo was a respectable hit in 1980, especially given the racy subject matter of male prostitution and murder; it earned nearly $23 million against a budget of $4.8 million during its theatrical run.[1] From there, Bruckheimer produced a handful of quality movies aimed at adult audiences, including Michael Mann's feature debut, the crime thriller *Thief*, and another collaboration with Paul Schrader, *Cat People*, which ultimately proved to be a forgotten flop.

Meanwhile, Don Simpson was unceremoniously fired as head of production at Paramount in 1982. His drug problem had become too noticeable for Paramount heads Barry Diller and Michael Eisner to look the other way. But Simpson had too much charm, too many great ideas, and far too much talent for them to simply push him out the front door and never look back. They allowed Simpson to remain with Paramount as a producer, and they handed him a screenplay written by Thomas Hedley, Jr., and Joe Eszterhas called *Flashdance*.[2]

To help him produce the film, Simpson once again called Jerry Bruckheimer to come in and help. There was no turning back once Simpson and Bruckheimer realized they had a certain undeniable chemistry, and a way of combining their opposing personalities to where the best of each person shone through.

Flashdance was a massive hit for everyone involved. It brought in nearly $95 million domestically and over $200 million worldwide, and wound up as the third highest-grossing film of 1983 behind *Return of the Jedi* and James L. Brooks' Best Picture winner *Terms of Endearment*. This was the starter pistol at the beginning of this Simpson and Bruckheimer team, and as would be the case more than once during the 1980s, each new project in line would simply dwarf the previous in box office receipts and cultural clout.

Beverly Hills Cop was originally an action movie intended for Sylvester Stallone, who was right in the middle of both the *Rocky* and *Rambo* franchise cash cows. Stallone rejected the film, however, mostly its comedic tone, and the screenplay fortuitously found its way into the hands of a young comedian named Eddie Murphy. Murphy would add his own comedic flair to the role of a fish-out-of-water cop from inner city Detroit investigating a murder in the highbrow, elitist world of Beverly Hills. And the rest is history.

Not only was *Beverly Hills Cop* a zeitgeist-capturing success, it was the number one movie of 1984, besting both *Ghostbusters* and *Indiana Jones and the Temple of Doom* with its robust $234 million haul.³ The success of the film changed everything for Eddie Murphy, and for Simpson and Bruckheimer, who were the new power couple in Hollywood producing. They could get any project they wanted off the ground; the next one would not only be off the ground, but it would ascend into the stratosphere.

In the midst of *Beverly Hills Cop* production, Jerry Bruckheimer paid a visit to the dentist's office for a cleaning. While in the waiting room, he stumbled upon an article in *California* magazine about the state's naval fighter pilot program and weapons testing school. The cover photo, showing the inside of a cockpit of a fighter jet with two accompanying planes flanking both sides in the background, struck a chord in Bruckheimer. He had a thought: this was *Star Wars* on earth.

But as Bruckheimer read further into the article, he noticed these kids in the program had colorful nicknames for each other, and the program was rich with jargon and tough talk. To Bruckheimer, the article oozed with cinematic potential; he knew he had something to work with here, so he walked into his office and tossed the copy of the magazine down on Don Simpson's desk.

The name of the article: *Top Guns*.

It took a few years, and a few hit movies, before Simpson and Bruckheimer were able to get the green light on *Top Gun*. Jeffrey Katzenberg, who ironically took over the head of production from Don Simpson when he was fired, held reservations about the project even as the screenplay was being hashed out. Simpson called Ehud Yonay, the journalist responsible for the article, and began brokering a deal. Yonay would get story credit, and Simpson and Bruckheimer hired newcomer Jim Cash and novice writer Jack Epps, Jr., to shape a screenplay around Yohan's piece.

Before the screenplay, however, Simpson and Bruckheimer knew they had some bigger fish to fry. They had to have the navy's full participation, and their input and guidance for most of the film. They needed the F-14 Tomcat fighter planes, otherwise there would be no movie. The navy was accommodating, and the producers hired U.S. naval aviator Pete "Viper" Pettigrew to serve as the picture's chief technical adviser. Pettigrew was one of dozens of naval aviators, pilots, technical consultants, and accommodations the navy lent to production.

As for the original Cash/Epps Jr. screenplay, there are certain elements that never made it to the screen. In an early draft, Maverick falls in love with a former gymnast, Kristen, who has a family-related grudge against hotshot pilots. The machinations of the action plotline are similar—Maverick squares off against other ace pilots in a series of simulated battles—but the third act involves a more detailed hostage situation involving North Korea, and Maverick being wounded though ultimately surviving a dogfight.

Simpson and Bruckheimer admired elements of the duo's work, but they wanted another writer to come in and streamline things. Simpson wanted the film to be flashy, stylish, and perpetually energetic above all else. He wanted a slick product for the masses. This was a rock and roll video with militaristic fetishism masquerading as a movie. They brought in Warren Skaaren, who did some nips and tucks and finally found his way into the working screenplay.

Skaaren, who was given associate producer credit for the film and not writing credit, removed the gymnast storyline, and figured out a way to put Maverick's romantic interest at the Top Gun academy. One of his early drafts had Maverick developing a romance with a female naval officer, but the navy stepped in and said such a relationship was forbidden, therefore could not be included as a plot element. Instead, Skaaren made the character a doctor of astrophysics, an intimidating, intelligent woman with the ear of the Pentagon who is on the base to evaluate the program and the pilots. This allowed the movie to seamlessly transition from the aircraft carrier rescue set piece in the opening scene, to the action at the academy and the romantic idolization of the United States Navy, its toys, and its boys' club.

The character of Goose, Maverick's partner and best friend, is a casualty in both versions of the screenplay, but the Iceman character is not fleshed out nearly as much in the Cash/Epps Jr. draft. Skaaren built up Iceman as an adversarial equal for Maverick, a fighter pilot perhaps even more confident and deserving than our hero; it would prove to be a shrewd move. Beyond that, the dialogue was punched up, the mythos of the institutions glamorized, and Simpson and Bruckheimer knew they had something potentially game-changing once Skaaren submitted his fixes.[4]

While Skaaren and Simpson and Bruckheimer pored over re-writes, the producing team kept sending updated pages to a young actor named Tom Cruise. He was one of the fresh young faces of 1980s Hollywood, a charmer with a crooked grin and just enough mystery to give the Maverick character the perfect balance of confidence and insecurity.

Tom Cruise stopped the pop culture clock for a moment when he slid across the floor in his briefs in 1983's *Risky Business* to the sound of Bob Seger's "Old Time Rock and Roll." He followed up with *All the Right Moves*, a mediocre teenage story where Cruise plays a star football player. Ironically enough, when *Top Gun* was in its earliest days of pre-production, Cruise was in the middle of working on Ridley Scott's fantasy drama *Legend*. Jim Cash had Cruise in mind for Maverick from the beginning; Bruckheimer knew he was right for the role of Maverick as well, but Cruise consistently rejected their offers. Desperate for something to push negotiations over the top, Jerry Bruckheimer called in military support.

Bruckheimer phoned navy admiral Peter Garrow and asked for a favor:

take Tom Cruise for a ride in a fighter jet. Admiral Garrow obliged, and Cruise got the chance to go up in a Blue Angels jet, still donning his ponytail from *Legend*. Despite the vomit and the dizziness, Cruise was sold on the project and called Bruckheimer immediately to let him know he was ready to begin production.

With Tom Cruise signed on to play the hero, Maverick, it was up to Simpson and Bruckheimer to find the right director. They needed someone who leaned heavily on style and flair, someone with a hard-charged energy. Bruckheimer knew whom to call, thanks to a memory he had from a rafting trip down the Grand Canyon.

Tony Scott was dispirited after *The Hunger*'s lukewarm reception. He couldn't secure funding for any new projects, but continued to create commercials. Roughly a year after *The Hunger* unceremoniously bowed out of theaters, Jeffrey Katzenberg set up a twelve-man rafting trip down the Colorado River, through the Grand Canyon. Along for the ride were Bruckheimer, Simpson, and Katzenberg invited Tony Scott—an avid outdoorsman—to tag along.

One night at the campsite, Scott used some of the down time to scale a thirty-foot rock wall without ropes, gloves, or the use of safety equipment. Tony Scott was a thrill seeker, and Bruckheimer was familiar with his hyper-

(From left) Don Simpson, Jerry Bruckheimer, and Tony Scott survey the scene on the set of *Top Gun* (Paramount Pictures, 1986).

stylized commercials, having remained close to the commercial industry even as he transitioned to film production. One of Scott's commercials, which felt especially relevant for the picture, was a Saab advertisement where Scott filmed one of the automobiles racing a fighter jet down a runway before the jet eventually takes off into the air and out of frame.

The memory of the river trip, and the flash of action in the commercial, both stuck with Bruckheimer, who pushed Tony Scott into the role despite the studio's desire to bring in a proven commodity. Bruckheimer eventually got things his way, and Tony Scott was hired.[5]

Jeffrey Katzenberg still was not sold on the film as constituted, however. He couldn't see what Simpson and Bruckheimer had in store for the project, and the recent failure of a pilot episode of an Air Force-set television show had Katzenberg, Eisner, and production heads at studios across the industry convinced that audiences did not care about aviation or pilots. It took Don Simpson getting on his knees, begging Michael Eisner to give them just one more chance to get it right. Eisner agreed, and the producers were granted a stay of execution.

Not long after this stay was granted, however, Jeffrey Katzenberg and Michael Eisner left Paramount for Disney. The corporate shakeup threw projects at Paramount into limbo, and one of those "homeless" projects was *Top Gun*.

Enter Ned Tanen, formerly the president of Universal Studios during the late '70s and early '80s—one of the studio's more robust eras. Tanen agreed to step in and fill the at least half of the void left by Katzenberg and Eisner, serving as president and CEO, but he needed a president of production. Dawn Steel, a marketing executive who advocated and helped push both *Flashdance* and *Footloose* across the finish line as blockbuster successes, was named president of production. The new heads of Paramount Pictures were ready to get some projects up and running, and it didn't take long for them to sit down with their biggest and most exciting new producing team.

Simpson and Bruckheimer showed Tanen and Steel everything they had in place; they read the latest version of the screenplay, they knew Cruise and Scott were on board, and all they needed to know was the budget. Bruckheimer guessed around $14 million, and he got the green light. Just like that, after the begging and pleading, the powerhouse producers were ready to take their next step toward Hollywood domination.

* * *

Tony Scott went through a series of false starts when he first agreed to direct *Top Gun*. His personal vision of the film—an '80s version of *Apocalypse Now*, Scott's own attempt at a dark military drama—did not gel with what Simpson and Bruckheimer had in mind for him; that sort of foreboding, violent story was not really in the script either. For days, Scott struggled to see what the producers saw in the project. Eventually, it clicked. Scott knew what they wanted: rock stars in a rock and roll movie in the sky. The epiphany allowed Scott to see the forest through the trees, and it helped him cast the rest of the film.

Scott and the producers initially offered the role of Charlie, Maverick's love interest, to Ally Sheedy, who had gained notoriety the last few years for roles in *War Games*, *The Breakfast Club*, and *St. Elmo's Fire*, the last two grouping her in with the hot new "Brat Pack" of Hollywood. Sheedy scoffed at the part, convinced audiences would not be interested in seeing Tom Cruise sitting in a stationary cockpit pretending to fly fighter jets.

Back at square one, Scott suggested a young actress named Kelly McGillis, whom he and Bruckheimer and Simpson had all seen in the 1985 Peter Weir thriller *Witness*, where she played Rachel, an Amish love interest to Harrison Ford's detective John Book. McGillis was a star on the rise, and in her Scott saw a maturity and collegiate nature that would perfectly juxtapose the boy's club of the Top Gun flight school. McGillis agreed to the role, and casting moved on to Maverick's adversary at the school, Iceman.

Val Kilmer wanted nothing to do with Iceman, or with *Top Gun* in any way, when Simpson, Bruckheimer, and Scott came calling. The only problem was, Kilmer had signed a three-picture deal with Paramount, and by 1985 he had fulfilled two thirds of that commitment with *Top Secret!* and *Real Genius*, two comedies; he basically had to do the film to honor his deal with the studio. Kilmer continually turned down meetings with Scott and the producers before eventually, reluctantly, giving in. After leaving that meeting, Scott cornered him in front of the elevator and assured him the film was going to be a blast to shoot. Scott's energy helped soften Kilmer's stance. From there he approached the film with an open mind, and he and Tony Scott would forge a friendship that would last more than two decades.[6]

The rest of the cast was populated with rising new stars, and reliably brilliant character actors. A young actor named Anthony Edwards was cast to play Goose. Outside of a handful of television roles, Edwards only appeared in a small part in the film *Fast Times at Ridgemont High*, and as Gilbert, one of the leads in the college comedy *Revenge of the Nerds*. But Edwards clearly had an affable quality and a casual charm that worked perfectly for the role. To play Goose's wife, Carole, in a small but crucial performance as far as the emotional impact of her husband's death would be concerned, Scott and his casting director, Margery Simkin, selected a rising young blonde actress named Meg Ryan. At the time, Ryan was primarily a TV actress, with only two film credits: *Rich and Famous*, and *Amityville 3-D*. But, like Edwards and Cruise and even Kilmer, Scott and Simkin knew the effervescent young beauty would be memorable in the pivotal role.

Not only did Cruise, Edwards, Kilmer, and the rest of the piloting members of the cast have to sell the dramatics of the action, they had to undergo intensive naval training. For four days, the actors were put through a survival course that included parachuting into a swimming pool, unbuckling from a cockpit that was submerged in water, practicing ejections, and spending time in an oxygen deprivation chamber to become familiar with the sort of elevation navy pilots dealt with on a regular basis.

On June 26, 1985, principal photography began on *Top Gun*. And then, Tony Scott was fired.

It was the first of a few speed bumps for Scott, and it would not be the last firing. He had filmed the opening credits sequence, a montage of aircraft carrier takeoffs, landings, and crewmen doing their jobs, all in slow motion with graduated filters and a dark, foreboding visual language similar to *The Hunger*. The dailies spooked Paramount, who suspended Scott for 24 hours, forbidding him to shoot anything else until everyone could all agree to put aside the slow motion and the ominous, smoke-filled action shots in favor of a more straightforward approach. Scott agreed, more eager to work than sacrifice this golden opportunity to hang on to his vision; still, he found a way to put some of these shots in the opening credit sequence.

The work in question was some of the more complicated, intricate bits of choreography, technological acuity, and collaboration between Paramount, the cast and crew, and the U.S. Navy.

The involvement of the navy proved to be invaluable to the film's authenticity. Often times, the real pilots would bring a sense of competition to the set, pushing the actors to do their best work. The navy was also more than willing to bring in technical advisors, like the aforementioned Pete Pettigrew, to ensure the film was as accurate as it could possibly be.

Not everything was smooth sailing, however. The navy was around to help, but they were not going to alter the course of their operable aircraft carriers in the Pacific Ocean so Scott could capture the proper amount of daylight to shoot his scenes; they still had a schedule to keep. But Scott already had a penchant for fighting back, no matter what the cost. In this instance, the cost was quite literal, as Scott had to write a personal check for $25,000 to the navy to have the captain of the aircraft carrier temporarily readjust its coordinates for one glancing look at the sunset.

The second time Scott was fired was because of Kelly McGillis; more accurately, it was McGillis' character, Charlie. Both the producers and the navy were concerned the character was being too overtly sexualized. Not that her attractiveness was an issue, but the "cheap" way she was being shot rubbed people the wrong way. Scott pushed back, and was again suspended until he and Simpson and Bruckheimer found compromise.[7]

Not only was the navy concerned with the Charlie character, as the dailies continued to come in the technical advisors were convinced *Top Gun* was becoming a romance and abandoning the flight school portion of the story. They suspected the saccharine direction of Maverick and Charlie's affair would become the main focus of the film, and the drama of the aerial footage would be tossed aside.

Then there was the budget, another concern for Paramount, but there was a more dangerous worry percolating behind the scenes. Don Simpson, who had quickly gained a reputation in Hollywood as a man of excess in his personal life, was in the throes of a severe cocaine addiction during the shoot. Simpson would have wild mood swings on the set and sometimes barge into rooms demanding rewrites, his mind racing with ideas; it intensified to the point the producer checked in to a rehabilitation facility halfway through filming. When he checked himself back out, however, very little had changed, and he continued to plague the set. In 1985, Simpson's unwieldy behavior was tolerated; just over a decade later, it would play a major role in the destruction of his career and, ultimately, his life.

Eventually, Scott and his crew did get to the aerial footage, which proved to be a mountainous task of logistics, camerawork, and special effects. For coverage (the static wide shots of jets maneuvering through the air) the effects crew shot the planes from the outside of a leer jet as they dipped and turned. Scott also realized these maneuvers against nothing more than a blue sky would not give the viewer any sense of forward momentum or motion. The

Tony Scott directs Tom Cruise on the set of *Top Gun* (Paramount Pictures, 1986).

look would be too static to be engaging. To combat this, Scott had his team of trained pilots fly at a lower elevation in order to capture the hills and mountains on screen; it would give the jets, visually, the proper look, even though it was a more dangerous bit of piloting than the naval officers normally practiced.

Cameras were eventually mounted on the exterior of the jets, which gave the aerial scenes an immersive feel. Once the cameras were tested and ready, the pilots and the production would meet and set up a rigid, coordinate set of maneuvers for each day's shoot. Freelancing would be impossible to film. In these meetings, with strategies ironed out on a dry-erase board, Scott and his crew would push and pull with the pilots, arguing on and off and eventually finding common ground about what could and could not be executed in the jets. They were intense meetings, often contentious, but in the end Scott would find a way to get what he needed from the pilots.

For the interior scenes of dialogue inside the cockpit, the actors all went up in fighter jets, strapped into the rear-facing co-pilot seat, with professional naval pilots doing the flying. It was a challenge to focus on dialogue for the actors as they shot across the sky breaking the sound barrier and doing barrel rolls in midair. Several of the actors, Tom Cruise included, finished their scenes and landed with a full vomit bag in hand. For additional cockpit scenes the actors performed on a sound stage, locked inside a tube for hours, surrounded by screen projections of the sky and the reflections off the windshield.

For stunt flying and in order to film the plates (the sky footage for the sound stage) the producers hired Art Scholl, an aerobatic pilot who was the go-to for any aerial footage Hollywood needed. Scholl lived and breathed flying; he dedicated his life to flight instruction, stunt work, and competing for the United States in aerobatic competitions.

On September 16, 1985, Scholl was tasked with executing an inverted flat spin, which was not particularly difficult for a pilot of his expertise, although any of these maneuvers came with degrees of danger. While in the spin, Scholl radioed back to the base that "something" had gone wrong and he had a problem. He began to descend from 35,000 feet. At 25,000 feet, he radioed in again saying he had a "real problem." The plane never recovered from the spin he had started, and it plummeted into the Pacific Ocean. It was a tragic event, an ignominious end for a celebrated aviator, and it cast a pall over the shoot. In the end, the film would end up being dedicated to Scholl.

The *Top Gun* shoot wrapped in March of 1986, but Scott, Simpson, and Bruckheimer still had some heavy lifting. They needed a score, and they needed a soundtrack with new pop/rock songs. *Top Gun* was being packaged as much more than just a movie; Simpson and Bruckheimer intended to make it a triumph of modern marketing. Composer Harold Faltermeyer created the anthem of the picture, which would become iconic almost instantly, but they still needed a collection of new songs that had potential to be chart-topping hits.

Simpson and Bruckheimer invited more than a hundred pop stars, music writers, composers, and singers to a screening of the film and asked them to submit a song for a section of the film. After receiving over a hundred tapes with songs and rifling through them, the music department was at an impasse. They tried a new technique, and brought in music producer Giorgio Moroder to write the songs ahead of time. Moroder composed "Danger Zone" and "Take My Breath Away," and the producers once again to invited musicians to a private screening. This time, the musicians could play one of these songs for their audition tape. Kenny Loggins had a different idea, however.

Loggins, who had been a singer for the Nitty Gritty Dirt Band and Loggins and Messina in the 1970s, had recently transitioned into a solo artist, and a default movie soundtrack guru to boot. Prior to *Top Gun*, Loggins had performed chart-topping hit songs for both *Caddyshack* and *Footloose*. According to the behind-the-scenes documentary, rather than try to perform one of the two songs Simpson and Bruckheimer had commissioned from Moroder and subsequently blend in with dozens upon dozens of other tapes, Loggins and his writing partner Tom Whitlock wrote a produced a rock song called "Playing with the Boys," which was intended to accompany the beach volleyball scene. Everyone loved the song, and agreed it would fit in the scene. From there, Loggins fell into "Danger Zone." They needed a musician, and Loggins needed some rock and roll music for his tour, so it worked out perfectly for both sides.

Giorgio Moroder's love ballad "Take My Breath Away" found its way to a new wave band called Berlin, headlined by their lead singer Terri Nunn. Berlin's sultry, mournful take on Moroder's composition turned the song into one of the biggest hits of the year, and would go on to win both the Golden Globe and Academy Award for Best Original Song in 1987.

Compiling the soundtrack was all part of the plan for global dominance by Simpson and Bruckheimer. They even had Scott direct the music video for "Danger Zone," cashing in on the overwhelming popularity of MTV and the music video revolution. *Top Gun* was a film, at least at its most basic level, but beyond that it was set up to capture the culture and change the course of modern blockbuster cinema. The fact it did these things with such ease is borderline incredible.

There is no way to say *Top Gun* was a success without somehow, at the same time, underselling the impact the film had on American popular culture and, beyond that, the landscape of the United States in general. The hype machine had been working overtime in the months and weeks leading up to the film's release, and the general public was percolating in anticipation as the United States military waited on the windfall.

Top Gun opened to $8 million at the box office. Adjusted for 2018 inflation, that figure comes out to just over $20 million. It was not a remarkable start—solid but not earth shattering. What *is* impressive is the staying power. The ability for a movie to surge in ticket sales throughout its theatrical run is an art almost entirely obsolete in the current Hollywood environment of mega-budget franchise blockbusters juxtaposing minuscule independent films looking to get a foothold during awards season. Nowadays, a film is only as good as its opening-weekend number, due to the frequency of blockbusters and theaters having very little patience for word of mouth success.

In its second week, *Top Gun* jumped an unprecedented 15 percent to bring in almost $9.5 million. The increase carried on through Memorial Day weekend, and in the first week of June it saw yet another increase. Everyone involved with production, from the top down, had tapped into the culture, and crafted what was already one of the landmark new films of the decade when it bowed out of the cinemas with $176.8 million. Adjusted to 2019 dollars, that is over $437 million domestically.

Top Gun was a game changer. The biggest movie at the 1986 box office had further solidified the golden touch of Simpson and Bruckheimer; for Tony Scott, the success unlocked the magic green light ability that only the biggest, most successful filmmakers can access. The film itself is probably more fascinating to simply observe, heavy in style and thin in substance, although subtext exists below the brilliant, high-flying surface. The seductive box-office receipts were the only proof Simpson and Bruckheimer needed that they had found their filmmaker, a modish commercial auteur that fit right in with their plans for carving out a spot for their own brand of new-era blockbusters.

Sometime during the filming of *Top Gun*, Tony Scott donned a light red baseball cap, the red cap that he would wear practically into perpetuity, always sporting it on set, and often seen wearing it in the snapshots of his day-to-day life.

Scott was certainly relieved after *Top Gun* worked out for everyone. There was still the burning desire to tell the kinds of stories he wanted to tell, to flex his blood-soaked pulp muscles. That moment was just around the corner in Scott's career, but first, Simpson and Bruckheimer wanted him to take the reins of a burgeoning franchise, and shoot a sequel whose potential was as good as money in the bank.

4

The Three Corners of *Top Gun* Analysis

It took almost no time for *Top Gun* to ascend beyond a normal cinematic experience, fracturing into the ether and capturing the imagination of audiences across any number of cultural channels. The shot of Tom Cruise flashing that off-center grin and sliding the aviator sunglasses onto his face was instantly iconic; the steamy romance at the core—heightened by Tony Scott's languid style—reached female audiences. No matter what social circle people may have occupied in 1986, *Top Gun* meant something.

There are three ironclad interpretations of *Top Gun*, all of which are valid responses to Scott's film. The simplest, most straightforward way to see *Top Gun* is as Scott originally intended, a bit of rock and roll in the sky. The picture is, at its core, an action movie juiced up with pop songs, fast toys, and daredevils. It is an Alpha film, the strutting, sweaty id of Ronald Reagan's patriotic 1980s America, and it was the natural evolution of the blockbuster movie for the era.

Steven Spielberg's 1975 adventure/thriller *Jaws* is widely recognized as the first summer blockbuster. It was the first to earn $100 million at the box office, and it opened the door to creative, high-concept genre filmmaking. From the success of *Jaws*, George Lucas and *Star Wars* were born; Steven Spielberg dominated the pop culture landscape for the foreseeable future with hits like *Close Encounters of the Third Kind*, *E.T. the Extra Terrestrial*, and the *Indiana Jones* franchise.

In the mid–1980s Spielberg, who had already become the godfather of popular culture, was beginning to shift his focus to more dramatic work. His 1985 adaptation of *The Color Purple* earned ten Academy Award nominations, though it went home empty handed. There was an opening for the sort of high-octane summer fireworks spectacle Jerry Bruckheimer, Don Simpson, and Tony Scott were peddling with *Top Gun*. There was novelty and energy and a buzz emanating from the screen, and it was almost immediately the gold standard of new blockbuster filmmaking that would propel Hollywood into the next decade.

Thanks to *Top Gun*'s success, Bruckheimer and Simpson's brand of action cinema became the standard bearer, the producers becoming a brand all their own. Director Michael Bay—whose hyper-stylized triumvirate of the Martin Lawrence/Will Smith actioner *Bad Boys*, the Sean Connery/Nicolas Cage Alcatraz thriller *The Rock*, and the Bruce Willis–led adventure *Armageddon* were some of the biggest hits of the 1990s—ascended from the shadows of Maverick and Iceman, the natural progression of Bruckheimer and Simpson's addiction to adrenaline, fast machinery, and pyrotechnics. *Top Gun* is the tip of the spear when it comes to the aesthetics and kinetics of late twentieth-century blockbusters.

It is also the tip of the spear concerning Tom Cruise, and his place as an eventual blockbuster mainstay through the rest of the '80s and the entirety of the 1990s. Cruise was a young, hot star in the early '80s, but *Top Gun* was the star maker.

Part of what allows this initial, chaste interpretation of the film to exist is due, at least in part, to the second popular analysis: *Top Gun* is nothing more than a bit of jingoistic propaganda, crafted by the military and funneled through the lens of Hollywood, where it could reach the most eyes. There is some truth to this judgment on Scott's film, however cynical it may be.

From the opening weekend, in various locations across the country, naval recruiters would set up booths outside screenings of *Top Gun* in hopes that the extra dose of adrenaline and patriotism affecting the youth after exiting the theaters would boost their numbers. While the navy could not directly advertise the movie in their marketing tools, they could adjacently use the film to their advantage. The navy did not track the actual numbers, but they did notice an uptick in general interest across the board.[1]

Plus, the fact that the navy was so intricately involved with production— their reach expanding beyond mere technical advisement into affecting the narrative storytelling in order to paint the military branch in the most favorable possible light—adds validity to this reading. The romantic entanglement between the Cruise and McGillis characters was scrubbed, and the interpersonal conflict among members of the academy softened, all in an attempt to make *Top Gun* appealing to anyone who might consider a career in the Armed Forces. On one hand, the support the navy provided was invaluable to authenticity on a technical and visual level; on the other, certain messages were sanitized.

The severity of such a bleak interpretation depends on personal opinion of the obligations of films and the influence of popular culture. It may not have been Tony Scott and his producing partners' original intention to create one long ad campaign for the navy, but the process unavoidably shaped the

4. The Three Corners of *Top Gun* Analysis

Val Kilmer (left) and Tom Cruise square off in *Top Gun* (Paramount Pictures, 1986). Anthony Edwards is behind them.

story. There is no crime in this result other than opportunism, which some may consider egregious enough to dismiss *Top Gun* altogether; however, that would be ignoring some groundbreaking technical achievements on display.

The third take on *Top Gun* pushes the film's subliminal message into the forefront. Tony Scott knew—especially in the volleyball scene, set to Kenny Loggins' "Playing with the Boys" and featuring a handful of sweaty, shirtless naval officers—that *Top Gun* had potential to bring in the female audience. His intention was to channel a "female gaze" by showcasing the chiseled chests of his stars on the volleyball court and in the locker room. What he had not anticipated was the impact *Top Gun* would have on the homosexual demographic.

In the decades preceding *Top Gun*, the film has become something of a cultural touchstone for metaphorical homosexual narrative in cinema. The flesh of the men on display is obvious, but pair it with the macho posturing and tension springing from male competition—especially between Maverick and Iceman—and the film can easily head down an entirely different path. Lines of dialogue—like Maverick telling Iceman he can "watch his back any time"—suddenly become obvious allegories for latent male homosexuality.

The aforementioned volleyball scene is the clearest piece of evidence to support this interpretation of the picture. Loggins' song, "Playing with the Boys," is enough support, but look even closer and you will notice that all of the onlookers are men. True, this is a film set in a naval academy, and in that case there likely would not be any women present in that setting, but the volleyball game appears to be on a nearby public beach, making the all-male audience to the game further sell the homoerotic analysis.

Just as the first interpretation of *Top Gun* is a product of the second, so this may be partially a product of the navy's influence. Originally, Tony Scott wanted Kelly McGillis to lean into her sexuality and accentuate her physique, but the navy pushed back. They did not want such a sexually charged character to exist in their world, where distractions can be deadly. McGillis was subsequently "softened" in that regard, her short skirts replaced with a bomber jacket and a more bookish, non-threatening impression. Her female sexuality is stripped down to its most essential elements, therein creating a void for the homoeroticism to take center stage.

Legendary film critic Pauline Kael was keen to the subtext from the beginning, citing the homoeroticism in the steamy locker rooms and the sun-baked beach as clear indicators of said subtext. Writer Jack Epps, Jr., had no intention of the film becoming an iconic "gay" movie over the years, but can see where the reading comes from now.[2]

Top Gun can be all of these things, or none of them, but the fact it has been dissected to this extent is proof of its undeniable cultural impact. There are more takes on the film in the ether of film analysis, but none make as strong a case as these three. *Top Gun* was, quite literally, a launching pad for Tony Scott, who would return to this world of heavy machinery and the Bruckheimer/Simpson orbit throughout the rest of his career. In between, he would also manage to tell the kind of stories he wanted, to varying degrees of success or failure.

5

Beverly Hills

Martin Brest had few credits to his name in 1983, when Don Simpson and Jerry Bruckheimer approached him with the screenplay for *Beverly Hills Cop*. The script had endured a long road of rewrites and unfinished drafts spanning the better part of a decade. Brest had the micro-budget comedy *Hot Tomorrows* and *Going in Style*—a hit comedy starring George Burns, Art Carney, and Lee Strasberg—on his ledger, but he had just been fired from *War Games* and had an industry scarlet letter hanging around his neck.

Simpson and Bruckheimer still pursued Brest, who was gun shy after the termination. Eventually, after the flip of a coin decided his fate, Brest agreed to direct.

Beverly Hills Cop was originally written as a vehicle for Sylvester Stallone, who was peaking as a movie star with his *Rocky* and *Rambo* franchises in full swing. Stallone eventually left the project for a number of rumored reasons. Stallone's exit proved to be a stroke of luck for everyone involved. It allowed Simpson and Bruckheimer to change the tone of the film for the better, and bring in a young firecracker comedian named Eddie Murphy to play Axel Foley. Murphy had shown off his acting chops in *Trading Places* and *48 Hrs.*, and was an immediate injection of energy into the entire project.[1]

A TV series based on Axel Foley and *Beverly Hills Cop* had been given the green light before Brest's film had ever been released. Everyone involved knew *Beverly Hills Cop* was going to be a hit—perhaps not the highest-grossing movie of 1984 as it turned out to be, but a hit nonetheless.

Brest's action comedy made Eddie Murphy a superstar overnight, fully opening up Hollywood for the comedian in an instant; the last thing he wanted to do, then, was return to television, a place from whence he just came. In the mid-1980s, the divide between the prestige of filmmaking and the assumed base intellect required to be a "TV actor" was deep and wide. There was a hierarchy among film and television actors that has since disappeared in the modern "Golden Age" of television. Murphy had escaped the confines of television with *Beverly Hills Cop*, and did not want to go back to play Axel Foley in a long-running series. Simpson and Bruckheimer knew they could not move forward with a different actor playing Axel on television, so they acquiesced to their star, and the series became the tent pole summer blockbuster sequel.

Rather than inviting Martin Brest back to direct, Simpson and Bruckheimer opted to bring Tony Scott—their fresh new superstar director—on board. Their relationship had gone so swimmingly throughout most of the arduous *Top Gun* shoot (at least, not counting those suspensions he suffered from time to time. Those were primarily between Scott and the studio, not Simpson and Bruckheimer), and Scott had so succinctly captured their vision for the film, it made perfect sense to bring him in to direct another major tent pole film. They asked him to hop over to *Beverly Hills Cop II* while he was putting the finishing touches on *Top Gun*, and he willingly agreed.

With Murphy back, the trio of supporting players—Judge Reinhold, John Ashton, and Ronny Cox—was eager to return and tell the next story in the franchise. That story, as originally constructed by the Larry Ferguson and Warren Skaaren screenplay, had Axel traveling to Paris with Rosewood and Taggert (Reinhold and Ashton, respectively) after Bogomil (Cox) is caught up with some nefarious characters and shot; the trio of detectives travel to Paris to tend to an ailing Bogomil and find his assailants. The script was virtually completed and the pieces of production were falling into place when they ran into a familiar problem: Eddie Murphy.

Following the success of *Beverly Hills Cop*, Murphy was the best and brightest new star in Hollywood. But he had been taking it slow for the most part. He tried his hand at music, producing a video for his one hit single "Party All the Time," and his *Cop* follow up, the supernatural comedy/adventure hybrid *The Golden Child*, was slated for a December 1986 release.

Murphy was comfortable in Southern California. He had no interest in traveling to live in Paris for two months; he was having too much fun living the Hollywood life. Also, Murphy knew how crucial he was to not only the film's eventual success, but to its existence at all, so he used his leverage to ensure the sequel would stay in Beverly Hills. Everyone agreed to keep it Stateside, for lack of a better option. Murphy and his friend Robert Wachs, who had produced *The Golden Child* and his stand-up movie *Delirious*, worked on the story and greatly influenced its direction.

In the fall of 1986, production began on *Beverly Hills Cop II*, and Tony Scott's manic energy and confidence would soon rub off on everyone involved.

Scott had never been one to sleep in, especially in these early years of his blossoming film career. His days typically began at four in the morning with a few espressos, the first of a dozen or so cigars he would smoke throughout the day—"nervous sticks," he called them—and two hours working through storyboards for that day's shoot. Bringing his intricate storyboards with him only instilled more confidence in the actors, and it made their job that much easier. Tony Scott was proving to be a pleasant filmmaker on set, tough but fair, and an absolute machine when the cameras were rolling.

According to Judge Reinhold in *The Making of Beverly Hills Cop II*, twelve-hour days, from five in the evening to five in the morning, were not enough to keep Scott from finding time to get in a jog at 7 a.m.[2] His energy was infectious during the shoot, even while Scott was a bit intimidated by the star power of Murphy. He also felt the pressure that came with taking over material that had been so successful, and putting his own action-oriented spin on it. The action was priority one this time around, because that was what the creative hive mind of Simpson/Bruckheimer/Scott wanted.

No longer was this a small action comedy with a comedian, it was a necessary blockbuster for Paramount with a top tier box-office draw in the lead, and major expectations in place. Scott met this challenge head on and embraced the creative collaboration between him and Murphy, who brought dozens of his own ideas to every scene. Murphy was so active and creative within a scene, Scott was forced to employ two cameras for every shot so as not to miss any of Murphy's character decisions. It was one of the first productions to employ this multi-camera technique on a consistent level, but has since become commonplace.

Murphy, Reinhold, Ashton, and Cox were all back on board, but a new slate of villains needed to step in and punch up the action. For his lead villain, Tony Scott sought out Jürgen Prochnow, a German actor whom Scott had seen in Wolfgang Petersen's epic 1981 submarine thriller *Das Boot*. It was one of Scott's favorite films, and Prochnow was arguably the most compelling cast member of the ensemble. He agreed to play Maxwell Dent, the ringleader of a band of armed robbers.

To play his wife, Scott and his producing partners agreed on hiring Brigitte Nielsen to play Karla Fry, Maxwell's fiancée and deadly accomplice. The tall Danish actress had recently made a name for herself on a number of fronts. She starred alongside Arnold Schwarzenegger in one of his lesser known films, the 1986 fantasy adventure *Red Sonja*; that same year, Nielsen married Sylvester Stallone following a brief courtship after the two met on the set of *Rocky IV*. The couple would then star in the 1986 action thriller *Cobra*, a critically disparaged film that was nevertheless a hit for Stallone, and has since found a certain level of cult status.

Nielsen was a rising star, and she fit Scott's vision. He wanted an actress who would be imposing, an opposite presence from the rapid-fire delivery and slight frame of Eddie Murphy. It all made sense on paper, and visually it translated effectively to celluloid, but the casting decision would prove to be damaging for both Nielsen and Scott in the long run.

For years, films had tried and failed to shoot scenes on the property of the Playboy Mansion. Hugh Hefner's hedonistic oasis in the middle of southern California was an enticing setting for any number of hopeful film productions, but Hefner had always declined all requests. The magazine pioneer *did* enjoy the first *Beverly Hills Cop*, however, so Hefner was easily swayed this time around. He allowed Scott and his crew to shoot one of the movie's set pieces on the grounds of the mansion.

Beverly Hills Cop II opened May 20, 1987, and the middling to poor critical reception was secondary to the ticket sales. Words like "pointless" and "laughless" were used to describe *Cop II* in the newspapers. Critics may have lambasted Scott's film, but it was critic proof on its way to a $40.6 million haul over the Memorial Day weekend (it had also opened the Wednesday before Memorial Day, padding it's business even further). It was number one at the box office for three weeks, and wound up with $153.6 million, the third highest grossing film of 1987 behind *Three Men and a Baby* and *Fatal Attraction* at one and two, respectively.[3]

Critics may have been on the nose with their lukewarm reception, but none of it mattered. Eddie Murphy's star power was at its absolute peak, and Tony Scott found himself as one of the most bankable new directors in Hollywood. It came with a price this time, however.

During filming, Scott and Brigitte Neilsen had begun a reckless love affair. It wasn't a secret for long, as word got back to Sylvester Stallone and Scott's wife at the time, Glynis Sanders, whom Scott had just recently married in 1986. The tabloids descended on Scott and Nielsen, and the involvement of Sylvester Stallone—one of the biggest actors in Hollywood at the time—only intensified the feeding frenzy. The affair ended both marriages, and it never became anything more than a careless mistake between actor and director, as Scott and Nielsen went their separate ways.

Axel Foley (Eddie Murphy) meets Hugh Hefner in *Beverly Hills Cop II* (Paramount Pictures, 1987).

Scott knew he had to get back behind the camera, but was not ready to make another tent pole blockbuster for Simpson and Bruckheimer. He had done two for them, and now he had the clout to get his own blank check and do one on his own terms. Armed with the wounds of a tumultuous personal life, Scott was ready to return to his roots, to go dark. Tony Scott was looking for *Revenge*.

6

Scott and Leary

Around this time, Tony Scott became friends with a psychologist named Timothy Leary and his wife, Barbara Chase.

Leary, born in Massachusetts in 1920, tried his hand as a student at Holy Cross, West Point, and the University of Alabama, none of which gelled with his anti-authoritative personality. Eventually, he enlisted in the Army to fight in World War II, where he earned his bachelor's degree; he parlayed that into a doctorate of psychology from the University of California at Berkeley, where he taught during the 1950s before making his way over to Harvard in 1959.

In 1960, Leary tried hallucinogenic mushrooms in Mexico, and his world completely changed. He had already been pushing back against the conventional, traditional approached to psychology that was stagnating research at universities; his new trip had convinced him that the universities were doing it wrong. He began advocating for the use of the hallucinogenic drug Lysergic acid diethylamide (LSD) in therapy sessions. He began his research at Harvard as a clinical psychologist, where he would take LSD while encouraging his students to do the same. Leary's radical approach to psychology eventually got him in trouble when he gave LSD to a student outside of the graduate research program; it was simply an excuse for the university to fire Leary, who was on his way out anyway.

Shortly after being fired from Harvard, Leary discovered a new platform to promote his mind-expanding hallucinogenic drugs in the form of the rising American counterculture movement, which had sprung up across the country as a reaction to the military industrial complex and the increasing activity in Vietnam. Youth across America were discovering marijuana and free love, and Leary suspected LSD would expand these curious minds even further. But Leary was a showman, and he wanted to find a way to market it to the masses. His peer, Canadian philosopher Marshall McLuhan, a brilliant media theorist who predicted the Internet some three decades before it happened, pushed Leary to think of a snappy phrase that would catch on. One day, the phrase came to him, "Turn on, tune in, drop out," which became a mission statement in the "hippie movement."

This movement involved a nebulous, ever-expanding cross section of American youth, and it was a rich ground for drug exploration; the (often) wayward youth who made up the majority of this new wave embraced Leary's teachings, and gravitated to his eccentric personality and unflappable energy. He became, along with poet Allen Ginsberg and writer Jack Kerouac, a symbol of the mental and spiritual liberation of which people were seeking in a world at war.

In 1967, as the hippie movement waned and recklessly propelled towards the Charles Manson orchestrated Tate/La Bianca murders, which would come to represent the symbolic end of free love, Leary began to embrace his outsider persona a little too fervently. He was arrested with marijuana possession in Texas, and was persistently on law enforcement radar as an outspoken advocate for narcotics. President Richard Nixon called him "the most dangerous man in America."

Leary was in and out of jail for minor marijuana charges time and time again, but he kept busy writing. He also decided to run for governor of California before a new trumped-up marijuana charge sent him to jail for a decade.

Then, he escaped.

In an incredibly physical escape, Leary managed to scale the barbed-wire fence and, with the help of friends, fled to Algeria. He bounced around for a few months, from Algeria to Switzerland to Afghanistan. He was captured in Afghanistan and extradited back to the United States, where in 1973 he was convicted and sentenced to five years at California's Folsom Penitentiary, where he developed and wrote *Exo-Psychology*, his book breaking down his eight-circuit model of consciousness.

Three years later, California governor Jerry Brown granted Leary's release, and he moved to Benedict Canyon to finish *Exo-Psychology*. He also married his fifth wife, an aspiring filmmaker named Barbara Chase, in 1978; the two had a son, Zach.[1] But Leary's personal life had been perhaps a bigger mess than his professional endeavors; his first wife committed suicide in 1955, followed by two divorces, and the suicide of his daughter in 1990. Leary and Chase's marriage would last more than a decade before ultimately unraveling.

During the years he lived with Barbara and his children in Southern California, Leary found himself in tight with some of the more powerful people in Hollywood society, many of whom viewed the psychologist as a rebellious icon standing up to the oppressive government. He made friends with Talking Heads lead singer David Byrne, actor Johnny Depp, and he became the goddaughter to a young actress named Winona Ryder.

Leary and Barbara also became friends with their neighbor, Tony Scott. At the time, Scott lived down the street from Leary and Blum, and despite his flashy Ferrari and his cigars and his adventurous lifestyle, Leary still took to the director's infectious spirit. He could see through the tough Tony Scott exterior, a façade created to get funding for the types of movies he wanted to make, and he knew Scott was a kind man. It's why Leary asked Scott and his then-girlfriend, Tania, to be godfather to Zach, who needed guidance beyond what his father—now in his late 60s—could provide.

Scott graciously accepted the offer, and he made it a point to be a positive influence in Zach's life. Every morning, in his routine of waking up, storyboarding, mainlining espresso, and getting in a jog as the sun came up, Tony Scott would visit Zach at home and drop off his dog to play with theirs for the day. When Zach turned 16, Scott gave him the money to buy his first car, and in the following years Scott would bring him on movie sets from time to time.

The friendship between Scott and the Leary family remained strong for the rest of Timothy Leary's life, all the way through to his death in 1996—he had been diagnosed with inoperable prostate cancer the previous year. Leary had gotten so close with the director, that he made Scott the executor of his family trust. It was an unlikely bond between two men who could not have been more opposite in regards to external personalities, but two men who clearly shared something deeper, beyond their individual public perceptions.

Part III

Embracing the Edge

7

Sex, Violence and Revenge

Jim Harrison had been a novelist a mere eight years when he published *Revenge*, his violent novella, in *Esquire* magazine on May 8, 1979. Four months earlier, Harrison had published his first novella, *Legends of the Fall*, which had been a huge success for the magazine and the writer. *Revenge* carried that torch of success in the late spring, and it became an enticing commodity for several studios and a handful of directors in Hollywood.

Sydney Pollack, Jonathan Demme, and Francis Ford Coppola each showed interest in *Revenge* at different stops along the development trail. At one point, an early draft of the screenplay had been written specifically for Jack Nicholson to star; this, like the interest from the aforementioned trio of directors, fell through for one reason or another. The idea remained just that, an idea, for almost a decade.

The rights to the story belonged to Ray Stark, a legendary Hollywood producer who was currently head of a studio he started, Rastar Pictures. Though it never hit the mainstream of production company prestige alongside Paramount, Universal, and the like, Rastar did produce a handful of hits, including the *Smokey and the Bandit* franchise, the big-screen adaptation of *Annie* in 1982, and the Roy Scheider helicopter thriller *Blue Thunder* in 1983, which became somewhat of a cult classic on home video. In 1986, Stark and Rastar produced Francis Ford Coppola's time-jumping romantic drama *Peggy Sue Got Married*, which became a surprise hit with $41 million in ticket sales, over double the budget.

As successful as Stark had been throughout his career, rarely were his films as dark or threatening—or as sexually explicit—as *Revenge*. Stark's career primarily consisted of cheery family films like *Annie*, whimsical comedies like *Funny Girl* and *The Sunshine Boys*, or romance stories like *The Way We Were*. The departure from what Stark knew as a producer may have kept this project in limbo just long enough for Tony Scott to come knocking.

Scott had read the Harrison novella, and kept the material tucked away in a corner of his memory. The story was forbidding and filled with dread, steeped in lustful sex and grim violence; it was more in line with Scott's own sensibilities as a filmmaker. He was pleased with the success he'd had and goodwill he had garnered with Don Simpson and Jerry Bruckheimer after *Top Gun* and *Beverly Hills Cop II*, but Scott also knew that goodwill was the currency he needed to be able to go off on his own, and at least try his hand at making the sort of movie he wanted. That desire was what convinced Ray Stark to give Scott the green light.

The screenplay had also caught the eye of Kevin Costner while it bounced around Hollywood. The California-born Costner had spent the first half of the 1980s climbing the acting ranks. The wholesomely attractive actor, with universality to his accessible handsomeness, appeared for a flash in Ron Howard's morgue comedy *Night Shift* in 1982. A year later he appeared to get his big break in Lawrence Kasdan's drama *The Big Chill*, a story about a group of college friends who reunite when one of their friends commits suicide. Costner played the friend who killed himself, Alex, and he appeared in flashbacks. In the end, however, what turned out to be a potential breakout role never happened, as Costner's entire thread was cut from the final print.

Kasdan and Costner were friends, and the director wanted to make things right after completely removing his part in *The Big Chill*. He cast Costner in his next film, a Western called *Silverado*, where Costner would share the screen with Kevin Kline, Scott Glenn, and Danny Glover. Much like Steve McQueen stole the show from Yul Brynner in *The Magnificent Seven*, Costner was dynamic as Jake, Scott Glenn's rabble-rousing younger brother. He over-

Tony Scott directs a scene in *Revenge* (Columbia Pictures, 1990).

shadowed the great performers around him, and the moderate success of *Silverado* was the push Costner needed to accelerate his career trajectory.

By 1988, when the pieces of *Revenge* were falling into place, Kevin Costner was on a track not unlike Tony Scott—though his recent run of success was arguably more substantial at the time. Costner had just finished a four-picture run of hits: Brian De Palma's hyper-stylized gangster film *The Untouchables*, the political thriller *No Way Out*, and a pair of baseball pictures that would become instant classics in *Bull Durham* and *Field of Dreams*. He was one of the hottest actors in Hollywood, and he had the sort of star power to push a small film like *Revenge* over the edge and into full-on production.

Jim Harrison worked on the screenplay with Jeff Fiskin, and the story was then retrofitted for Costner, who also served as executive producer. He would play Cochran, the navy pilot who retires to Mexico to work with his friend, Tibey, on the grounds of his picturesque ranch. While on the ranch, Cochran falls into a dangerous affair with Tibey's wife, Miryea. To play Miryea, Tony Scott had one name and one name only in mind: Madeleine Stowe.

By 1988, Stowe had been a working actress for a decade, appearing as one-off characters in dozens of television shows. She had a starring role in the 1981 miniseries *The Gangster Chronicles*, and had just recently been getting film roles when she made a splash in John Badham's surprise action/comedy hit, 1987's *Stakeout*. Her star, too, was on the rise when she agreed to join *Revenge* as the alluring object of Kevin Costner's insatiable lust.

To play Tibey, Scott and his producing team of Costner, Hunt Lowry, Stanley Rubin, and Jim Wilson all agreed that legendary actor Anthony Quinn would fit the role perfectly. Quinn, who was 73 when filming began, had been acting since the late 1930s. He had two Academy Awards—both for supporting roles in 1953's *Viva Zapata!* and the 1956 Vincent Van Gogh drama *Lust for Life*—and had the sort of gravitas Scott needed in the role. Tibey must be personable, charismatic, but also capable of extreme violence if pushed too far; Quinn fit the profile better than anyone else Scott briefly considered.[1]

Production took place in Durango, Puerto Vallarta, Mexico City, and various desert locales across Mexico. Scott leaned into his signature style for the story, utilizing harsh back lighting, high contrast, and more than enough billowing drapes and smoke effects. The lavish aesthetics of the story helped intensify the sex and violence, a decision that stirred up friction between Scott and producer Ray Stark.

Stark was clearly out of his comfort zone from the jump, and when he began watching the dailies he was upset by the sexually explicit nature of the love scenes between Costner and Stowe. The bloodshed didn't help ease Stark's concerns either, and he and Scott began butting heads over what sort of film *Revenge* would ultimately be. Unfortunately for Scott, he did not have final cut on his films yet, so Stark's word eventually overruled his own.

A candid shot of (from left) John Leguizamo, Kevin Costner, and Miguel Ferrer on the set of *Revenge* (Columbia Pictures, 1990).

Oddly enough, however, Stark did not want to cut out the explicit scenes as much as he wanted to space them out. He felt adding extended moments of dialogue and inserting character backstory would slow the pacing of the film and allow the sex and violence to feel more earned. It may have sounded good, but Scott's vision was specific; this was supposed to be a lean, tight thriller from start to finish. The two argued about the direction of the film for a while, but the argument proved futile after some time and Scott placated Stark by extending scenes, adding dialogue, and slowing down the overall propulsion of the film.

The tinkering and the conflict behind the scenes caused the theatrical version of the film to come in at over two hours in length, heavy with laborious dialogue scenes and aimless navel gazing. Scott and editor Chris Lebenzon, who had worked with Scott on both *Top Gun* and *Beverly Hills Cop II*, tinkered with the movie to try to help the pacing. Regardles, Stark's lack of confidence in the finished product convinced him to push the film's release date all the way to February 1990—no man's land.

Revenge opened to poor reviews and general audience disinterest. Critics were especially turned off by the misogynistic violence and bleak atmosphere. Debuting in third place at the box office with just over $6 million, the film bowed out of theaters in only four weeks with a final tally of $15.6 million, $20 million shy of its budget.[2] It was a disastrous showing all the way around.

If there was a bright side it was that the film made such little impact on the culture in general, it didn't damage Scott's industry clout he had thus far accumulated after two monumental hit films.

In fact, when *Revenge* finally hit theaters, Scott had already been pulled back into the world of Don Simpson and Jerry Bruckheimer; and this time, Tom Cruise was in charge.

8

Thunder Roadblock

Nineteen eighty-six was a busy year for Tom Cruise, a year where he went from actor to icon seemingly overnight. But *Top Gun* was not the only major film for him that year; as production on *Top Gun* came to a close in March of 1986, Cruise had already begun work on *The Color of Money*, Martin Scorsese's long-gap sequel to Robert Rossen's pool-hall drama *The Hustler*.

Cruise played Vincent, a young hotshot billiards player hustling from one pool hall to the next with his girlfriend, Carmen (Mary Elizabeth Mastrantonio) and Paul Newman, who returned as "Fast" Eddie Felson.[1] *The Color of Money* was the second hit movie for Cruise in 1986, and it was also where he and the iconic Paul Newman became friends. Newman, who probably loved the sport of auto racing as much as the craft of acting, if not more, brought Cruise—himself a burgeoning adrenaline junkie after the time he was able to spend in fighter jets on the *Top Gun* set—along with him to Daytona Motor Speedway to drive a stock car around the track a few times.

Just like with *Top Gun*, Cruise's experience behind the wheel of a racecar was the only motivation he needed to reach out to his old friends, Don Simpson and Jerry Bruckheimer, and pitch a NASCAR movie that would basically be *Top Gun* at Daytona. Simpson and Bruckheimer, recognizing the possibilities in combining the kinetic action of auto racing with the million-dollar Tom Cruise smile, had virtually no hesitations about moving forward; they contacted Tony Scott, who was everyone's obvious choice to direct.

Scott was still tinkering with *Revenge*, but likely saw the writing on the wall and realized his vision for the film would be completely upended by Ray Stark's interference. Teaming up with Simpson, Bruckheimer, and Cruise once again must have been one of the easier decisions in Scott's career. Just like that, they were off and running.

In hindsight, they should have taken things a bit slower.

When production began on *Days of Thunder*, there was no screenplay. There was, however, Tom Cruise driving cars at high rates of speed; the story would arrive eventually. Simpson and Bruckheimer had faith that the movie was already a guaranteed success, but that did not keep them from bringing in a legend to pen the script.

Robert Towne, one of the renegade voices of the New Hollywood movement that defined American cinema in the 1970s with the screenplays for *Bonnie and Clyde*, *The Last Detail*, *The Parallax View*, and his Oscar-winning script for Roman Polanski's *Chinatown*, had remained prolific throughout the 1980s, and had just written and directed the 1988 thriller *Tequila Sunrise* when Simpson and Bruckheimer brought him on board for their racing picture.

Towne, Simpson, and Bruckheimer toured the NASCAR circuit to research the lives and characters surrounding the sport, and eventually the bare bones of a screenplay began to take shape. Towne began building a story, but Simpson and Bruckheimer decided to begin principal photography before Towne had finished a workable draft.

As the characters came into focus for Towne, he found inspirations for all the major players in the world of NASCAR. Cruise would mimic professional racer Tim Richmond, and his crew chief, Harry Hogge, was inspired by real-life crew chief legend Harry Hyde. To play Hogge, the producers brought in Robert Duvall, a legend in his own right who had won Best Actor six years earlier for *Tender Mercies*, and who had just recently starred in the adaptation of Larry McMurtry's Western saga *Lonesome Dove*, one of the most successful TV miniseries of all time.

To play the racing team owner, Rick Hendrick, the producers hired Randy Quaid, a hardworking actor and Oscar nominee for 1973's *The Last Detail*. Finding a way to fit in a love interest for Cruise's character, Cole Trickle, was a bit tougher.

The world of NASCAR was, much like the U.S. Navy during *Top Gun*, almost exclusively a world of macho men and macho posturing. Towne and Cruise found inspiration in Kelly McGillis' character from *Top Gun*, a strong, intelligent woman sent to evaluate the fighter pilots. This time around, the strong, intelligent female who fights to keep these male egos in check would be a neurologist, Dr. Claire Lewicki, who comes into Cruise's world after a near-fatal crash on the track.

Nicole Kidman had been working as an actress in Australian TV and film for the better part of the 1980s. Her most notable film to cross over into U.S. theaters was *Dead Calm*, Phillip Noyce's minimalist thriller set aboard a sailboat co-starring Sam Neil and Billy Zane. The only convincing Kidman needed to come aboard *Days of Thunder* was one lap around the track in a racecar. She was sold.

Days of Thunder also needed an adversarial presence to challenge the cocksure Cruise character. It was Iceman in *Top Gun*; here, it was Rowdy Burns, a seasoned vet on the track who lives to torture young Cole Trickle before the aforementioned near-fatal crash eventually unites the two men. Michael Rooker was an intense young actor from Alabama who had just recently begun to find his way into more notable films in the late '80s. He first captured attention on the independent film circuit with his disturbing turn as the title character in the 1986 micro-budget horror/thriller *Henry: Portrait of a Serial Killer*.

Rooker spent the next few years grabbing bit parts in some noteworthy films, from the baseball drama *Eight Men Out*, to Michael Mann's first attempt at *Heat*—his 1989 TV version called *L.A. Takedown*—to the Al Pacino/Ellen Barkin hit thriller *Sea of Love*. He had the perfect roguish charm and gruff handsomeness to step in as Rowdy Burns, and counterbalance Cruise's slick matinee idol sheen.

Days of Thunder was an early opportunity for Tony Scott to, once again, put together a strong supporting cast of actors who would soon become stars, something he had participated fully in on the *Top Gun* set. Scott's casting decisions would eventually become one of his strongest, most prophetic talents as a filmmaker. John C. Reilly, who was still years away from stardom brought on by his collaborations with Paul Thomas Anderson on *Boogie Nights* and *Magnolia*, played one of Cole's pit crew members; Cary Elwes, previously the hero in *The Princess Bride*, was hired to play the slithering,

Tony Scott (left) and Tom Cruise discuss a scene for *Days of Thunder* (Paramount Pictures, 1990).

antagonistic new driver, Russ Wheeler, who sends Cole into a psychological tailspin; even Don Simpson nabbed a role as a rival racer named Aldo Bennedetti.

Simpson, Bruckheimer, and Scott received complete cooperation from NASCAR, much in the same way they received comprehensive advisement from the navy during *Top Gun*. In the nuts and bolts of the production, and in the kinetic energy of the story, the two films were almost identical; where they differ is in the screenplay, which Robert Towne was writing and re-writing on a daily basis. In an interview with *Empire*, Scott recalled Towne "writing scenes at night, we would shoot in the morning," adding it was "a dangerous way to work."[2]

Towne not only aped characters and personalities from the real world of NASCAR to create his cast on the page, he used stories from the racers and pit crews and car owners to help him shape the narrative. By all accounts, Robert Duvall's Harry Hogge was almost identical to the real man, Harry Hyde, who was a pit crew chief on the circuit for more than two decades. Fred Dalton Thompson, who just recently began cornering the market on surly middle-aged authority figures in action films like *The Hunt for Red October* and *Die Hard 2*, was cast as Big John, a clear imitation of Bill France, the real chairman of the NASCAR racing circuit until 1972, when he turned over operations to his son. The scene where Thompson dresses down Cole Trickle and Rowdy Burns was the recreation of an actual meeting between Bill France and two star racers at the time, Dale Earnhardt and Geoff Bodine, whose rivalry was one of the biggest running stories of the sport during the 1980s.

The production was hectic from top to bottom, both in subject matter and frenetic planning and execution. The days would stretch late into the night, into the early morning, and the production budget began to swell past $50 million. Some of it was due to the complicated nature of the action scenes; some was Scott's obsessiveness. He and Simpson and Bruckheimer constantly pushed and pulled against one another to get the shots they needed, when they needed them, in order to stay as close to the schedule as possible.

There was also the weather issue. *Top Gun* was shot almost exclusively in San Diego, where the weather is fairly reliable, but the *Days of Thunder* production hopped from various racetracks in North Carolina, South Carolina, Florida, and Tennessee (among other places) during the winter, where the weather proved more volatile. It would be cold, rainy, gray, or sunny from day to day, causing havoc with continuity. Plus it only compressed the schedule even more, and greatly abbreviated the window for postproduction.

Principal photography eventually wrapped in early May; the film's release date was June 27, less than two months away. That left Scott and a team of editors roughly six weeks to cut a staggering 240 hours of footage down to under two hours.[3]

Scott and his team managed to get *Days of Thunder* cut down at the eleventh hour, and the film hit its release date at a lean 117-minute runtime. The publicity machine surrounding the movie had been churning for weeks, touting the return of the *Top Gun* team in a story about daredevils flying across the ground rather than through the sky. It was a tight package loaded with expectations and a certain blind confidence that the box office would make the arduous production worthwhile.

Days of Thunder opened over the extended July 4th weekend at number one, with a healthy $15.5 million in ticket sales. Reception was lukewarm at best, however, with many critics pointing out the transparency of the film as a cliché-filled marketing machine. Audience interest quickly waned. The freshness and verve of *Top Gun* was understandably diluted this time around, with crowds feeling they had seen this story before, and in a much better movie.

The box office diminished week-to-week following the holiday weekend. Days of Thunder ended its theatrical run with $82.7 million against an approximate $60 million budget. The foreign take bumped the total gross up to just a shade under $158 million. It was not a flop per se, but it felt that way for Simpson and Bruckheimer, who were certain they had another box-office

(From left) Tony Scott, Don Simpson, Robert Towne, Jerry Bruckheimer, and Tom Cruise pose for a photograph on the set of *Days of Thunder* (Paramount Pictures, 1990).

powerhouse on their hands, a movie that would be at or near the top of the highest-grossing films of 1990 (it ended the year at number thirteen).[4] When marketing and distribution totals were factored in, the box office take shrank considerably.

The failures of *Days of Thunder* fell at the feet of Simpson and Bruckheimer—at least in the eyes of Paramount Studios, who severed their relationship with the producers in the fall of 1990, the very same year the producers had signed a five-picture, $300 million-deal with the studio. Simpson and Bruckheimer would, however, land on their feet at Disney just one year later.

As for Scott, he had recently begun dating Donna Wilson, a beauty pageant queen from North Carolina, who played a minor character in *Days of Thunder* named Darlene. Their relationship proved sounder than Scott's previous marriages, or affairs; this one would stick. Scott would also find himself in the middle of exciting new voices and inspirations in Hollywood; he would reach a turning point in his directing career, one of a handful of shifts in style and substance. He had no idea these next few years would both redefine and solidify his legacy as a truly visionary action filmmaker.

9

Tony Scott and Shane Black, in Over Their Heads

In 1987, Shane Black made a name for himself in Hollywood when he wrote the screenplay for *Lethal Weapon*. The electric buddy/cop action film starring Mel Gibson and Danny Glover energized the anemic genre, and made Black a star screenwriter overnight. Black's sardonic wit and ability to balance action, humor, and examine machismo through a fresh lens, set him apart from the pack of action screenwriters at the time. He sold the *Lethal Weapon* screenplay for $250,000, and after the success of the film he became one of the most sought after action screenwriters in Hollywood. It was a given he would return to write *Lethal Weapon 2* after the first film became a smash hit.

In the months following the landmark success of *Lethal Weapon*, however, Black went through an existential crisis. He struggled with his newfound fame, and often doubted his own abilities as a screenwriter in spite of *Lethal Weapon*'s success. That doubt and fear crept into his first draft for *Lethal Weapon 2*; in fact, hero Martin Riggs (Mel Gibson) dies at the end of his version, a sacrifice for Black's personal anguish. Warner Bros. balked at his draft, urging him to lean more into the humor and save Riggs in the end. Anticipating failure, Black quit the project and decided on a simple story credit; Jeffrey Boam was brought in to finesse the story for the studio and the bulk of his work is what ultimately made it to the screen.

And then, Black went through a tough relationship breakup and didn't write for two years. He was wallowing in self-pity, reading crime novels and wasting away in his Los Angeles home. Thankfully, time began to heal the emotional wounds, and he eventually found the ability to channel his misery into his writing. From the ashes of his broken relationship, Joe Hallenbeck was born.

Hallenbeck was similar to Martin Riggs, a former real-life hero who has been broken by tragedy, barely hanging on to any semblance of a life. The story Black crafted, involving professional football, gambling, and corruption, also paired the downtrodden antihero with an African American partner; this time, it was not a comfortably middle-class family man like Roger Murtaugh, but a fellow down-on-his-luck former hero, an exiled pro quarterback named Jimmy Dix.

Black's original script for *The Last Boy Scout* was vastly different from the final product. In his first drafts, Joe Hallenbeck is booted from the Secret Service for beating up the son of Senator Calvin Baynard, after the son kills a mother and her child in a drunk driving accident. The beaten son would eventually become the puppet master behind the entire story. As for the villainous football team owner Shelly Marcone and his henchman, Milo, they had a more detailed backstory. Milo, for example, kidnapped women and made snuff films when he wasn't killing people for Marcone, a subplot that seems bizarrely out of place with the rest of the linear thriller plot.

The snuff film subplot was where Hallenbeck's wife, Sarah, came into the original story. In this first draft, Milo kidnaps Sarah to be the victim in one of his movies, only to have Joe rescue her in the end. Sarah also killed Milo in the original third act, which involved a boat chase and helicopter crash. Most of these details never saw the light of day in the end, but the bones of the story were in place, and Black knew he had a winner.[1]

A bidding war broke out over *The Last Boy Scout* screenplay in 1990. Geffen Pictures, a subsidiary of Warner Bros., offered $1.5 million, but Carolco and Tri-Star countered. Geffen and Warners eventually ratcheted their price up to $1.75 million, but Carolco countered once again with a staggering $2.5 million bid, a record for any screenplay at the time.

Despite the record-breaking offer from Carolco, Black decided to stay with Warner Bros. and Joel Silver, who he had worked with on *Lethal Weapon*. Almost immediately, Warner Bros. brought Black in and told him he needed to drastically alter his record-breaking screenplay. They hired Joel Silver to produce, and to oversee rewrites, as he and Black had been batting this story around for a few years.

By the time *The Last Boy Scout* crossed his desk, Joel Silver had already cemented himself as one of the most successful new producers in Hollywood, in an action genre that was becoming more producer driven each year. In fact, Silver's trajectory is similar to that of Jerry Bruckheimer and Don Simpson, though Silver had his breakout a few years prior.

Walter Hill's 1979 New York street gang thriller, *The Warriors*, was Silver's first feature as an executive producer. It brought him a decent level of notoriety, but his collaboration with Hill on *48 Hrs.* three years down the road would set him on an all-new trajectory. Silver also produced both *Streets of Fire* and *Brewster's Millions* with Hill; the former was not a success at the time but has since found a cult following, the latter a solid and surprising comedic turn for the duo.

From *Weird Science* to *Commando* to, in 1987, producing a pair of action classics in *Lethal Weapon* and John McTiernan's jungle action/thriller *Predator*, Joel Silver had his finger on the pulse of modern action filmmaking.

When he and Shane Black first flirted with the story of *The Last Boy Scout*, Black was working on it under another title: *Die Hard*. Silver knew that would be a perfect title for the new action film he was producing with director John McTiernan and an unknown star in TV actor Bruce Willis. He talked Black into letting him have the title; Black agreed, and changed his title to *The Last Boy Scout*. It would still not see the light of day for a few years.

In the meantime, *Die Hard* made a big star out of Bruce Willis, and it stoke the wildfire that was Joel Silver's drug-fueled ego. Fox wanted a *Die Hard* sequel, but Willis had another project higher on his priority list, a caper comedy passion project called *Hudson Hawk*. Silver agreed to fund *Hudson Hawk* if Willis did *Die Hard 2*; he agreed, and *Die Hard 2: Die Harder* became an even bigger box-office smash than the original.

Silver secured funding for *Hudson Hawk*, and during that shoot he approached Willis with the screenplay for *The Last Boy Scout*. Willis was not particularly interested in the first draft, which focused on him saving his wife. He had just come off two *Die Hard* films where he was tasked with rescuing his wife, and the motivation felt stale to him. Silver assured him the script would change accordingly. Black began his rewrites, shrinking the presence of the wife character, Sarah, and keeping her out of harm's way. He also removed the disturbing subplot involving Milo and his snuff films, therin streamlining the story considerably. Eventually, Willis was happy with the script and agreed to shoot *The Last Boy Scout* once he wrapped *Hudson Hawk*.

With Willis secured, Silver needed to find a director. Early on in the search, he offered Tony Scott a chance to direct, but Scott initially passed on it because he had already begun working on his next film, a war movie set in the Middle East. Almost as soon as he initially declined Silver's offer, funding for his war film fell through and Scott was free. He greatly admired Black's original draft of *The Last Boy Scout*, and even though the shooting script was almost unrecognizable from what Scott had read, he was eager to work with a new power producer and a new cast of rising stars. Tony Scott could manage anything, or so he thought.

Silver hired casting director Marion Dougherty, a legend in her field who had worked with the producer to put together the terrific *Lethal Weapon* ensemble. Dougherty had been working in Hollywood since the late 1950s, and was responsible for putting together casts for such classics as *Midnight*

Cowboy, *The Friends of Eddie Coyle*, and *Lenny*. When she began working with Warner Bros. in the 80s, she was responsible for giving Glenn Close her first breakthrough role in *The World According to Garp*; she assembled the aforementioned *Lethal Weapon* cast for the studio, and she cast Tim Burton's *Batman* in 1989.

First and foremost this time, Dougherty was tasked with finding the right partner for Willis' down-and-out Joe Hallenbeck. The character was Jimmy Dix, a former quarterback for the fictional L.A. Stallions who was railroaded out of the league and is struggling with an addiction to painkillers. Her search eventually brought her to Damon Wayans.

Wayans, one of six siblings, was a comedian who had just started to gain another level of notoriety when Dougherty called him in to audition for the Dix role. His first part in the movies was a brief but amusing cameo in *Beverly Hills Cop*; the following year, Wayans landed a part on the *Saturday Night Live* cast. His stint on the sketch comedy show lasted only a year, and from there he continued to land bit parts in successful films like *Hollywood Shuffle*, *Roxanne*, and *Colors*, showing a knack for making the most of his small parts. Then, in 1990, his older brother Keenan Ivory Wayans brought him on board a new, more hip, more urban-centric sketch comedy show, where his comedic talents flourished and his star power became apparent.

In Living Color made a star out of Damon and Keenan Ivory Wayans; it also put a rubber-faced Canadian actor named Jim Carrey on the map. The pilot aired in April of 1990, and it didn't take long for the show to be a hit. Damon was the star, writing and acting in all of his own skits and showing audiences the sort of magnetism he had as a performer. To Dougherty, Wayans' energy and jocularity was a perfect juxtaposition to Willis and his disheartened, sardonic former hero.

Dougherty brought in Marg Helgenberger to play Sarah, Joe Hallenbeck's adulterous wife. Helgenberger had been a working TV actress for a few years, and was beginning to move over into film, having just appeared in Steven Spielberg's *Always*. Scott liked Helgenberger in the role, but Bruce Willis, who was reveling in his new power in Hollywood, held a meeting with Silver, Scott, and Dougherty, and demanded they replace Helgenberger with Chelsea Field.

Field had a similar trajectory to Marg Helgenberger, having recently transitioned from TV series into film; she had previously appeared in a small role in *Commando*, a Joel Silver production, where she played a flight attendant. For whatever reason, Willis wanted Field in the role, and not Helgenberger. He pushed until he got his way, no doubt holding his importance to the entire project over the heads of Silver, Scott, and Dougherty; Helgenberger was out, and Chelsea Field was the new Sarah. It was the only time Dougherty had ever experienced such abuse of leverage.

(From left) Danielle Harris, Bruce Willis, and Damon Wayans try and save the day in *The Last Boy Scout* (Warner Bros., 1991).

The rest of the casting went without Willis interfering. For the brief but crucial part of Billy Cole, the running back who goes on a shooting spree in the middle of a game before turning the gun on himself, Dougherty and Scott went through dozens of professional football players before circling back around and landing on one of the first auditions: a martial artist and aspiring actor named Billy Blanks, who would go on to find fame in the late 90s with his collection of "Tae Bo" workout videos.[2]

Noble Willingham, who had been a mainstay in film and television for two decades, was cast as the greedy and murderous owner of the L.A. Stallions, Sheldon Marcone. To play Marcone's sneering and bloodthirsty henchman, Milo, Dougherty and Scott went against type and cast a stand-up comic and character actor named Taylor Negron, who had almost exclusively appeared in smaller roles in comedies like *Fast Times at Ridgemont High* and Rodney Dangerfield's *Easy Money*, where he played Dangerfield's son.

The rest of the cast was filled in around the quintet of lead roles. Child actress Danielle Harris, who had recently starred in back-to-back *Halloween* sequels, was brought in to play the Hallenbeck's foul-mouthed teenage daughter, Darian. Bruce McGill, a busy character actor most well known as "D-Day" in John Landis' frat-house comedy classic *Animal House*, was cast as

Mike, Joe's investigative partner and the one caught red-handed having an affair with Sarah.

Everything was in order when principal photography on *The Last Boy Scout* began on March 11, 1991. Scott had three months to shoot, with six months allocated for post-production, and Warner Bros. had a release date virtually set in stone: December 13. The rigid schedule and firm date added some pressure to the shoot, but it was nothing in comparison to the sort of headaches a film set of Alpha males with strong egos, their own ideas, and little time for creative collaboration, would eventually create.

Scott attacked the shoot with the same verve and vigor he had on all of his films, even while Willis and Joel Silver tried to control everything. Bruce McGill recalls his brief time on set: "I shot in warm weather," McGill said, "so [Tony] was wearing these African tracking shorts, and always with an expensive cigar. He was very physical, often without a chair, but kneeling like a guy in the bush." No matter how immersive and physical Scott's approach was, however, he could not stave off the impending battle of egos that would soon become a problem.

Production grew more and more contentious as time went on. Willis and Damon Wayans began to butt heads on the set to the point where they despised working with one another; the disdain played well into the first two acts of the film, where Hallenbeck and Dix struggle to get along. Both Joel Silver and Bruce Willis continually interjected with opinions on the direction of certain scenes; often times, the two would rewrite scenes on their own, on the fly, and demand Tony Scott shoot what they had done. That isn't to say Silver and Willis were fast friends, but quite the opposite. The two strong-willed Hollywood players perpetually bickered, so much so that this production would be the end of what looked like, at one time, to be one of the most lucrative and successful unions of actor and producer in the history of cinema.

Tension mounted in the middle of the shoot when Willis' vanity project, *Hudson Hawk*, hit theaters with a resounding thud. Critics lambasted the comedy; it opened in third place Memorial Day weekend of 1991, and promptly sank like a stone. It limped out of theaters in less than a month with an abysmal $17.2 million in ticket sales, roughly 26 percent of its absurd $65 million budget. The colossal failure of *Hudson Hawk* stung both Joel Silver and Bruce Willis, who continued to fight over the direction of scenes in *The Last Boy Scout*, both demanding their own changes and nervously in need of a hit movie. Willis felt one of the best ways to do that was to put his own directorial spin on the work of his fellow actors from time to time.

Willis and Bruce McGill had been friends dating back more than a decade, when Willis was still bartending in New York City. By the time they reunited on set of *The Last Boy Scout* set, McGill had been working in the industry for over a decade. Willis, on the other hand, had become a superstar with blockbuster hits, a high-profile celebrity marriage to Demi Moore, and a string of Planet Hollywood restaurants he shared a stake in with Sylvester Stallone and Arnold Schwarzenegger. He was more confident throwing his clout around, and giving a few unsolicited directing tips to McGill in the process. "We get [on the set]," McGill said, "and he was the star of the movie, and I'm just this stage actor who did some movies. Bruce [Willis] was assertive and he was asserting himself in a way that sometimes did become obnoxious. Never to me. Our relationship didn't change much, although he did give me a piece of direction.... Behind my impassive face I thought 'are you fucking kidding me?'"

Tony Scott was threatened with termination more than once, but that was nothing new for him. Despite having three different creative voices pushing him, Scott was still strong enough to keep his style firmly in tact. Scott persisted through the ninety-one-day shoot, and when the dust settled, he approached his team of editors with what seemed like an endless assemblage of celluloid.

Scott's films were notorious for accumulating miles and miles of footage because of his penchant for using multiple cameras in each scene. While the technique had become a bit more commonplace in the years since *Top Gun*, nobody did it to the excess of Scott, who made excess the modus operandi of his entire career. *The Last Boy Scout* had an astounding bit of footage for a team of editors to chop down into a coherent film.

According to Mark Helfrich, by the time he and his team got their hands on the film, it had already been chopped up and edited. Apparently, Joel Silver was not pleased with the work from the initial cuts, so he reassembled the celluloid and handed off to Helfrich and a group of editors to try to make sense of everything. It made the process that much more difficult, as there were splices all over the film.[3]

Helfrich, Stuart Baird, and Mark Goldblatt eventually nipped and tucked and found their way to the theatrical cut of *The Last Boy Scout*. It may still be incongruous or hasty at times, but the fact that a trio of editors was able to shape the mess of film and edits into a streamlined and coherent action movie is an impressive feat.

The Last Boy Scout opened number two at the box office behind Steven Spielberg's big-budget Peter Pan adventure, *Hook*, with a respectable $7 million in ticket sales. The following weekend it dipped to third as Steve Martin's *Father of the Bride* remake snuck in between it and *Hook*, but sales would bounce back the third weekend with a solid 48 percent increase.

The Last Boy Scout ended its theatrical run a shade under $60 million. It did not set the world on fire, and it was not anywhere near the hits Silver, Willis, and Scott had enjoyed in their careers. At the same time, however, the fact that this Frankensteinian mishmash of ideas and egos had doubled its alleged budget of $30 million was impressive.

The fact the movie itself turned out so well is a miracle.

* * *

Despite the arduous shoot and miles of footage to edit down, Tony Scott still managed to create a singular vision with *The Last Boy Scout*. Through all the fights and the threats, Scott and his editors cobbled together a hyper-reality of macho pasturing, guns, and football, and they may have also inadvertently created a more accurate portrayal of a modern, "casual" dystopia than any other film at the time.

Black's lurid neo-noir screenplay—however chopped up it may have been in the end—exists in a dystopia, make no mistake. This is a world where football is the poisonous fruit of the masses and violence is commonplace; a mass shooting on a football field in the middle of the game was outlandish, fantastical in 1991. The way Scott and cinematographer Ward Russell shoot this opening football game could not be more dour, more bleak, soaked to the bone by oppressive rain and lit with a garish glow from spotlights that seem to rise and fall like the spotlights of prison watchtowers.

The world of *The Last Boy Scout* exists on a heightened plane of reality in which Joe Hallenbeck, the hangdog private detective, and former football star Jimmy Dix, confront assassins and madmen in alleyways and parking lots and in the hilltop home of Sheldon Marcone, the film's central villain. The police are neutered, rendered practically useless, which can be interpreted as a casualty of a failing societal infrastructure. Scott and Ward Russell lean in to the neo-noir aesthetics ripe for this story, creating a lawless Los Angeles where these downtrodden heroes must fight against oppressive, corporate evils.

The "reality" here, where cars can fly through the air and land in a swimming pool before exploding in a fireball, where a disgraced quarterback can hurl a football some eighty yards in the air to hit a senator in the face just in time to save him from a sniper's bullet, is intentionally elevated to a point where the only true interpretation of the film is a world where the timeline fractured into this unforgiving, nihilistic society. It is a bleak analysis of a film full of jokes, but even the humor cuts to the bone.

Nothing seems to function properly in *The Last Boy Scout*, a true indicator of a dystopian society. Political power, represented here by Chelcie Ross' Senator Calvin Baynard, is sour and corrupt and in bed with the fraudulent puppet master of the most popular sport in America. Only Hallenbeck and Dix are able to find solutions, wading through the waters of paranoia and ineptness. Local government and law enforcement is failing, and the streets are littered with nefarious hit men, and the domestic lives of our heroes are unwelcoming and fragile.

Killers and gangsters seem ubiquitous in *The Last Boy Scout*, but they aren't entirely the reason for this dystopia. At every turn, in every corner of the frame, are men who have lost touch with any shred of human decency, unable to relate to the women in their life. It's an epidemic not belonging exclusively to the hired guns, but every male character in the picture. There is not a healthy relationship between a man and a woman anywhere to be found here, only a lack of intimacy and trust. Women are rejected, cheated on, shot, nearly drowned in an attempted rape, and Joe's daughter, Darian (Danielle Harris), is a foul-mouthed brat. On this plane of existence, women are merely objects, and an obsession with sports and misogyny has broken the functionality of the world.

In most dystopian films there is a hero to rise above the ranks of a disparate people. The hero is Schwarzenegger in *The Running Man*, Clive Owen in *Children of Men*, Keanu Reeves' Neo in *The Matrix*; here, it is Joe Hallenbeck and Jimmy Dix correcting the malady of the modern world. They endure a gauntlet of violence and brutality, to come out on the other end as saviors of a rotten society.

There are places where *The Last Boy Scout* could have been improved upon; certain edits create incongruity—there is an especially egregious moment at Hallenbeck's house where night becomes day from one scene to the next. The film also can't shake the influence of half a dozen creative minds all in the same room, all with their own ideas. The dissent is there, but for the most part it manages to ingratiate itself within the hard-boiled nature of the characters and the anarchic violence. More often than not, troubled productions show their scars in the finished product. *The Last Boy Scout* may have its scars, but unlike most tortured shoots they are masked by one of the more effective neo-noir films of the 1990s.

It is, like so many Tony Scott films, something that will never be made again. The blatant misogyny of the male characters, the general treatment of women, and the bleak gun violence would never float in the modern era, in a world that just might represent the world of *The Last Boy Scout* a little closer than we might want to admit.

10

A Marriage of Style and Sound

Tony Scott had a frequent visitor on set of *The Last Boy Scout*, an eager young screenwriter and aspiring director—a movie geek with a mean streak—who had been invited to visit. The gawky motor mouth with the sharp chin and the encyclopedic knowledge of genre film was currently working on a rewrite of *Past Midnight*, a B-picture drama starring Rutger Hauer and Natasha Richardson, for New Line Cinema, and he jumped at a chance to see Scott at work.

The 28-year-old kid would ask Scott questions about shots, about set design, and Scott was always willing to share tips and tricks with an aspiring young filmmaker. Scott never forgot the challenges he faced in becoming a director, a chip he carried on his shoulder into perpetuity, so he was never going to turn away an inquiring mind. Shortly after *The Last Boy Scout* wrapped, Scott invited the kid out to a party where they began discussing screenplays. The kid had written a few, and he offered Scott a pair to read: *Reservoir Dogs*, and *True Romance*.

Scott read the scripts in one flight from the U.S. home to Europe, and as soon as he landed he told the kid, Quentin Tarantino, he wanted to direct both. But Tarantino already had his sights set on directing *Reservoir Dogs*. Scott obliged, and dove head first into *True Romance*.

Tony Scott also jumped into the deep end of Beverly Hills real estate in 1992. While his career to this point may have been a series of ups and downs, the Simpson/Bruckheimer collaborations set him up for the rest of his life, even while he was collecting Ferraris and paying the navy $25,000 of his own money to move an aircraft carrier a few degrees for the perfect shot. With that money, Scott purchased Bella Vista, a 10,000 square-foot villa with Spanish architecture and roofing, complete with a pair of guesthouses, pathways, pools, and lush gardens.

Bella Vista had been built for King Vidor, one of the pioneers of filmmaking with credits as far back as 1913's *Hurricane in Galveston*. In 1927, John Barrymore, legendary actor and patriarch of an acting legacy in Hollywood, purchased the property and lived there until his passing in 1942.

When Scott purchased the home, it included five bedrooms, a pub, and a floor-to-ceiling library with a study; there was also a room in the attic that Barrymore allegedly used as an opium den.[1] It was now home for Tony Scott and his girlfriend, Donna Wilson, and it personified the boisterous filmmaker's hedonistic lust for life. Whatever was to come, Scott had achieved his goal; he was making art his way. He had stepped out of his brother's shadow in the last few years, and was set to evolve as a director. While his personal life may have found at least some sense of structure and calm, Tony Scott was ready to take more risks as a filmmaker; that meant not taking his foot off the accelerator.

Of all the early screenplays in Quentin Tarantino's catalogue, *True Romance* was the most autobiographical. That isn't to say Tarantino lived a life of guns and drugs and Mexican standoffs while writing *True Romance*, but the characters all took on different aspects of his life and personality. Clarence, the hero of the story, worked at a comics store (Tarantino worked at a video store in California) and loved Kung Fu movies and Elvis; Dick Ritchie, the eager wannabe actor shuffling through auditions in Hollywood mirrored Tarantino's own attempts to break into the industry; Alabama, Clarence's call-girl Juliet, was Tarantino's fantasy come to life.

To play Clarence, Tarantino had someone more weathered, more worn down by the real world, in mind. He had written the role for a dogged character actor like genre mainstay Robert Carradine, but Scott wanted youth. He wanted the film to move, and he knew a fresh new face would breathe life into the story. Scott and his casting directors sent a copy of the screenplay to Christian Slater, one of the hottest young stars in Hollywood at the time.

Born in New York, the fortunate son of a soap opera acting father and casting director mother, Christian Slater began popping up in soap operas and in bit roles on TV series in the early '80s. For the next few years he would work his way up the ladder, into bigger roles in TV movies before his breakout film role in 1985, when he played Binx, the rebellious outlaw brother to Helen Slater's (no relation) titular character in *The Legend of Billie Jean*. Slater had an edge as a young performer, and was immediately compared to a simmering young Jack Nicholson, a comparison he sometimes embraced in his early years before eventually finding his own groove as a thespian. Three years later, after a handful of film and TV roles, Slater had his second breakout film, *Heathers*, where he played the sociopathic antagonist JD opposite Winona Ryder's Veronica.

After *Heathers*, Slater began filling up his schedule. He was in the skateboarding thriller *Gleaming the Cube*, the family adventure *The Wizard*, and

10. A Marriage of Style and Sound

eventually he found his way into more adult-oriented fare; in 1990 he joined Emilio Estevez and Kiefer Sutherland in *Young Guns II* as "Arkansas" Dave Rudabaugh, which indoctrinated him into the "Brat Pack," an unofficial collection of young movie stars in which Estevez and Sutherland were included. That same year, Slater slipped back into the angst-ridden teenager clothes to play pirate DJ Mark Hunter, a.k.a. "Happy Harry Hard-On," in the small independent hit *Pump Up the Volume*. Slater had cornered the market as a heartthrob with an edge, a handsome young man with a potential mean streak.

The next year, Christian Slater stepped into the next tier of actors in Hollywood, playing Will Scarlett in the summer blockbuster *Robin Hood: Prince of Thieves*. He landed a role in *Star Trek VI: The Undiscovered Country*, another hit in the fall of 1991. Slater was in Minnesota filming the dramatic tearjerker *Untamed Heart* when he got a copy of the *True Romance* screenplay. He was caught off guard by the idiosyncrasies of Clarence—his tendency to talk to an imaginary Elvis, his brooding loneliness, his distinctive passions—and came in to audition.

After landing the role, Scott and Slater began hashing out the character, an odd collection of ticks and traits that actor and director needed to shape into the right character for the story. Slater saw the character as light and breezy, but Scott felt he needed to have a darkly comic side, not simply carry on like a breezy kid just free of his teen years. The two men watched *Taxi Driver*, another story of a loner who wants to save the object of his desire, and a story with striking similarities to Tarantino's screenplay; Slater began to understand the balance of darkness and light he needed to bring to this part after seeing Travis Bickle steadily unravel on the streets of New York.

To play Alabama, Clarence's unwavering object of desire and the key character for the entire picture to work, Tony Scott wanted Drew Barrymore, who had been a child movie star turned femme fatale in potboilers like *Poison Ivy* and *Sketch Artist*. Tarantino again had a different view of these characters; he had actress Joan Cusack in mind. Barrymore's schedule did not line up for the shoot, and Cusack didn't fit in Scott's new iteration of the script. An emerging young star named Patricia Arquette had gotten wind of the screenplay, however, and she was interested in tackling the role.

Born into a family of actors, Patricia Arquette lived in a commune with her mother, her father, and her four acting siblings: Rosanna, Richmond, Alexis, and David Arquette. She fled the commune for California when she was fifteen to live with her sister, Rosanna, who had recently found success as an actress. It took her a few years before Patricia finally cracked the Hollywood code, starring in both *A Nightmare on Elm Street 3: Dream Warriors* and *Pretty Smart* in the first few months of 1987. From these two features,

Arquette continued to work consistently on television and in film, but she was still waiting on the big breakout. She saw that opportunity in Alabama Worley.

Scott knew Patricia Arquette from *Wildflower*, a TV movie from 1991 directed by Diane Keaton. In the melodrama Arquette played Alice, the youngest of three sisters who is partially deaf, epileptic, and under the watch of an abusive stepfather. Scott knew she had the right amount of innocence and a unique beauty that would give Alabama some vibrancy. He and the casting directors Risa Bramon Garcia and Billy Hopkins hired Arquette, and she began researching the role, meaning she lived with a few different Florida prostitutes periodically and came back to the set with a character she would never break.

It was also clear Arquette was perfect for the role the first time she and Christian Slater met at audition. There was an undeniable chemistry, and an attraction that would soon carry over from the screen into the two actors' lives for a brief while. With the heroes in place, it was time to fill in around them; that meant finding the first act adversary, Alabama's former pimp, Drexl Spivey.

Drexl is a devious and sleazy pimp who hangs on to his Apache lineage to try to appropriate African American culture. The part was, like so many parts throughout, small but absolutely crucial to the film. Drexl, like the characters Vincent Coccotti or Floyd on the couch in California, had only one or two scenes; but those scenes were pivotal moments, and they needed memorable performances to stand out.

One afternoon, Scott had tea in London with his friend, Gary Oldman, and they discussed the part. At this point, the English-born Oldman had made his mark as a chameleon, shifting from Sid Vicious in 1986's *Sid and Nancy*, to Lee Harvey Oswald in Oliver Stone's sprawling 1991 conspiracy epic *JFK*, to Count Dracula in Francis Ford Coppola's operatic take on Bram Stoker's epistolary novel. He had the sort of shadowy face and lean frame that could fit into virtually any cinematic scenario. Based solely on Scott's description, "Drexl's a pimp who thinks he's black," and without seeing a screenplay, Oldman agreed to play the part.[2]

In the middle of casting, buzz was beginning to build around Quentin Tarantino and his Sundance, Cannes, and Toronto Film Festival hit, *Reservoir Dogs*. The film was a small sensation, putting Tarantino on the map as an important new writer/director in the industry, and it opened doors for the casting of *True Romance*. Actors wanted a chance to star in something with Tarantino's name on it, because they saw the sort of attention he paid to each and every character.

Brad Pitt begged Tony Scott to play Floyd, the stoner roommate of Dick Ritchie, Clarence's friend and a wannabe actor living in California. At the time Brad Pitt had just gone from humble, aspiring Midwestern actor to the newest sex symbol in Hollywood, thanks to his brief but memorable appearance as the young thief who seduces Geena Davis in Ridley's *Thelma & Louise*, which just so happened to grab six Oscar nominations. Despite the star-making turn, Pitt was not quite the bankable matinee idol he would soon become when he wanted to play Floyd.

After *Thelma & Louise*, Pitt played a wannabe rockabilly musician in *Johnny Suede*, and an inept detective in the painfully misguided real-life/cartoon mash up *Cool World*. Both films were disastrous. He retrenched a bit in Robert Redford's *A River Runs Through It* and the disturbing serial-killer drama *Kalifornia*, but neither had been any sort of sizeable hit. Pitt saw gold in Floyd, a character that has since become iconic in the pantheon of "stoner" characters in film. He recognized the part was rife with comedic possibilities, not to mention the fact that it is Floyd who sets the entire climax in motion thanks to his willingness to talk to whoever shows up at the door.

Val Kilmer was eager to rejoin Tony Scott. In the years since he broke out as Iceman in *Top Gun*, Kilmer was busy becoming a bankable star with an eclectic array of performances in Ron Howard's fantasy adventure *Willow*, Oliver Stone's drug-soaked Jim Morrison biopic *The Doors*, and the middling Michael Apted Native American reservation thriller, *Thunderheart*.

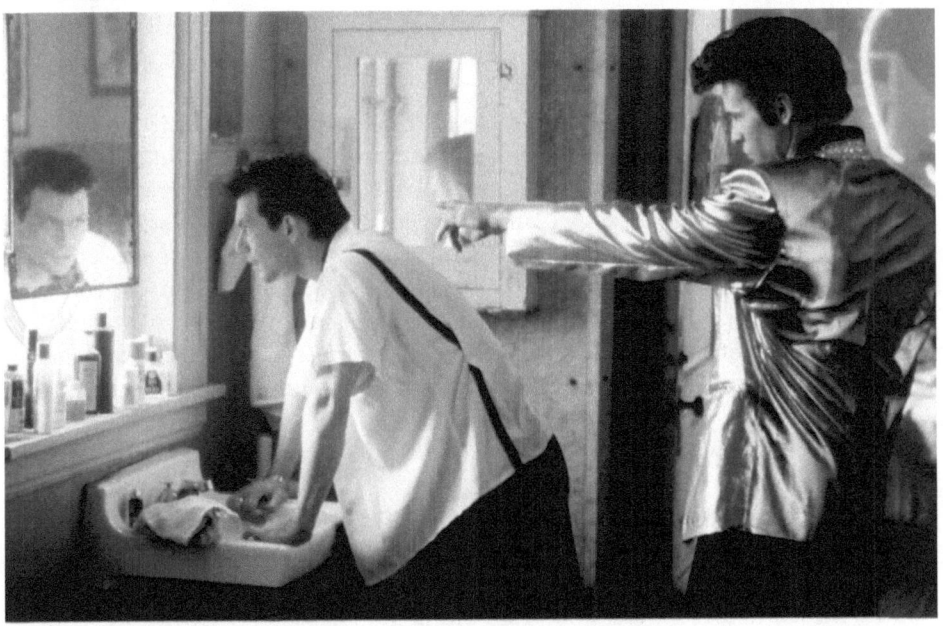

Christian Slater (hands on sink) schemes with Val Kilmer in a set photograph from *True Romance* (Warner Bros., 1993).

Kilmer wanted to play Clarence, and he leaned on Scott to let him have the part. Scott had a different plan in mind, however, a plan that had already steered him towards Christian Slater. Kilmer eventually gave in to Scott's wishes, and immediately turned the corner and begged to play Elvis, who would appear to Clarence only as a vision from time to time. According to Scott in a *Maxim* magazine interview, for months Kilmer would sing Elvis songs into his answering machine until he finally landed the role.

The new influential aura surrounding Quentin Tarantino and *Reservoir Dogs* was also partly responsible for Scott landing two acting legends—Dennis Hopper and Christopher Walken—to play minor characters that are gone by the end of the film's first act. Dennis Hopper had been one of Hollywood's most volatile troublemakers since he burst on the scene in his landmark American film *Easy Rider* in 1969. Hopper cultivated a career playing insane characters, many of whose screen insanity mirrored the unhinged lifestyle of Hopper himself. From a strung-out photographer in *Apocalypse Now*, to a nitrous-huffing madman in David Lynch's *Blue Velvet*, Hopper had streaked across Hollywood like a fireball, burning bridges and battling a severe reliance on drugs and alcohol. By the early '90s, time had eased Hopper's impulses. He had been sober for nearly a decade, and had recently played a disheveled alcoholic father in the crowd-pleasing basketball film *Hoosiers*. The role here as Clarence's father, a recovering alcoholic and former police officer now working as a night-security officer, felt like the natural progression of Hopper's character in *Hoosiers*, a portrait of another broken man trying to put the pieces of his life back together.

Christopher Walken had become the flipside of the Dennis Hopper coin by 1992. After winning Best Supporting Actor for *The Deer Hunter* in 1978, Walken had put together his own career playing emotionally distraught characters, idiosyncratic madmen, and cold-blooded killers. But where Hopper regularly went big, Walken's madmen played inward, smaller but never less threatening, tapping into a different type of psychopath. He fit the role of Vincent Coccotti, an icy Mafia hitman, better than anyone in Hollywood.

Tony Scott had one specific idea for a key character in *True Romance*, and in this character he saw an opportunity to playfully stick it to Joel Silver.

Lee Donowitz is the producer in the third act of *True Romance*, the egomaniacal, slimy mega producer who wants to purchase the suitcase full of cocaine Clarence inadvertently swiped from the apartment of a (now dead) pimp named Drexl. Tony Scott saw an opportunity to roast Silver, who had made his life hell on the set of *The Last Boy Scout*; he made sure to lampoon Silver's appetite for excess and ego fulfillment in Lee Donowitz. During auditions a twitchy, prolific, German-born character actor named Saul Rubinek read for the Donowitz part. Scott knew almost immediately that he had the

10. A Marriage of Style and Sound

Joel Silver mannerisms down, and Rubinek was hired. Bronson Pinchot, whose Serge in *Beverly Hills Cop* upstages Eddie Murphy in his one-and-only scene and had since become a sitcom star playing Balki Bartokomus on *Perfect Strangers*, was hired as Elliott Blitzer, Donowitz's spineless turncoat assistant.

The rest of the cast was populated with hard-edged character actors like Tom Sizemore and Sean Penn's brother, Chris (who also appears in *Reservoir Dogs*), who play DEA agents, Samuel L. Jackson—a character actor himself at the time—as a drug dealer who dies within the first ten minutes of the film, and New York actor Michael Rappaport as Dick Ritchie, Clarence's California connection. Like he had done in *Top Gun* and *Days of Thunder*, Scott assembled a cast of future stars in supporting roles, a talent he had gotten better and better at each time out.

There was another meaty part in the background, a mob henchman named Virgil, who would play a crucial role in the film's most controversial scene. That part went to James Gandolfini, an unknown New Jersey-born actor who had found an early niche playing Italian heavies. Scott knew Gandolfini from the set of *The Last Boy Scout*, where Gandolfini played another henchman in what amounts to an elevated walk on performance, but even then Scott spotted something in the sneering young Italian actor that he knew would work in a more substantial part.

This time around, Scott needed Gandolfini to do some heavy lifting in one of the film's most intense scenes, and one of the most harrowing scenes in all of '90s cinema.

* * *

It was clear the *True Romance* set would have a different vibe from any of the sets Tony Scott had run thus far. While *Top Gun* was full of young talent, the production was big and slick and sun-bleached. *Beverly Hills Cop II* and *Days of Thunder* were in the same vein; Jerry Bruckheimer runs a tight ship. *Revenge* was small, *The Last Boy Scout* was a nightmare, and now Tony Scott found himself on the cusp of a new cinematic revolution. He was surrounded both by legends of film and a collection of amazing, eager young stars. The energy of the set was palpable for everyone. Tony Scott was right at home, burning through cigars, mixing it up with the cast, and according to Tom Sizemore in *Maxim* magazine, yelling, "Rock'n'roll motherfuckers!" before every take.

Patricia Arquette struggled from the outset with some of the language of Quentin Tarantino's screenplay. In an early scene her character, Alabama, is chatting up Clarence in a Detroit diner, sharing pie and coffee, discussing their turn-ons and turn-offs. Alabama's turn-off: Persians.

The front-facing racism in Tarantino's writing caught Arquette off guard and made her feel uncomfortable. It has since become an understood thread of Tarantino's storytelling tapestry, but when *True Romance* began shooting in September of 1992, the racial overtones and casually explicit conversational rhythms were daring new concepts for most actors, including Arquette. Eventually, the character took over for her, and she started to see the dialogue in context of the larger story, from the mouth of Alabama. This was the language of these characters, and the separation finally let her relax and ease into the role.

Early on, Tony Scott had two issues arise, both of which involved Elvis Presley. To kick start the movie and introduce Clarence as he is waxing philosophical on the attractiveness of the King to a female barfly (Anna Thomson at the time, now Anna Levine), Scott felt it was a foregone conclusion that the song would be a blues-infused Presley hit to bring us into this obsessed fan's world. The estate of Elvis Presley, however, had other plans; they would not license any of Presley's music for the film.

Scott approached a young singer/songwriter named Charlie Sexton to compose an original tune for the film. Sexton was only 24 at the time but had already built a steady career as a journeyman guitarist and a solo artist, with his 1986 record *Beat's So Lonely* reaching number seventeen on the Billboard chart when he was only eighteen.[3] He had the perfect delivery to execute an Elvis riff. Sexton came up with "Graceland," a rockabilly homage to the life of Presley sung in the same hangdog cadence, and Scott absolutely loved it. In the end, having an adjacent song about Presley and his Memphis home, rather than something like "Jailhouse Rock" or "Suspicious Minds," felt more in tune with Clarence at the beginning of the film, a kid miles away from any sort of interesting life to rival that of his idol; he may love Elvis, but he isn't yet cool enough to hear him.

The second issue involving Presley was the actor playing him. No matter how affectionate Val Kilmer was with his Elvis character, Scott knew he could not sell Elvis because it's a character that is almost impossible to portray accurately. Presley was too ubiquitous, and his mannerisms too familiar, for any fictionalized version of him to not unintentionally veer into parody; the only honest take on Elvis thus far had been John Carpenter's 1979 TV movie starring Kurt Russell, which focused more on the music and less on the character; Scott did not have that luxury with his version of Elvis, who was there strictly to, well, be Elvis.

Kilmer was all in on the part, and Scott enjoyed his energy and his performance, but the character was never quite coming off right because Presley's larger-than-life iconic persona was too dominant to see past; the same can be said for James Dean and Marilyn Monroe, two icons who shared the stage at the birth of the pop culture movement across the world in the mid–twentieth century.

Scott approached Kilmer with this conundrum, and he had a tough solution. Kilmer's performance was still integral to the story—Elvis is responsible for motivating Clarence to go confront and kill Drexl, after all, setting the entire plot of the film in motion—but Scott would shoot him mostly in the background. Headshots would become torso shots of the gold jacket and the horseshoe ring dangling off his pinkie finger, and the only glimpses of Kilmer's face would be in out-of-focus images directly behind Clarence or reflected over his shoulder in the mirror. Kilmer understood what Scott was saying, and according to Scott he never let up on playing the role.

Set building was minimal, and *True Romance* was shot on location in Detroit and in and around Los Angeles. Two major sets needed to be built: Dennis Hopper's trailer, and the primary Safari Inn motel room location. Hopper's trailer was built in halves, with removable walls and ceiling sections where light could be appropriately manipulated. To film the iconic confrontation between Hopper and Christopher Walken's Vincent Coccotti, Scott shot Hopper's half of the dialogue one day, with his side of the trailer background intact. The next day, he flipped everything and shot Walken's.

Hopper, whom Walken's Coccotti shoots point blank in the head at the end of the scene, was uncomfortable with the prop gun being pressed up against his forehead when it was fired. Scott, just as boisterous as Hopper, pushed back against the actor's protests, and decided to show Hopper just how safe the prop gun was. He put it to his own head and pulled the trigger, not accounting for the microscopic, rapid-fire recoil of the barrel. The pistol fired, and the slide popped Scott in the forehead, knocking him to the ground.

Bloodied and dazed, Scott composed himself on the ground where Hopper was standing over him shouting, "I told you so! There's no fucking way I'm doing that!" Once he was patched up and ready to shoot again, Scott sheepishly agreed with Hopper that the barrel did not need to be pressed right against his head.[4]

There is also a technique Scott employed to get Patricia Arquette in character, a technique that has since been rightfully outed as too aggressive, too demeaning, and frankly too abusive. It was an early scene, shot on the billboard outside Clarence's apartment—a set in California that Scott had used for a Marlboro commercial—and Arquette was having difficulty getting to the semi-hysterical emotional level she needed to be at for the scene to work. Imploring Scott to help, Scott slapped her across the face.

The slap became known, according to Scott on the director's commentary, as "The Persuader," and he used it at least one other time during the shoot. While Arquette began requesting it because of the effectiveness, it is certainly something that no longer has a place in Hollywood. In 1992, however, it was an acceptable form of motivation.

The dialogue and storytelling of *True Romance* was brilliant, but it also had a handful of scenes lifted from standard narrative tropes. There was the character professing love, the showdown with the villain, the deal negotiation, the standoff, all familiar threads audiences have seen time and time again. This motivated Scott to set up scenes in creative places with unusual settings, in order to keep the audience fully engaged. It was the reason he shot Alabama's declaration of love on the billboard, and it was what eventually motivated him to shoot the drug negotiations between Clarence, Alabama, Dick, and Donowitz's hapless assistant, Elliott Blitzer, on a rollercoaster.

Scott was trying to think of a unique place for the negotiations when he spotted a commercial for an amusement park. It gave him the idea, just as it does for Alabama in the film. The rollercoaster scene plays beautifully, and Pinchot felt genuinely ill, as he was not a fan. But Michael Rappaport, as Dick Ritchie, had the worst trouble making it through the scene. The first day, Rappaport was too terrified to speak his lines. To try to make it though the next day, Rappaport took an overabundance of muscle relaxers. The first time they ran the scene, then, Rappaport was too inebriated to remember his lines; the third time through, finally, he figured out how to pull himself out of his mildly euphoric state while delivering his dialogue.

The scene in the Safari Inn where James Gandolfini's character, Virgil, beats Alabama within an inch of her life, has become a moment that is equal parts iconic—mostly because of Alabama's triumph in the end—and equal parts horrifying to watch unfold. Scott, Gandolfini, and Arquette knew the scene would be difficult to shoot and tough to stomach, but Scott was convinced the severity paid off in the end. The fight is brutal, unforgiving (and, written mostly in step with what happens on screen), but comes with an incredible moment of catharsis. It was the darkness and the violence placed upon this sweet, innocent young girl that propelled the moment; just as crucial for Scott, however, was the fact that Alabama saves herself and ultimately kills Virgil. Having her rise up and remain resourceful enough to fell Gandolfini's brute in the end would redeem the horrific nature of the scene, at least partially.

The final showdown and shootout inside Lee Donowitz's hotel suite was shot inside a derelict Los Angeles hotel. In order to give Donowitz's room depth and dimension, Scott knocked down the walls between three rooms to build the suite; this also allowed Scott to use a patio outside one room for a crucial scene in the movie. When they were shooting this climactic battle, Scott had convinced himself of something he'd been thinking about from day one.

In Tarantino's screenplay, Clarence dies in the shootout and Alabama escapes with the money. Tony Scott had grown attached to this couple over the past few months and weeks, and he admired their characters and their journey together; killing Clarence felt like cruel punishment for Arquette's

Alabama, who had endured more than enough punishment by this point. He wanted to change Clarence's fortune, but Tarantino disagreed.

Tarantino saw *True Romance* as one of his early punk films, and he thought killing off his on-screen persona in Clarence would be the best punk move he could pull behind the scenes. Despite his protests that Scott was succumbing to audience placation, that he was "selling out" as he put it in the *Maxim* interview, he gave his begrudged blessing. Clarence was saved, but not before taking a bullet in the eye and allowing Scott to carefully milk that emotional moment where the audience thinks he may have died.

Tony Scott and company wrapped production on *True Romance* in December, sixty-five days in. The shoot proved that Scott had mastered the art of efficiency and managing large sets and even larger casts. After the nightmarish slog that was *The Last Boy Scout*—a troubled shoot Scott still managed to get in on time—the vibrancy and youth of *True Romance* was a welcome change. Scott fit right in, and the synchronicity of these actors and their director is clear as the ensemble comes together in near perfect fashion.

And yet, *True Romance* fizzled at the box office when it opened September 10, 1993, even though critics generally praised Scott's efforts. Roger Ebert said it was "the kind of movie that creates its own universe, and glories in it."[5] Words like "visceral" and "dynamite" peppered other reviews, but something

(From left) Brad Pitt, Michael Rappaport, Christian Slater, and Patricia Arquette pose for a photo during the *True Romance* shoot (Warner Bros., 1993).

did not translate to full theaters. *True Romance* checked in at number three on opening weekend with just over $4 million, roughly $300,000 behind the other wide release, *Undercover Blues*; the Harrison Ford and Tommy Lee Jones film adaptation of *The Fugitive* would enjoy its sixth consecutive weekend at number one with $8.3 to add to its then $144 million total.[6] The Bruce Willis speedboat thriller *Striking Distance* opened the next weekend, pushing *True Romance* even further down the line. After a three-week run, it closed with a meek $12.3 million, not even enough to cover the $13 million budget.[7]

True Romance proved to be a tough film to market in 1993, in the aftermath of the epic blockbuster decade of the 1980s and the burgeoning computer revolution of the new '90s blockbusters. If it was to be a film aimed at teenage boys, the hard R rating certainly kept away the 15-and 16-year-olds who may have been interested.

At first glance, with romantic drama mainstay Christian Slater in the lead, and in the days before internet advertising and trailer promotions found target demographics, *True Romance* would have been easily shrugged off by young male filmgoers looking at marquees trying to decide what to see that afternoon. There was a perfect storm of circumstances that, in the box office performance, outweighed the shiny new Hollywood toy that was Quentin Tarantino. Had the film been released in the modern era, it would have absolutely found the sort of success for which everyone involved was hoping.

True Romance found a strong second life on VHS and eventually DVD. As Quentin Tarantino's career hit the next level, captivating the audiences with his 1994 film *Pulp Fiction* and pushing through to the twenty-first century, an entire new era of film fanatics made their way back to Scott's film. Profits came down the road, and notoriety and success was a slow burn for everyone involved. It took time, but *True Romance* eventually found the proper appraisal in the court of pop culture opinion.

11

Scott, Tarantino and the Birth of the '90s Crime Aesthetic

The creative explosion of the 1970s introduced a new generation of film fans to Francis Ford Coppola, Martin Scorsese, Steven Spielberg, and dozens upon dozens of fresh new faces like Al Pacino, Robert De Niro, and James Caan in front of the camera. But the decade of great creative flourish and ingenuity hit a brick wall when excess eventually laid waste to unbridled creative freedoms in Hollywood. The '80s was time for studios (at least they thought it was time) to pull the reigns back in and begin working on a new model, something more controllable and marketable than the likes of Cimino or Coppola, who burned through money to satiate their vision; the return on investment and the accompanying headache was not worth the initial investment anymore.

The 1980s fully embraced the summer-movie season, which had been kick started by the success of Steven Spielberg's *Jaws* in June of 1975. *Star Wars* followed suit in 1977 with a record-breaking Memorial Day weekend opening, but when Spielberg's *Raiders of the Lost Ark* hit in June of 1981, the summer season was solidified as the go-to location for big studio tent pole films. Franchises would begin to dominate the box office in the 1980s with the *Indiana Jones* films and Robert Zemeckis' ingenuity in *Back to The Future*, among others. Nineteen eighty-nine witnessed the rebirth of superhero cinema with Tim Burton's *Batman*. Action movies belonged to the biceps of Arnold Schwarzenegger and Sylvester Stallone; Best Picture winners were historical epics like *Gandhi*, *Out of Africa*, and *The Last Emperor*, or adult-oriented blockbusters like *Terms of Endearment* and *Platoon*. Independent cinema was practically nonexistent, relegated to the Venice Film Festival, or the Cannes Film Festival, where small films made on no budget with no star power would struggle to find widespread distribution in the United States.

Independent film had been marginalized to the point were very few outsiders were getting their chance. But in 1985 when Robert Redford debuted the Sundance Film Festival, an unprecedented new surge of talent, similar to the early 1970s, would begin to showcase their work and change the industry.

On January 21, 1992, the Sundance Film Festival in Park City, Utah, was abuzz with anticipation about a fierce little crime drama from a video-store clerk turned director named Quentin Tarantino. In the preceding years, Sundance had grown from a small festival screening films both old and new when it began in 1985, to a sounding board for the burgeoning independent-film wave that was slowly infiltrating studio pictures in Hollywood. In 1989, Steven Soderbergh's *sex, lies, and videotape* captured the essence of a new brand of realism, a strong rebuttal to the general bombast of the 1980s.

Soderbergh's film would go on to become the most financially successful independent feature of its time, and it cemented Sundance as ground zero for a new revolution in American cinema. The arrival of *Reservoir Dogs* three years later—a subversive crime thriller, told in the aftermath of a robbery gone wrong, that looked and felt like something American audiences had never seen—was the first step towards a new crime aesthetic that permeated a decade of genre filmmaking. But the first time it was screened at Sundance, everything was a complete disaster.

Tarantino screened *Reservoir Dogs* for an exclusive audience on January 21, and the lens was a mismatch with the projection, distorting the corners of every frame on the screen. What's more, just as the climactic standoff between the surviving members of the cast was reaching its fever pitch, the lights in the auditorium came on prematurely, stopping the finale in its tracks. Fortunately, Tarantino was able to screen *Reservoir Dogs* again, only a week later at the festival, and from that screening he was off and running.[1]

Two years later, *Pulp Fiction* would take Tarantino's status and push it beyond all comprehension. His time-jumping crime noir hit like a bolt of lightning at the Cannes Film Festival, and it tussled with *Forrest Gump* through awards season; Tarantino would win Best Original Screenplay at the 1995 Academy Awards, and his very unique, idiosyncratic rhythms both as a director and writer would be imitated to obscene levels for years to come.[2]

Tarantino's one-two crime drama punch is often credited for birthing a new '90s aesthetic, especially in crime and action pictures. Films got dirty, and real, and the violence and language would begin to sting again. *Natural Born Killers*, a screenplay Tarantino wrote and Oliver Stone directed, also came out in 1994 and is regularly grouped together with *Reservoir Dogs* and *Pulp Fiction* when discussing this new wave of independent crime cinema. What is often left out, and should not be for a myriad of reasons, is Tony Scott's *True Romance*. After all *True Romance* was, at one point in the writing process, one part of the whole.

Early on, while Tarantino worked at the video store and spent his free time churning out pages of his screenplay, the stories of Clarence and Alabama, a handful of the criminals in *Reservoir Dogs*, and Mickey and Mallory Knox in *Natural Born Killers*, were all interwoven. Eventually, with the page numbers undoubtedly swelling to comical proportions, Tarantino broke apart the films into these four screenplays, keeping much of the connective tissue in tact. This is why, in *Reservoir Dogs*, Harvey Keitel's Mr. White mentions Alabama as a partner in crime and a "nice little thief"; it's why Seymour Scagnetti is a parole officer in *Reservoir Dogs*, and his brother Jack (Tom Sizemore) is an unhinged cop in *Natural Born Killers*; it is why Mr. Blonde, a.k.a. Vic Vega (Michael Madsen), and John Travolta's Vincent Vega in *Pulp Fiction* share the same last name. At one point, Tarantino flirted with the idea of doing a Vega Brothers film, but that never materialized beyond interview sound bytes.

True Romance belongs in the conversation with these other films because of the connectivity to this world, and the way the puzzle pieces fit together. But beyond that, Scott's film became a sort of clearing house for an entire decade of stars. *Reservoir Dogs* had its fair share of fresh new faces—Steve Buscemi, Michael Madsen, and Tim Roth being chief among them—and some old-school talent with Keitel and Lawrence Bender. The same could be said for *Pulp Fiction* and *Natural Born Killers*, films that resurrected John Travolta, introduced Samuel L. Jackson as a force, and reconfigured the trajectory of Woody Harrelson and Juliette Lewis. *True Romance* has arguably the most substantial cast of all, overflowing with actors on the cusp of stardom.

The aforementioned Samuel L. Jackson is, in fact, seen briefly in an early scene before he is murdered by Drexl, played by Gary Oldman, who would spend the better part of the 1990s embodying unhinged madmen in films like *The Professional* and *The Fifth Element*. He may not have been a discovery, per se, but he was finding a new niche as a wild-card villain. Supporting players from James Gandolfini, to Michael Rappaport, to Tom Sizemore, to even a baby-faced Brad Pitt all found their grooves in the years following *True Romance*, after their names were attached to a "cool" bit of intellectual property. Even well-established legends in the industry like Christopher Walken and Dennis Hopper found a resurgence in Hollywood after popping up in such a fresh new world of astute dialogue, hip cultural accouterments, and brutal violence.

That isn't to say *True Romance* was on the same level of success as any of the other three pictures, which is an unfortunate mishap, a stroke of bad luck that seemed all too familiar in Scott's career outside of his Don Simpson/Jerry Bruckheimer collaborations. It's an issue with marketing and timing more than anything else. The studio did not have a grasp on how to push these new, hard-boiled pop thrillers on the masses in 1993. *Reservoir Dogs* had been a success, sure, but somewhat of an underground success, finding its true sea legs as a cultural launch pad thanks to VHS rentals and a groundswell of support for this new aesthetic. The film was a callback to the independent wave of the 1970s, but with a modern flair, and a certain level of self-awareness that earned the adoration of those who sought it out at their local Blockbuster. By the time Tarantino was gaining any media traction, *True Romance* hit theaters in September of 1993, square in the darkness before the dawn that would become *Pulp Fiction* the following spring.

Had *True Romance* been released in April or May of 1995, directly in the afterglow of Tarantino's masterpiece, with audiences feverishly seeking out anything and everything Tarantino's fingerprints were on, the marketing could have taken care of itself. There is little reason to believe a hard-boiled crime fantasy from "the writer of *Pulp Fiction*" and "the director of *The Last Boy Scout*" would not have filled seats for weeks. Alas, it did not happen that way, and *True Romance* opened without the fanfare it deserved.

Thankfully time, combined with the tendency for modern film critics and audiences to re-appraise and reconfigure the importance—or lack therof—of just about any previous film imaginable, has given the film a second lease on life. *True Romance* has since planted its flag as a pioneer film of a decade where countless writers and directors and producers tried to capture the look and feel of Scott and Tarantino's (and Oliver Stone's) pictures. There is a legitimate argument to be had that *True Romance* is the second best of the quartet, perhaps in a parallel universe finding its place as an equal to *Pulp Fiction* in every way.

Reservoir Dogs works like a stage play, *Pulp Fiction* like the dog-eared novels its title adores, and *Natural Born Killers* plays like a bad night inside the mind of a cocaine-addled madman who obsesses over the depravity of the American Media Machine. They are more esoteric than *True Romance*, which has a solid dose of so many tones and themes, and is imbued with a sympathetic touch of its director. Scott rescued Clarence and Alabama from the cruel, nihilistic fate Tarantino originally had planned, and the result is something that stretches retroactively across the film. Scott aces the romantic playfulness of the central story, and seamlessly blends into it a film that is equal parts *Bonnie and Clyde* and *The Getaway*, filtered through a high-contrast new aesthetic. The film shows us loneliness and love, fear and anger, flawed characters and final stands, it is a mixture of hope and despair that also manages to feature one of the very best assembled casts in the history of filmmaking. Our main characters are relatable, believable in love, and we connect on a level deeper than with any characters in the other three pictures. To deny Tony Scott of *True Romance* is to ignore the one element—empathy—that sets it apart from the rest.

In the years following the Tarantino renaissance, and even in the wake of *True Romance*—whose failures at the box office also began to correct themselves in the video stores—crime dramas and street-level thrillers with labyrinthine plots and pop-culture prophets were the new fast track to a green light for young writers eager to become the next Tarantino, or upstart studios trying to become the next Miramax, the pioneering independent studio directly attached to the ascendance of Tarantino, Kevin Smith, and basically an entire cross section of the '90s zeitgeist. In the shadow of *Pulp Fiction* was where lackluster efforts like *Things to Do in Denver When You're Dead*, *8 Heads in a Duffel Bag*, and *2 Days in the Valley* all tried and failed to capture the magic of Tarantino's opus. At the same time, terrifically entertaining films like Christopher McQuarrie's *The Way of the Gun*, Doug Liman's *Go*, and the kidnapping thriller *Suicide Kings*—starring *True Romance* and *Pulp Fiction* alum Christopher Walken, no less—were spawned in this new wave.

Pulp Fiction is always cited as the fulcrum of the movement, and rightfully so, but *True Romance* deserves at least a portion of the credit. Scott's professional career had been a competition between him and his brother, and even when he dared step outside the box—and when he clearly saw something so many other filmmakers at the time could not recognize in these fresh young faces he routinely cast in his pictures—they weren't connecting with audiences in the same way as Ridley's films for reasons that were often outside his creative control. It would not be the last time Tony Scott was out in front of a new filmmaking aesthetic.

And it wouldn't be the last time his contributions were overlooked.

PART IV
High-Tech Decade

12

Tension Under the Sea

For whatever reason, be it poor marketing or disagreeable egos or meddling producers with conflicting ideas on direction, Tony Scott's career outside of his collaborations with Don Simpson and Jerry Bruckheimer was proving to be an uphill climb at the box office. *The Last Boy Scout* was a moderate hit, but on either side of this minor miracle were *Revenge* and *True Romance*, two substantial flops at the time.

Scott's highest-grossing films by the end of 1993 were, to no one's surprise, *Top Gun*, *Beverly Hills Cop II*, and *Days of Thunder*. They may not be his better films from a pure quality standpoint, ironically enough, but they were moneymakers with the backing of Simpson and Bruckheimer who, in 1993, were busy kick starting their own production company under the ever-expanding umbrella of Walt Disney Studios.

Simpson and Bruckheimer's first picture for Disney—under the Mouse's more adult-oriented studio branch, Touchstone—was the R-rated Denis Leary Christmas comedy *The Ref*. A terrific yuletide comedy, *The Ref* was inexplicably released in March of 1994 and disappeared from theaters in a few weeks. But Simpson and Bruckheimer were already planning a one-two punch of new high-octane action pictures for Disney while *The Ref* was stumbling through the spring of 1994.

For one movie, Simpson and Bruckheimer hired a young, prolific music video director named Michael Bay. *Bad Boys* was the picture, and it would join together Bay's new hyper-kinetic aesthetic—the obvious evolutionary step from Tony Scott's own rapid-fire techniques at the time—with two young actors on the cusp of superstardom: Will Smith and Martin Lawrence.

Simultaneously, the producers had a submarine project percolating. Much like Jerry Bruckheimer happened upon a magazine article that became the inspiration for *Top Gun*, Don Simpson caught a few minutes of a documentary on The Discovery Channel called *Sharks of Steel*. It was the only spark of intrigue Simpson needed to begin putting a story together; he had a knack for building terrific stories from a single idea. Both he and Bruckheimer agreed the story should be more about tension and suspense, less about explosions and high-flying stunts—though they would be there as well. The producers also reached out to their friend and frequent collaborator, Tony Scott, who was more than willing to tackle a submarine thriller.

The story needed to put two characters at odds, and create a chamber drama inside the claustrophobic walls of a submarine. Simpson and Bruckheimer tasked writer Michael Schiffer—whose two previous feature writing credits were the dynamic police/gangland drama *Colors*, directed by Dennis Hopper and starring Robert Duvall and a baby-faced Sean Penn, and the inner-city school drama *Lean on Me*—to pen the script. These two films may appear vastly different on the surface, but all of Schiffer's work dealt with the nature of community and the importance of clear communication in the midst of stressful situations. With an assist from a friend, Richard P. Hendrick, and weeks of extensive research, Schiffer eventually arrived at his first draft for *Crimson Tide*.

Schiffer's work was strong, the technical jargon worked, and the story's tension felt organic; however, Scott and his powerful producing partners felt the dialogue could be punched up in a few places. They needed this story, full of naval officers wearing the same attire, primarily shot in dark light and shadows, to flesh out some of these characters so as to give them some individuality.

Scott suggested Quentin Tarantino. It was natural that he would think of his *True Romance* collaborator to heighten some of the stodgy, technical dialogue. This was in the first half of 1994, and Tarantino was right on that cusp of superstardom. In the afterglow of *Pulp Fiction*'s early Cannes praise, Tarantino took the time to add a few conversations and exchanges in the *Crimson Tide* script. One of his contributions to the final cut is the famous *Silver Surfer* argument between Rivetti (Danny Nucci) and Bennefield (Eric Bruskotter), which has managed to always stand out amid the macho posturing.

Aside from Tarantino's contribution, the screenplay also passed through the hands of Robert Towne, the Oscar winning screenwriter of *Chinatown* who had previously worked with Scott on the *Days of Thunder* outline. Simpson and Bruckheimer sought Towne's expertise with one scene early in the film, when Captain Ramsey and Commander Hunter are discussing the pros and cons of war; they wanted Towne to fill the scene in with necessary foreshadowing. The conversation needed to set up the later conflict, which would in turn be the crux of the entire film, so Towne peppered specific dialogue into the scene to help raise the stakes as the film carried on, and these two characters began pushing back against one another in this early moment to set the stage.[1]

With a screenplay in place, Scott, Simpson, Bruckheimer, and casting

12. Tension Under the Sea

director Victoria Thomas began to assemble the sizeable cast of characters. To play Captain Ramsey, the wiry and stubborn officer of the old school, they needed to go big. They needed a steely-eyed legend in the industry that could fill the shoes of an unbending submarine captain. Simpson and Bruckheimer were convinced that they needed Warren Beatty.

The mid-1990s were a tricky time for Warren Beatty. For more than three decades, Beatty had been one of the kings of Tinseltown, having landed squarely on the A-list after the grass roots success of *Bonnie and Clyde* in 1967, in the earliest days of the New Hollywood renaissance. He worked with auteurs like Robert Altman on *McCabe & Mrs. Miller* and Hal Ashby on *Shampoo*, while also working with populist filmmakers like Alan J. Pakula in *The Parallax View*; in 1978, he directed himself in the blockbuster fantasy/comedy hybrid *Heaven Can Wait*.

In 1981 Beatty fully transitioned from a ladies man—the matinee idol with the glint in his eye and sex appeal that went for days—to a serious filmmaker when his Communist revolution melodrama *Reds* grabbed a dozen Academy Award nominations and won three, including a Best Director statue for Beatty. He still embodied that roguish charm, but now he had the accompanying prestige. For several years, Beatty remained dormant, only to re-emerge alongside Dustin Hoffman in director Elaine May's notorious, big-budget 1987 calamity *Ishtar*.

In 1990 Beatty directed an esoteric comic book adaptation of *Dick Tracy*, which was met with middling reviews, but a terrific marketing campaign—plus the inclusion of Madonna, arguably the biggest star on the planet at the time—ensured solid box office returns. The following year he earned his fourth Academy Award nomination playing the Las Vegas gangster Bugsy Siegel in Barry Levinson's *Bugsy*. The film collected ten nominations, won two, and was also the set where Beatty would meet Annette Bening, whom he would marry and remains so to this day.

Beatty was beginning to age into a different actor when the *Crimson Tide* producers courted him, a member of the old guard now rather than the dashing lead. It was not agreeing with him. The notoriously fickle star was hesitant to commit to the Ramsey role. Simpson and Bruckheimer continued to press him, but they also set up a backup plan in case Beatty declined: Al Pacino, recent Oscar winner for *Scent of a Woman*.[2]

With Beatty and Al Pacino circling the project, interest in the other characters picked up steam. Brad Pitt lobbied to play Hunter, and was an early favorite to take the role; once Beatty and Pacino both shuffled their feet too long, however, all three actors were scrapped in the hopes that square one would actually help everything stay on schedule. Undeterred from this casting setback, Scott and his team simply reached out to the next legendary actor in line; they pitched the movie to Gene Hackman.

Of all the possible Oscar winners Simpson and Bruckheimer approached for the Ramsey role, Gene Hackman's filmography was arguably most impressive. After winning a Best Actor Oscar in the spring of 1972 for *The French Connection*, Hackman was a ubiquitous presence in great films the rest of the decade, showing a surprising range in his performances. He played big in *The Poseidon Adventure* and bruising in *Scarecrow*; he withered and sunk inward in Francis Ford Coppola's paranoia-fueled thriller *The Conversation* and Arthur Penn's sweat-soaked noir *Night Moves*; he showed off his comic chops both as an uncredited scene stealer in Mel Brooks' *Young Frankenstein*, and as the hammy comic-book villain Lex Luthor in Richard Donner's big-screen adaptation of *Superman*.

Hackman remained busy in the 1980s, though he struggled to find a hit for a few years. War dramas like *Under Fire* and *Uncommon Valor* missed their mark, and a few more dramas came and went before Hackman reestablished his prominence in 1986, playing coach Norman Dale in the iconic basketball drama *Hoosiers*. From there, Hackman had his hits (*No Way Out*, *Mississippi Burning*), and his misses (*The Package*, *Loose Cannons*). In 1993, his standing as a legend of cinema was forever cemented when he won Best Supporting Actor for playing the sadistic sheriff Little Bill Daggett in Clint Eastwood's melancholy western masterpiece *Unforgiven*. The win came more than two decades after he received his first Oscar for *The French Connection*.

Hackman seemed like a natural fit as Captain Ramsey, a gruff and outwardly confident man, so much so that the initial plan to bring in either Warren Beatty or Al Pacino is difficult to even imagine now. Hackman accepted the role, and casting turned their attention to Lieutenant Commander Hunter, Ramsey's adversary. Scott had a handful of eager young actors wanting to take the role opposite Hackman, including Val Kilmer—never too far on the outskirts of a Tony Scott film—and Andy Garcia. Simpson and Bruckheimer had a different idea; they wanted Denzel Washington.

Washington was much like Gene Hackman had been in the mid–1970s, a superstar and a brilliant actor in the middle of his first hot streak, except he had matinee-idol handsomeness and a million-dollar smile to accompany his acting chops. Washington had unmatched magnetic energy. After winning Best Supporting Actor in 1990 for *Glory*, Washington would go on to earn another Oscar nomination for Spike Lee's 1992 biopic, *Malcolm X*; he had just recently starred in *Philadelphia* opposite Oscar winner Tom Hanks, and alongside Julia Roberts in Alan J. Pakula's adaptation of John Grisham's *The Pelican Brief* when Simpson and Bruckheimer hired him to play Hunter.

Denzel Washington was not terribly excited about having Quentin Tarantino on the payroll, however. The actor took exception to some of the dialogue Tarantino added to the screenplay, citing its racist leanings, something Washington had taken issue with in the writer's first two films; both

Reservoir Dogs and *Pulp Fiction* freely used the "N" word in several scenes, though the additions he made to *Crimson Tide* did not.

Whatever the case, Washington didn't appreciate it, and when Tarantino visited the set the actor confronted him in front of the cast and crew. Tarantino sheepishly tried to move their heated conversation into a more private section of the set, but Washington was not interested in that. Eventually, the argument died down and Washington returned to work, but he would hold a grudge for seven years before finally reaching out and burying the hatchet with the director.[3]

With the two leads set, casting now needed to fill in the periphery with unique and memorable faces. Thanks to the extensive casting needs, *Crimson Tide* soon became, unbeknownst to anyone at the time, a breeding ground for young new talent and future superstars in Hollywood. It was another Tony Scott casting coup.

Scott brought James Gandolfini over with him from *True Romance*. The two had seemed to get along well—as most people did with Tony Scott on his sets—and Gandolfini was the sort of unforgettable face that would stand out in the mass of khaki-clad machismo filling the background behind Hackman and Washington. Viggo Mortensen, not yet a star, snagged a pivotal supporting role, and character actors like George Dzundza and Matt Craven were given meatier parts than usual. Steve Zahn landed a brief supporting

(From left) Matt Craven, Tony Scott, and Denzel Washington work through a scene on the set of *Crimson Tide* (Hollywood Pictures, 1995).

performance, and a young actor named Ryan Phillippe would appear in his first on-screen role.

To shoot the film, Scott reached out to Dariusz Wolski, a Polish-born cinematographer who had done some work for Ridley and Tony's commercial company, RSA. Wolski had also shot a film Tony admired greatly, the 1993 Gary Oldman thriller *Romeo Is Bleeding*. "I did a commercial with [Tony]," Wolski said, "and he said 'I want to talk to you about something else ... have you ever shot a movie on a submarine?' I said 'no,' and he said 'me neither.' We were jumping into very deep waters."

Everyone in charge of production on *Crimson Tide* had just assumed they would get full cooperation from the navy once again. Scott, Simpson, and Bruckheimer developed a strong working relationship with the navy during the *Top Gun* shoot, where the navy were only too willing to lend their support building a propaganda machine around the picture. This time, however, the subject matter was too murky for them to get involved. The entire basis of the film is a disagreement on the rules of engagement while humanity hangs in the balance, followed by a mutiny. The navy objected to the depiction of mutiny aboard a nuclear sub, and refused to assist Scott and his team. They did secure the consultation of Captain Skip Beard, U.S.N., who spent months coaching Hackman, Washington, and the rest of the cast on the way to salute, on the technical jargon, and the general demeanor of submarine crews.

Tony Scott was left scrambling to find a submarine for the exterior shots he wanted. He tried to rent submarines from both the British and French navy, and was unsuccessful. That's when Scott's resourcefulness—and his adventurous streak—kicked in, and he decided to do a bit of high-wire guerrilla filmmaking to capture what would be his only external shot of the Alabama.

Scott and his team traveled to Hawaii, where submarines would regularly depart and dock at the naval bases. He set up in a boat with a camera, and had the second unit crew in a boat and helicopters waiting to shoot the submarine once it hit the open ocean. In order to be prepared, Scott assigned a crewmember to wait outside the base where they could spot the submarine leaving and relay the information back to Scott.

A chaotic scene ensued, as Scott and the boats and helicopters surrounded the sub. The captain of Scott's boat communicated with the submarine, and they ordered Scott to cease filming immediately. However, since Scott and his crew waited to get into open waters, there were no laws prohibiting their presence. The submarine captain veered sharply away from Scott's cameras and began to submerge; it was exactly what Scott had hoped for, and he had his dramatic establishing shot of the USS *Alabama* as it dives beneath the surface.[4]

The rest of the film was far more organized and contained than Scott's rogue adventure in Hawaii. The remainder of the film was set almost entirely inside the submarine, while special effects coordinator Al DiSarrio, Jr., and his team were able to tackle the crucial exterior underwater shots of torpedoes firing and execute a key scene involving an exploding, imploding submarine hit by Alabama's torpedo launch. Using a combination of controllable "dry" models surrounded by smoke and clever lighting, and "wet" models immersed in water where prop torpedo's were launched, the effects team were able to capture a true-to-life kind of submarine explosion that had not been shown on screen in any of the previous submarine films.[5]

Elaborate interior sets were built on a soundstage to accompany the real vessels. A large platform set of the control room was built on a hydraulic machine called a gimbal. The gimbal would tilt and rotate up and down to simulate the submarine surfacing, diving, or sustaining damage from a torpedo. The quarters were cramped, but the set was run just as tightly as the corridors of the submarine; the bigger issue, according to Wolski, was the use of multiple cameras in tight quarters. "Lighting of a certain area affects another area," Wolski said, "so that was really tricky. You just have to invent stuff to deal with it."

Scott and Wolski developed a strong working relationship throughout; any disagreements or fights on set were to serve the greater good of the picture. "His style was very very, how would you say, intense ... he was always pushing visually, pushing action. Every argument we had, or every confrontation about how to do things ... it was never personal. It was all about what was best for the screen. Whatever was good on the screen, that's what mattered ... there was no ego."

He was also not about to bend to the new rules of Hollywood, where smoking was no longer permitted on sets. This would not fly for Scott, who had an almost transcendent love for his cigars. "We came on the [sound] stage, and the stage manager said there was no smoking ... so Tony basically said he is not going to make the movie if he can't smoke ... they hired an extra fire marshal to stand next to him so it was safe."

"But I was a heavy smoker back then," Wolski added, "so I could always cheat a couple of cigarettes behind his back, hiding myself in his cloud of smoke."

Before production ended on *Crimson Tide* Tony Scott married his girlfriend, Donna Wilson, on November 24, 1994. A week later, he officially wrapped production on *Crimson Tide* and hit the editing room with Chris Lebenzon, whom he had worked with on *Top Gun*, *Beverly Hills Cop II*, *Revenge*, and *Days of Thunder*.

On April 7, 1995, Don Simpson and Jerry Bruckheimer introduced American audiences to Michael Bay with *Bad Boys*, and the razor-tongued police pairing of Will Smith and Martin Lawrence. *Bad Boys* was an immediate success and spent two weeks at number one. A month later, Simpson and Bruckheimer were pulling double duty, doing both a victory lap for *Bad Boys* and a promotional tour for *Crimson Tide*, which was set to open May 12 and had with it all the buzz and anticipation of a solid summer blockbuster.

When *Crimson Tide* hit theaters, it captured the top spot with $18.6 million. Reviews were some of the best of Scott's career. At *Entertainment Weekly*, Owen Gleiberman called it "the kind of sumptuously exciting undersea thriller that moves forward in quick, propulsive ways."[6] Most praises of the film revolved around the moral implications of the central conflict, and the way Scott, Washington, and Hackman keep a tight grip on the tension filling the entire picture. It felt like the perfect balance of Scott's action aesthetic and a smart screenplay.

Crimson Tide held strong, falling to second place in its second weekend only to see a brief resurgence in ticket sales over the subsequent Memorial Day weekend. It ended its nine-week run with $91.4 million against an estimated $53 million budget. Adjusted for 2018 sales, the film sits at a robust $192.9 million, a sizeable hit no matter the decade.[7] In the meantime, *Bad Boys* bowed out of theaters with almost $69 million against a $19 million budget, a solid enough hit to spawn a massive blockbuster sequel in 2003.

Don Simpson and Jerry Bruckheimer were now, unequivocally, the most powerful producing team in Hollywood. As for Tony Scott, he only continued

Denzel Washington and Tony Scott take a break on the set of *Crimson Tide* (Hollywood Pictures, 1995).

to showcase his specific set of skills, his ability to capture kinetic action with a stylistic flair, and for the studios his ability to shoot a film on a tight schedule no matter the setbacks was arguably the biggest tool in his belt. Scott was becoming more than an action director; he was becoming a brand.

Crimson Tide is a story of men pushing back against other men, an arm-wrestling match suspended in midair, never moving one way or another. It is a tense situation aboard the USS *Alabama*, perfectly conveyed by two masters at the very top of their game. The plot machinations of Crimson Tide have long since receded from the collective memory; what remains is the allure of an intellectual showdown between Gene Hackman and Denzel Washington.

This is a film that exists for, above all else, these two Alphas in the industry to stand face to face, and debate the very nature of war as inherent human nature. The gears of the plot are secondary. This is Scott's most cerebral action thriller, a film less concerned with bombast and more focused on verbal sparring.

"There's a really beautiful story," Dariusz Wolski said of the shoot. "We were heading to Catalina to shoot this open scene (on top of a submarine bridge and deck set) where they are smoking cigars on the top of the bridge … there was a bit of a concern about the swell, and the multiple cameras. Finally we show up, we load up everything, put the cameras, four cameras, dolly tracks, etcetera … the sun gets really low, beautiful. We rolled four and a half pages with four cameras for literally an hour and a half in the perfect light…. Everyone is completely high on oxygen because we are liking the fresh air. We haven't seen the daylight for four weeks."

They managed to get through the shot, and the crew was overjoyed with the beauty of the scene. "It's the most exhilarating experience ever," Wolski said, "having done a great scene, everything looks great. We come to shore, and Tony keeps twitching, and he says 'fuck.'" Wolski was confused by the response, and asked Tony what was wrong, because the shoot had gone so perfectly. "He goes 'I'm not sure, that's just too easy.'"

"That's the most beautiful way to describe him."

13

The Simpson Tragedy

Part of what made Don Simpson and Jerry Bruckheimer work so well together were their opposing personalities and radically different approaches to filmmaking, and to the industry altogether. Jerry Bruckheimer was always the technician, the critical thinker, and the genius marketer on the back end; Don Simpson was the free-spirited creative mind of the two, with more influence on storytelling and aesthetics. At the same time, Simpson always felt like a Hollywood outsider, and he leaned into that rogue mentality in work and in life.

The personality differences weren't limited to their working relationship. Bruckheimer never fell into the party scene of Southern California in the 1980s, a world of cocaine and excess and sexual deviancy that had a tendency to ruin lives and careers from time to time. Rumors abounded of Simpson's sexual proclivities, and his addiction to the darker avenues of human satiation, a man consumed by the late-night seediness permeating Hollywood. Don Simpson fully embraced this hedonistic scene from the beginning, when he first made his way down to California from Alaska, and became a tragic cautionary tale early in 1996.

In 1995, when Simpson and Bruckheimer began filming *The Rock*, Michael Bay's second film with the producing pair, an action blockbuster set on Alcatraz Island, Don Simpson's reputation as a hard-partying drug abuser had started to affect every facet of the producer's life and career, just as it had done more than a decade earlier when he was fired from Paramount. It was an open secret that Simpson was spiraling out of control. Simpson would miss production meetings, he would reject detoxification and rehabilitation programs, and he continuously ignored the advice of friends to seek help. On top of the drug abuse, Simpson was struggling with his own body image, trying crash diets and undergoing numerous plastic surgeries in order to help him battle his fluctuating weight. It was a problem he perpetually fought against, even during his most intense times of drug abuse.

If the narcotics and the troubling lack of self worth weren't enough to pollute Simpson's ability to function as an elite Hollywood producer, he was also close friends with legendary tabloid fodder, Hollywood Madame Heidi Fleiss, and had a penchant for prostitutes that some feared was putting his life in danger almost nightly.

Jerry Bruckheimer was out of answers for Simpson's dangerous and erratic behavior by the time *The Rock* began pre-production in the summer of 1995, and in August the partnership would suffer a fatal blow in a scene that seems pulled directly out of a salacious Los Angeles film noir.

While Simpson rejected detox inpatient drug-rehabilitation programs, he hired a personal physician, Dr. Stephen W. Ammerman, to allegedly help him shake his drug addiction. The problem was, however, Dr. Ammerman had a history of drug abuse and was seen by many in Simpson's orbit to be nothing more than a freeloader looking for an easy avenue to high-end narcotics. This theory proved to be true on August 15, 1995, when Dr. Ammerman was found floating in Simpson's pool, dead of an overdose.

Ammerman's death was the final straw for Bruckheimer; the two men agreed to end their partnership once production on *The Rock* was wrapped; they announced the breakup in December, midway through the shoot. Though they stayed cordial with one another, and Bruckheimer remained supportive of Simpson's difficult struggle to get sober, their partnership was over and the greatest pair of producers to come along in the modern era of Hollywood was set adrift on their different paths.

Don Simpson (left) with Jerry Bruckheimer on the set of *Crimson Tide* (Hollywood Pictures, 1995).

The struggle would destroy Don Simpson almost immediately. In the weeks after the public divorce, friends of Simpson were worried as his weight spiked and he was clearly battling severe depression. Filmmaker and friend James Toback was the last person to speak to Simpson on the phone, the night before his death. On January 19, exactly a month after the professional split with Jerry Bruckheimer, 52-year-old Don Simpson was found dead on the bathroom floor of his Hollywood hills home.[1]

The results of Simpson's autopsy confirmed what everyone already knew, that the producer had died of a drug overdose. Simpson's system was packed with prescription medications, antidepressants, cocaine, morphine, and Valium.[2] Simpson's drug habit had reached as much as $60,000 price tag per month at the time of his death.

No matter what Jerry Bruckheimer, or Tony Scott, or anyone in Don Simpson's life at the time, had expected given Simpson's excessive lifestyle, the news was still a crushing blow. Even in the throes of his fatal addiction, Don Simpson had friends, and he was a friend to so many in the industry. It may have shaken the foundations of the hedonistic Hollywood lifestyle, but only temporarily. Business had to keep moving, and specifically for Jerry Bruckheimer the business of making mega-budget action blockbusters was moving at an incredibly accelerated speed in the late 1990s. Bruckheimer carried on the mantle he and Simpson had built over the last dozen years plus of success, and he parlayed it into an even stronger second act.

14

The Fan and Subverting Hero Worship

Tony Scott had a chance to direct *The Rock*, but he decided that in the successful wake of *Crimson Tide* was the perfect opportunity to explore a story involving darkness and violence, his first passion as a filmmaker. When news of Don Simpson's passing found Scott, he had recently shot a Brazilian advertisement for ice cream starring none other than Sharon Stone, and he was in the final few weeks of production on his latest film, a thriller set against the backdrop of professional baseball. The subject matter was curious for Scott, who was not particularly familiar with baseball and didn't have any relevant experience as a fan of the sport; however, Scott's desire to dive headfirst into a dark thriller shortly after filling up multiplexes with another Simpson/Bruckheimer vehicle was a pattern the director had settled into over the last decade. For whatever reason, he settled on *The Fan*.

Top Gun and *Beverly Hills Cop II* pushed Scott towards *Revenge*. From the mediocre success of *Days of Thunder*, Scott went smaller and darker once again with *The Last Boy Scout* and *True Romance*; *Crimson Tide* was another blockbuster for the trio, so it felt only natural for Scott to want to dive headfirst into a threatening story of psychosis and obsession run amok. Nevertheless, the baseball angle would prove to be a hindrance.

Peter Abrahams had already authored an impressive catalogue of airport paperback thrillers when he published *The Fan* in 1995. Like the bulk of Abrahams' work, *The Fan* was well received critically and it found its way into the right hands in Hollywood. The book told the story of Gil Renard, a knife salesman whose personal and professional life is collapsing around him on all sides. He finds solace in rooting for his favorite White Sox player, a superstar free agent signee named Bobby Rayburn. Eventually, Gil loses his grip on reality, and decides *he* is the one who can fix the hitting slump in which Rayburn finds himself. His method proves murderous.

Producer Wendy Finerman, a young industry professional fresh off the monumental success of *Forrest Gump*—which took home six Oscars in March of 1995, including a gold Best Picture statue for Finerman—knew there was obvious cinematic merit in Abrahams' novel. She hired a television writer named Phoef Sutton, whom she had been working with on another project at the time, to adapt the book into a screenplay.

Sutton, who worked on two different Bob Newhart sitcoms and twenty-one episodes of *Cheers* in the '80s and '90s, had recently adapted the Cornell Woolrich novel *Mrs. Winterbourne* for the screen when he was hired to adapt *The Fan*. "[Finerman] showed me the book (it hadn't been published yet) and asked me if I'd be interested in adapting it. As I'm a huge baseball fan, I leapt at the chance. Also, since I'd mainly done comedy up to that point, I thought it would be a good change of pace."

Sutton reached out to legendary Baltimore Orioles shortstop, iron man Cal Ripken, Jr., to help him with his research.[1] Most of the questions from Sutton involved the nature of his celebrity—there was arguably no bigger professional baseball player at the time—and how he handled the public with his fans and his own children. Ripken's input proved invaluable in the early drafting days.

The net was cast far and wide for Gil Renard. Jack Nicholson flirted with the project before ultimately passing on it; Al Pacino was considered for the

Wendy Finerman and Tony Scott have a laugh on the set of *The Fan* **(TriStar Pictures, 1996)**

role, but not for long. Brad Pitt, who continued to push for another chance to work with Scott, wanted to play Gil despite being offered the role of Bobby Rayburn. He got neither part. The script eventually found its way to Robert De Niro, who jumped at the opportunity to play another complicated psychopath.

Robert De Niro had his most recent Martin Scorsese collaboration, the Las Vegas gangster epic *Casino*, and his first (and to this day, only) film with Michael Mann, the sprawling Los Angeles crime drama *Heat*, both due out in the fall of 1995 within weeks of each other. De Niro was still on top of his game in the mid-1990s, having recently starred in *This Boys Life*, the underrated coming-of-age gangster fable *A Bronx Tale* (which he also directed), and Kenneth Branagh's adaptation of *Frankenstein* in the years leading up to the one-two punch of headlining films from Martin Scorsese and Michael Mann at virtually the same time. He may have been spent when he agreed to play Gil Renard, but De Niro never let on during his legendary preparation process.

In De Niro, Tony Scott met his match as far as homework was concerned. Much like Scott's obsessive early-morning storyboarding sessions and insatiable bloodlust for detail and authenticity in every frame of each one of his films, so was De Niro's approach to playing even the most unhinged characters. Like Gil Renard. Scott and De Niro combed through Sutton's screenplay and accumulated pages of notes for his character; De Niro interviewed police officers and stalking experts, and he researched serial killers and infamous celebrity stalkers; he interviewed a knife salesman, and he tapped into the collection of madmen he had played in his own career to try to bring something compelling to the character.

Another person who did not get the Gil Renard part, despite lobbying for the role, was Wesley Snipes. In the decade preceding, Snipes had amassed a mixed bag of great films, iconic roles, and flat, forgettable action movies. For every brilliant turn in *New Jack City* or *White Men Can't Jump*, Snipes had forgettable police potboilers like *Rising Sun* or *Boiling Point*. Snipes had *Money Train*, his second collaboration with Woody Harrelson—and a pale comparison to the first collaboration with *White Men Can't Jump*—releasing on November 22, 1995, the same weekend as De Niro's *Casino*, when he was hired to play superstar slugger Bobby Rayburn.

Cal Ripken was so beneficial to Pheof Sutton, he was brought in to serve as the film's primary consultant. That meant meeting with the actors, and even serving as Wesley Snipes' hitting coach. His meeting with Robert De Niro was a three-hour lunch where the two discussed baseball in great detail. It was research for De Niro, and it was all a little strange for Ripken because the method actor was in the middle of researching obsessive fans and was listening to tapes of John Bardo.

Robert John Bardo is one of the most infamous celebrity stalkers in American history. After growing up in a military family that moved frequently, Bardo exhibited signs of obsessive stalker tendencies in his teens before fixating on a young television and burgeoning film actress named Rebecca Schaeffer. Bardo tracked down Schaeffer through investigative techniques that were much looser in the late 1980s. On July 18, 1989, John Bardo knocked on Rebecca Schaeffer's front door and shot her dead; he was sentenced to life without parole in a California penitentiary. It was one of many celebrity stalkers De Niro researched during pre-production.

Sutton had other actors in mind for the cast, though he had no say in the end. "I wrote it with specific actors in mind," he said, "though they turned out to be a very different from the actual cast. Denzel Washington for the baseball player and Johnny Depp for the fan. The idea we had for the baseball player was that he be someone who has always been a 'Golden Boy,' who has never faced any hardships in his life before this. Snipes seemed like he'd fought his way up from the streets. Not the same thing at all."

The two biggest supporting roles were Rayburn's agent, Manny, and Jewel Stern, an antagonistic sports radio talk show host always bouncing around the periphery of the main action. Ellen Barkin, who had seen her fair share of success and failure over her then seventeen-year career, was hired to play Jewel.

Barkin ascended from un-credited walk on parts in TV movies in her early 20s, to playing the first-billed female character in Barry Levinson's male-centric drama *Diner*, which then led to a string of supporting roles in dramas like *Tender Mercies* and genre films like *The Adventures of Buckaroo Bonzai Across the 8th Dimension*. In the sweat-soaked 1986 crime thriller *The Big Easy*, co-starring Dennis Quaid, Barkin found the perfect femme fatale niche that she would embrace for the next several years. Mary Lambert's *Siesta* was a similar role, but in 1989 Barkin captured the very essence of the "dangerous woman" archetype as Helen Cruger, a possible serial killer who seduces Al Pacino's lonely New York detective in *Sea of Love*.

While *Sea of Love* was not an earth-shattering hit, it definitely boosted Barkin's visibility in Hollywood. Never one to be painted into a performative corner, Barkin swung and missed at a pair of comedies—*Switch* and *Man Trouble*—before landing the role as Caroline, the mother to an adolescent Leonardo DiCaprio in the hard-edged family drama *This Boy's Life*. Along with Barkin and DiCaprio, the film co-starred Robert De Niro as an overbearing and increasingly dangerous stepfather. *This Boy's Life* was critically well received, and is an important building block in the early evolution of Leonardo DiCaprio, one of Hollywood's last-remaining movie stars.

Fast forward two years and Ellen Barkin would again find herself sharing the screen with Robert De Niro. This time, however, practically all of their interactions would take place over the phone, as De Niro's increasingly unstable Gil Renard uses Jewel Stern's radio show to communicate with Bobby Rayburn.

Finding the right actor to play Manny was tricky; the character had to be slimy, but likeable enough to not turn off the audience entirely. John Leguizamo, who had just graduated from stand-up comedian and bit player in movies like *Out for Justice* and *Regarding Henry* to rising funnyman and legitimate character actor, made sense for the role. Leguizamo portrayed Benny Blanco, the arrogant and careless young gangster in Brian De Palma's brilliant 1993 gangster picture *Carlito's Way*, with a mixture of cocksure menace and carelessness that could easily transfer over to this stereotypical, bloodsucking sports agent.

To play Bobby Rayburn's rival on the San Francisco Giants, Scott and casting director Ellen Lewis hired a burgeoning young character actor named Benicio Del Toro. Some of the other teammates were actors; some were actual baseball players, like John Kruk, the Chicago White Sox power-hitting first baseman in 1995.

Kruk was suspicious of Tony Scott's baseball acumen from the get go. Scott encouraged foul language for "authenticity" purposes, and he asked Kruk—a relatively immobile, rotund left-handed fielder playing first base—if he could play shortstop, which made little sense in the context of actual baseball. Nevertheless, Kruk went along with the shoot and said his lines, even though most of them wound up on the cutting room floor in the end.[2]

Scott brought along Dariusz Wolski from *Crimson Tide* set to shoot *The Fan*, which would be an entirely different experience from the tight submarine sets. Now, the canvas was the entire city of San Francisco, and a few scenes on stages in Los Angeles. "The script was in progress," Wolski said, "constantly evolving, and we worked very long hours."

Before production began on *The Fan*, Phoef Sutton was fired.

"I wrote the first draft of the script," Sutton said. "They hired Tony Scott, Robert De Niro and Wesley Snipes off that version. Once Tony was hired I was immediately replaced as writer. That's the way it goes in this business. I didn't meet Tony until just before production." Frank Darabont, fresh off his Academy Award– nominated film *The Shawshank Redemption*, was hired to come in and do re-writes.

Even though he was replaced, Sutton was then brought *back* in to do rewrites on Darabont's work. "After the Darabont rewrite, I was asked to do production rewrites on Darabont's draft. This was slightly confusing for me, since many of the characters and attitudes had been changed from my version, but I did my best."

Aside from the indecisiveness with the micro aspects of the screenplay, the shoot ran relatively smooth—as Tony Scott's productions typically did—save for one brief run in with the San Francisco Police Department.

It was near the end of filming, when Scott and the cast and crew were shooting outside Coop's (Charles Hallahan) office, next to a set of train tracks for San Francisco's railway system. A portion of the crew was on the tracks, which caught the attention of a police officer that happened to be passing by and knew nothing about the filming. He attempted to disrupt the shoot, and after a brief back and forth between the officer and a now incensed Robert De Niro, De Niro hopped in the Humvee that Gil drives in the scene and sped around the police officer, stopping feet from the train tracks and stomping away to his trailer.

The officer wrote De Niro a citation for reckless driving; De Niro's stunt double, Joseph Manuella, came out of the trailer and signed the ticket.[3]

"There was something about Tony and his incredible respect for Bob De Niro," said Wolski. "He was in complete awe of him, and I think they really got along very well."

"I think," Wolski said, "[*The Fan*] was one of the hardest movies I've done. The script, the schedule, changing locations ... we re-routed traffic on the freeway once to the point where the chief of police who was [Scott's] buddy came over and said 'what the hell are you doing? It's rush hour.'" Tony explained to the chief that the lighting was right, and it must be done. "He was a man who always got away with a lot, he just pushed so hard and always got away with it."

Major League Baseball did not get along well with *The Fan* when they saw what Scott had done with the material. Officials with the league read an early draft of Sutton's script and approved use of the San Franisco Giants logo, uniforms, and facilities. In between that first draft and the cut they screened in July of 1996, Tony Scott sank his teeth into the story and brought the darkness to the forefront. The result was a film amped up with more violence and more objectionable dialogue than what had been conveyed in the initial script; MLB properties demanded cuts be made to tone down both the bloodshed and the foul language.

Scott agreed and he and his editors, Claire Simpson and Christian Wagner, nipped and tucked a few scenes to soften the edges. It was screened for officials again, and regardless of whether or not they objected to the finished product, they had very little in the means of recourse.

Unfortunately Major League Baseball's objections to *The Fan* were inconsequential. Test screenings were falling flat, and when the film hit theaters on August 16, 1996, a virtual wasteland for films in which studios have little to no confidence, critical reception was tepid at best. Critics were unsure how to take Scott's film, and were put off by the speed in which the story flies off the rails into a bizarre sort of horror film. David Ansen of *Newsweek* said, for instance, "Scott ... has no patience for, nor interest in, reality (or baseball, for that matter)."

On top of the critics dismissing the film, audiences did not seem particularly interested in a baseball thriller. The combination of a baseball movie in August—commonly referred to as "the dog days" of the baseball season, when fans and players slog through the heat anxiously awaiting cooler temperatures and (hopefully) playoff games—and the 1994 lockout that ended the baseball season still fresh in everyone's memory most definitely added insult to injury.

The Fan opened in fourth place with an anemic $6.3 million. The bottom fell out almost immediately, as in the second week ticket sales dropped almost fifty percent. After three weeks, *The Fan* was done at the domestic box office with a dismal final number: $18.6 million against an estimated $55 million budget.[4]

Zooming out on the film, the sport of baseball had just recently come out of a strike-shortened season in 1994, souring fans. Baseball was still struggling for popularity in America in 1996, as professional football began diverting attention to their league. In hindsight, it may not have been the best time for a baseball-themed thriller; compounded with the massive flaws and bad reviews, *The Fan* stumbled before ever getting out of the batter's box.

Sutton remembers the lukewarm reception at the premiere. "I was appalled," Sutton said of the final cut. "I recognized very few scenes and lines from my script. What's more, the audience reaction was not very good. Everyone left the theater rather depressed."

"I think the failure of the movie," added Wolski, "was that Tony was a little bit ignorant about the baseball game. It's such an iconic thing for Americans, and that's where he got caught.... I think he was much more preoccupied with the whole psychology of the stalker, and the baseball was just an excuse for that."

The pattern continued for Scott. His collaborations with Don Simpson and Jerry Bruckheimer, however canned and predetermined they may have been, were the hits that sustained him to this point in his career. Any time he stepped outside the system to make dark passion projects like *Revenge*, or a cutting-edge genre mash-ups like *True Romance*, the box-office numbers were not there. The only outlier to this point was *The Last Boy Scout*, and even that success paled in comparison to what Scott had accomplished with Simpson and Bruckheimer.

Time has since been kind to those idiosyncratic departures in Tony Scott's career; they carry the director's spirit in them, and for all their flaws (some more than others), they have infinitely more to say about their creator than something like *Beverly Hills Cop II* or *Days of Thunder*. Even *The Fan*, behind its obvious warts and out-of-control final act, is a more interesting examination of the filmmaker than the surface-level aesthetics he introduced to the world in *Top Gun*.

Tony Scott and his crew (unnamed) prep for a scene on *The Fan* (TriStar Pictures, 1996).

The Fan will never be reclassified, in the court of public opinion, as a misunderstood classic of the thriller genre. It's not one of the better films of the 1990s, it is not anywhere near the top of Robert De Niro's storied career, and it may very well be the answer least given if someone were tasked with naming all the films of Tony Scott's career. Its practically nonexistent box office all but doomed *The Fan* to disappear forever, and the film has clearly been left in the ditch of the decade as a failure underserving of reappraisal.

Yes, there are issues with *The Fan*, that is certain. There are editing flubs and inconsistencies, a somewhat shameless inclusion of the Nine Inch Nails song "Closer" to tie itself as closely as possible to David Fincher's 1995 serial-killer blockbuster *Se7en*, and the finale loses control of the story, devolving into an insanely overwrought showdown in Candlestick Park in the middle of distractingly torrential rain that is obviously coming from a machine. But at the heart of *The Fan*, Tony Scott and Phoef Sutton are subverting classical notions of hero worship, and in the process, indicting celebrity. It is a subversion told with characters in the most extreme circumstances, on intensely opposing ends of the social spectrum; it's exactly why Scott proves to be a perfect match for the material, despite the fact he knew very little about baseball.

14. The Fan *and Subverting Hero Worship*

The Fan is not a baseball movie, per se, but a thriller matching a damaged, working-class stiff suffering from fits of violent psychosis and self-aggrandizing delusions up against an aloof, disenfranchised baseball superstar with all the money in the world and barely enough heart and soul to put on a good face visiting sick children in the hospital. Scott does not immediately condemn Gil to the role of evil psychopath for the audience to root against; he allows Gil to earn sympathy, however fleeting, in the early scenes as he tries to juggle his dying career and his earnest son in terribly inept and dangerous ways. Gil is clearly unstable, but not so openly psychotic in the first half. Scott paints Gil as a poor sap and a man seething with anger as the nostalgia of his little league years fades under the weight of responsibilities for which he was never mentally prepared.

As for Bobby Rayburn, he is not simply a victim of Gil's violent breakdown. Before sympathy falls entirely into his corner throughout the second half of the picture, Rayburn's personality is painted in great detail. The story bounces from Gil's thread to Bobby's, where we see him and his agent, Manny, exhibiting cold, selfish behavior. Rayburn has little time for charity, he has no friends on the team from the beginning, and he exhibits minimal empathy for the people in his life outside of his son.

Once Gil comes fully unhinged, he loses all sympathetic beats and becomes nothing more than a knife-wielding madman to punch up the third act. Bobby Rayburn is now our hero, though we have been loaded with enough character pathos from both sides of the story to come to this finale with mixed emotions. There is no sympathy for Gil, but there is always pity. There is no wish for Bobby's son to die, but there is also a miasma of the athlete's unpleasant personality lingering over the final confrontation.

There is a simpler version of *The Fan* here, a version that most audiences took away from the film in 1996: villainous crazy person terrorizes heroic baseball player. But sometimes films need second glances. Seen through a new lens, with more of an understanding of mental illness and the troubling nature of celebrity culture coloring perception, *The Fan* works on a more elevated and introspective level than most of the "obsession thrillers" that came out in the late 1990s, the heyday of the subgenre.

15

Enemy of the State

Once again, Tony Scott saw one of his darker, more cynically-charged pictures flounder at the box office. Darkness was his passion when it came to his filmmaking, but no matter how brilliant or challenging (or occasionally poor) they may be, these movies weren't connecting with audiences—at least upon initial release. *The Hunger, Revenge,* and especially *True Romance* have seen sustained cultural relevance in certain circles. *The Fan*, however, has not yet seen any signs of resurgence, and likely will never find its retroactive moment in the sun.

But Tony Scott's collaborations with Jerry Bruckheimer worked on an absolute, objective level. And as the pattern of Scott's career continued, Jerry Bruckheimer just so happened to be gearing up for his first film as a solo producer in the wake of Don Simpson's tragic passing.

Jerry Bruckheimer Films and Touchstone Pictures, a studio label under the Walt Disney umbrella, were joining forces for the foreseeable future. The producer had hired an art director turned burgeoning writer/director named David Marconi to write a high-tech suspense thriller based on an idea Bruckheimer and Don Simpson had conjured up in the early 1990s when they were brainstorming. The paranoia-fueled thriller would involve the NSA terrorizing a nebbish everyman, and serve as a newly-fashioned homage to the government thrillers of the 1970s like *The Parallax View*, or *Marathon Man*, or *Three Days of the Condor*.

Bruckheimer sent the first draft of *Enemy of the State* to Tony Scott, who initially declined. The story did not grab him the way he wanted; the story was there, and it could be good, it just needed some punching up. Around the same time, Gene Hackman was rejecting the first draft of the script for many of the same reasons as Scott; Jerry Bruckheimer knew he made perfect sense as Brill, the shadowy, older, paranoid ex–NSA operative. The role was not a far cry from Hackman's 1974 Francis Ford Coppola classic *The Conversation*, where he played a deeply paranoid surveillance expert named Harry Caul—it's easy, in fact, to consider this film a continuation of Harry Caul in

Tony Scott (left) and Will Smith share notes on the set of *Enemy of the State* (Touchstone Pictures, 1998).

The Conversation. But Hackman's fit for the role would not matter if Bruckheimer couldn't get the screenplay polished.

He brought in Aaron Sorkin, a hot young writer who had recently found notoriety with his screenplay for the 1992 Rob Reiner military courtroom drama *A Few Good Men*, which he originally wrote for the stage and later for the screen. Sorkin penned the Alec Baldwin/Nicole Kidman thriller *Malice* in 1993, and the Michael Douglas/Annette Bening drama *The American President* two years later. The outspoken liberal renegade, a self-described "physical" writer with a penchant for telling stories dense with dialogue and razor sharp wit, also had a couple of television dramas in the works—*Sports Night* and *The West Wing*—around the time he was brought in to help Marconi's screenplay. And he wasn't the only up-and-coming screenwriter who was commissioned for input.

Sorkin worked for two weeks on the screenplay, fleshing out the characters and sharpening the dialogue. With his flourishes added, Bruckheimer went back to both Hackman and Scott, who were already eager to work with each other again after *Crimson Tide*, as long as the script was right. It was, and both men agreed to tackle the film. Tony Gilroy, fresh off the success of *The Devil's Advocate*, punched up the paranoia, and script doctor Henry Bean, who had written the two terrific thrillers *Internal Affairs* and *Deep Cover*, added a few finishing touches.

To play Robert Clayton Dean, the mild-mannered attorney swept up in a politically charged murder plot involving the NSA and satellite surveillance,

Scott and Bruckheimer both felt Will Smith was a perfect fit, even if the mild-mannered lawyer character was playing against type. By 1997, Smith had cemented himself as the new blockbuster superstar with the trifecta of *Bad Boys*, *Independence Day*, and *Men in Black* all raking in money hand over fist. Smith was ready to explore a darker side of his traditionally heroic characters, and he jumped at the chance to star alongside the legend, Gene Hackman.

From there, Scott had to find the two women in Dean's personal life, his wife and his former lover with whom he had an affair and who is now a crucial business contact. Regina King, fresh off her breakout role as Cuba Gooding, Jr.'s headstrong wife in *Jerry Maguire*, was the perfect strong personality to play the wife, Carla. "She wore the pants in the relationship," according to Scott. For Rachel, Scott wanted a more free-spirited, exotic look. He had wanted to work with Lisa Bonet on a project for a decade, ever since he saw her as Epiphany Proudfoot in Alan Parker's supernatural thriller, *Angel Heart* a decade earlier. She was the perfect contrast to Regina King.

To play the film's central villain, the sneering, murderous head of the NSA Thomas Reynolds, Scott saw a perfect juxtaposition for Gene Hackman's character in fellow Oscar winner Jon Voight. Following his Best Actor win for 1978's Vietnam drama *Coming Home*, Voight churned out dozens of films and television appearances over the next two decades. By 1997, he had transitioned into a sturdy genre foil, playing the villain in Brian De Palma's adaptation of *Mission: Impossible* in 1996, and the dastardly riverboat captain Paul Serone in the 1997 B-movie horror classic, *Anaconda*. Voight represented a version of Hackman's Brill character, if Brill had never turned his back on the misdeeds of the NSA.[1]

The bulk of the supporting cast, beyond the central characters, were NSA employees, bespectacled satellite gurus in vans and field officers chasing down Smith's character. After touring both the NSA and CIA, Scott realized these high-level operatives were not stodgy elder statesman, but young Ivy League professionals fresh out of the fraternity house. It redirected the casting, and it's what brought in the youthful likes of Barry Pepper, Seth Green, Jamie Kennedy Scott Caan, Jake Busey, and Jack Black, whom Scott had worked with briefly on *True Romance* and *The Fan*.[2] Once again, Tony Scott was filling his movie with faces that would become ubiquitous in years to come.

The screenplay was operable, but it still needed more technical polish in certain areas, and it needed a stable of reliable advisors. *Enemy of The State* was packed with surveillance jargon and the most advanced technological material on the market, as well as tactical military and police field techniques; Scott and Bruckheimer wanted authenticity as much as possible. Even though the story was compelling, the details of the tech processes on display were equally as important. They hired Steve Uhrig and Marty Kaiser, two surveillance experts for the CIA, to fill in the details of camera and audio technology. For Jake Busey, Scott Caan, and Barry Pepper, who play NSA field agents pursuing Smith on foot for the bulk of the film, Scott and Bruckheimer hired retired Navy SEAL Harry Humphries to make sure the actors were moving properly and were handling their weapons in a convincing fashion.

The film is set in and around Washington, D.C., and Georgetown, but Scott and his location scouts found valuable sets in nearby Baltimore, including an underground waterway they used as a tunnel, and the coalfields where Dean and Brill try to escape the pursuing NSA agents.

Production wrapped on April 6, 1998, and sights were set on a November 20 release date. Like all of Scott's shoots (save for *The Last Boy Scout*), filming moved quickly, efficiently, and the mood on the set was overwhelmingly positive. And, like all of Scott's films, the director handed off thousands of feet of footage to his longtime editing partner, Chris Lebenzon, who had worked with Scott on five of his previous films. The reels were eventually pared down to a taut, fluid action thriller checking in at just a shade over two hours long.

Armed with the star power of Will Smith, the legendary aura of both Gene Hackman and Jon Voight, and the clout of the Tony Scott/Jerry Bruckheimer portfolio, *Enemy of the State* opened to generally positive reviews and found that adult demographic as the holidays neared. The first weekend it collected $20 million, not enough to beat Nickelodeon Studios and their *Rugrats Movie*, which took the number one spot with $27.3 million. Animation always wins.

But *Enemy of the State* had legs. The second weekend dip in ticket sales was only nine percent, a monumental achievement (for context, *The Rugrats Movie* ticket sales dipped 23 percent, which is still a strong decline but much closer to average) as it made another $18.1 million. It remained in the top ten until the middle of January 1999, and ended its theatrical run with $111.5 million domestic take, and a worldwide tally of $250.6 million. It beat *Crimson Tide* in the end, and was Tony Scott's third-biggest film at the box office.[3]

Enemy of the State was another Bruckheimer collaboration, and another sizeable hit for Tony Scott. It was also, much like *Top Gun* and *True Romance*, at the forefront of a new filmmaking trend. The high-tech surveillance camera work in *Enemy of the State* would permeate popular mid-budget thrillers for years to come, the floating God's eye of satellite spies finding its way into the *Bourne* franchise and the new James Bond model. It was arguably the first time Scott's work—aside from the zeitgeist-capturing potency of *Top Gun*—was properly credited for being ahead of the curve.

This would be the fifth and final collaboration between producer and director, and the five films the men worked on together are also the five most financially successful films in Scott's career. The duo's paths would diverge following *Enemy of the State*; Bruckheimer would dive headfirst into franchise

Will Smith (left) and Gene Hackman in *Enemy of the State* (Touchstone Pictures, 1998).

filmmaking with Disney, and Scott would turn his attention to his family, and to Scott Free Productions.

* * *

In 1980, Tony Scott and his brother, Ridley, founded Percy Main Productions, a small production company named after his father's childhood home. In 1995, the company was rebranded as Scott Free Productions. The first film under their new production company name was Ridley's 1996 sailing adventure *White Squall*, starring Jeff Bridges and showcasing young up-and-coming stars Scott Wolf, Ryan Phillippe (who had just recently had his first role in *Crimson Tide*), and Jeremy Sisto. It had been four years since his last film, the disastrous Christopher Columbus historical epic *1492: The Conquest of Paradise*, which was the longest gap between films in Ridley's career.

White Squall was a flop too, but a well-respected picture that's had solid afterlife on home video. The second film for Scott Free was *The Fan*, which performed just as poorly as *White Squall*. Both films were summarily dismissed, though *The Fan* was probably derided more than *White Squall* in that regard. The third film under the production company, and Ridley's follow up to *White Squall*, would correct course somewhat, boosted by the star power and tabloid magnetism of star Demi Moore, although the box office was still thin.

15. Enemy of the State

G.I. Jane generated a great deal of buzz in 1997; part of it was Demi Moore, who famously shaved her head for the role, and part of it was the inside look of the Navy SEALs' training programs and the heated discussion of gender roles within the ranks of the U.S. Military. While it did hold the number one spot at the box office and generate social discussion for a moment, the final tally fell $2 million short of the $50 million budget. It was a paradox of success and shortcomings. But in three years, Scott Free Productions would have its landmark film, one that would propel them into the future as one of the more substantial production studios in Hollywood: Ridley's *Gladiator*, which would accumulate almost $500 million globally and win five Academy Awards, including Best Picture, in March of 2001.

For Tony Scott's first project as producer, he returned to the place his filmmaking journey began: *The Hunger*. Originally produced for British and Canadian television, Scott's new take on *The Hunger* was an anthology series of salacious, sexually charged late-night horror tales, a *Twilight Zone* for adult viewing. Scott directed the first episode of the series, titled "The Swords," and the first episode of the second season, "Sanctuary." Actor Terrence Stamp hosted the first season, David Bowie the second, and *The Hunger* eventually ran for these two seasons on Showtime before it was canceled.

In 1998, Tony produced *Clay Pigeons*, a small independent crime drama starring Vince Vaughn and Joaquin Phoenix. For a few years, Scott produced, adding the film *Where the Money Is*, and TV movie credits *RKO 281* and *The Last Debate* to his ledger in 2000. That same year, Tony and Donna Wilson Scott welcomed their twin sons, Max and Frank Scott, into the world.

With a new family at home and a new card from the Producer's Guild, Tony Scott found himself reenergized and ready to get back behind the camera. And he was ready to head right back into the world of high-level intelligence, surveillance, and shady government dealings he had just left with *Enemy of the State*.

16

Spies and Sports Cars

In the early 1990s, an aspiring young writer named Michael Frost Beckner finally got his foot in the door in Hollywood, selling three speculative, or "spec," scripts. One of those scripts, *Sniper*, landed in the hands of producer Robert L. Rosen, who then produced the film directed by Luis Llosa and starring Tom Berenger and Billy Zane. It was no rousing success, but *Sniper* made a little money for everyone involved and spawned a five-film franchise of direct-to-video sequels, four of which also starred Berenger.

As for Beckner, his next screenplay was *Cutthroat Island*, which became shorthand for big-budget studio disaster in 1995, alongside Kevin Costner's *Waterworld*. The film, directed by Renny Harlin and starring his wife at the time, Geena Davis, and Matthew Modine, was a swashbuckling adventure that hit at the wrong time, roughly a decade before Johnny Depp, Jerry Bruckheimer, and Disney made the genre chic again with *Pirates of the Caribbean*.

Beckner wrote a screenplay for a microscopic German film adaptation of *Prince Valiant*, and decided somewhere shortly after that it was time to get back to his roots, at least partially. He returned to the world of snipers and CIA operatives and espionage with his latest spec script, *Spy Game*.

The screenplay eventually found its way to Marc Abraham, a prolific producer throughout the 1990s with hits like *The Commitments*, *Air Force One*, and *The Hurricane* on his ledger. The story, about a cagey veteran CIA agent tasked with trying to get his protégé out of a Chinese prison before the agency disavows his existence, struck a chord, and Abraham and a team of producers green lit the project. They also knew precisely whom they wanted to play Nathan Muir, the older and wiser of the father/son dynamic: Robert Redford.

At 64 years old, the Academy Award–winning director was showing no signs of slowing down. In the 90s, Robert Redford directed four feature films; one of which—*Quiz Show*—earned him his second Best Director nomination in 1995. His career as an actor was still a force as well; Redford starred in Phil

Alden Robinson's vastly underrated tech caper *Sneakers*, Adrian Lyne's seductive adult melodrama *Indecent Proposal*, Jon Avnet's surprise romantic drama *Up Close & Personal*, and pulled double duty as actor and director in *A River Runs Through It* and *The Horse Whisperer*.

Not only was Redford's acting and directing career still going strong, Redford either produced or executively produced a dozen films during this run. And in 1989 his Sundance Film Festival, held in Park City, Utah, every winter since 1985, reached new heights of cultural relevance when Steven Soderbergh premiered his salacious, groundbreaking independent drama *sex, lies, and videotape* at the festival, changing the dynamic of the event and reshaping the expanse of cinema over the next decade.

The 1990s were the Golden Age for the Sundance Festival. Not only did it help usher in the new wave of "cool" crime cinema with Quentin Tarantino's *Reservoir Dogs*, the 1990 festival introduced the world to political documentarian Michael Moore and his Michigan General Motors exposé *Roger & Me*; the next year, a young director named Richard Linklater made waves with his handheld, observational comedy *Slacker*; in 1994 Kevin Smith debuted in Park City with his micro-budgeted black-and-white comedy *Clerks*; Todd Solondz, Darren Aronofsky, and Doug Liman all made their names during the decade. And Robert Redford's brand, and his aura in the industry, only intensified as he so graciously moved into his golden years.

With Redford on board as Muir it made the producers' choice for Tom Bishop, the fiery young protégé in trouble throughout the film, easy to coerce. They sent the script to Brad Pitt, who had just finished up a decade of superstardom to match any handsome young leading men in the history of Hollywood with the hit films *Interview with the Vampire*, *Legends of the Fall*, *Se7en*, and *Fight Club*, and off kilter thrillers like *Kalifornia* and *12 Monkeys*, the latter for which he received an Academy Award nomination for Best Supporting Actor. Pitt had also starred in *A River Runs Through It*, under the direction of Robert Redford, and he was more than eager to team up with the icon once again. He agreed to do the film in less than 24 hours.

Now, Abrahams needed a director, and they needed someone with experience. *Spy Game* was a globe-trotting, time-hopping thriller with complicated set pieces, convoluted sections of exposition, and the width and breadth of this shoot required an adventurous filmmaker who knew how to handle complex situations. Like his friend Brad Pitt—who had remained close to Scott over the years and flirted with another collaboration several times after *True Romance*—Scott wanted to work with Redford, so he agreed right away.

The third central character in *Spy Game* was Elizabeth Hadley, the woman who is captured by the Chinese government for involvement in an embassy bombing, the love interest of Pitt's Bishop, and the entire reason Pitt's character is in the Chinese prison to open the film. The female lead needed to be both beautiful and smart, with an edge and mysteriousness beneath her soft façade. Catherine McCormick, who had starred alongside Mel Gibson in his Scottish period epic *Braveheart* in 1995 and then steadily appeared in smaller films the rest of the decade, fit the bill. Her gaze was hard, but she could appear kind when needed, and Scott believed the physical attraction between her and Pitt was convincing.

There are dozens upon dozens of other roles in *Spy Game* as it travels (narratively, anyway) from the Vietnam War, to 1976 Berlin, to 1985 Beirut, to the early 1990s in Langley, Virginia, but they are all in support of the three leads. At one point, a romantic link between Redford's Muir and Hadley was in the script, but Scott felt it was too messy in the context of the story and it created an unwarranted tension between Redford and Pitt that was not necessary.

Spy Game was a new challenge for Tony Scott, as the film required dozens of locations with complicated set pieces. But the budget was not endless, which it probably needed to be to get all of the locations accurately captured on film. Instead, Scott managed to use one place for two or three locations. Certain scenes, for example, were done on a stage and in and around Oxford, England; but Scott needed the opening scene and subsequent moments in the film to take place inside the Chinese prison, and the budget was not there to fly everyone to China and fill an entirely new cast and crew on location. So, Scott used a prison on the outskirts of Oxford. The prison was new and clean and bright, so Scott and art and production directors Kevin Phipps and Norris Spencer decorated down the setting to resemble an unforgiving, unkempt hellhole.

Scott and his team originally used Tel Aviv to double for 1985 Beirut. However, the local staff grew contentious with one another as unrest percolated through the region. At one point, someone threw a Molotov cocktail into a set, destroying it. Not long after the incident, Scott and his producers knew they needed to pack up and find a new, safer place to shoot; but they could not take too long finding a new area to double for Beirut, as Brad Pitt had previously committed to film Steven Soderbergh's *Ocean's Eleven* reboot immediately after *Spy Game* was scheduled to wrap. Losing even a week of filming tightened the vice on production, so after quick glances at Istanbul, Tunisia, and Turkey, Scott settled on Casablanca, Morocco, less because it was a perfect fit and more because of the time crunch.

Throughout the shoot, Scott continued to double up locations and capture what he needed as pragmatically and utilitarian as possible. While shooting in Morocco, he found a perfect oasis of tropical trees and thick brush along the Sea of Galilee, in the middle of arid desert terrain, that stood in perfectly for the Vietnam sequences.

Scott also wanted to shoot the different segments and years of the story with different film stock, but digital adjustment was more affordable. For the Vietnam sequences, the footage was de-saturated to an uneasy, sepia tone. The Berlin scenes employed reversal stock techniques, which heightened the color and overexposed highlights to give it a washed out, high contrast sheen. Berlin was cold and blue, and the present day scenes more traditional. It helped divide the convoluted narrative structure into segments that were easier to differentiate—it was a similar technique Steven Soderbergh used in *Traffic* a year prior, but that was to shift settings, not eras.

At first, Tony Scott's eccentric directing approach perplexed Robert Redford; Scott was from a new school of high energy and multiple cameras and conventional scenes in the most unconventional ways possible. Before long, however, he was pulled into Scott's orbit and his bewilderment became intense curiosity; Redford became engaged with the process. He would ask questions about the lenses Scott used, and about his ritualistic early morning storyboarding sessions before every day's shoot. Redford was especially thrown sideways by Scott's decision to shoot a terse conversation between Redford and Pitt's characters on the roof of a building in Beirut (or, Morocco) with a helicopter circling them. It seemed like a bombastic approach to a simple conversation. Once Redford saw the dailies, however, he understood Scott's motivation; the swooping, spinning helicopter shots added a breathless sense of motion to the pivotal scene.

In the first cut of *Spy Game*, Tony Scott realized the film lost sight of Brad Pitt's character for far too long, so much so that the central motivation was all but forgotten as Pitt's character was off screen for more than forty minutes. To remedy this, Scott inserted a brief black-and-white flashback of Pitt giving Redford a flask, another brief shot of him being tortured in the Chinese prison, and he added time stamps to remind the audience that Redford's character was under the gun.[1]

And then, on September 11, 2001, terrorists attacked both the World Trade Center and Pentagon in the worst attack of its kind on American soil. The event not only sent the entire world into a tailspin of fear and paranoia, it changed the trajectory of pop culture for a brief moment in time. Films depicting the Twin Towers in Manhattan were edited. An early poster and trailer for Sam Raimi's *Spider-Man* featured the superhero using the Twin Towers and his web shooting to save the day. Following the attacks the posters were removed and the trailer edited. Other films, like Arnold Schwarzenegger's terrorist-based action/thriller *Collateral Damage*, were delayed indefinitely; some movies—an action film starring Jackie Chan as a hero who takes on terrorists in the World Trade Center, for example—were scrapped altogether. Songs were removed from the radio, TV shows had to adjust on the fly ... for a few weeks following 9/11, pop culture's place in a new world of global threats and societal unease was up in the air.

(Left to right) Tony Scott breaks down a scene for Robert Redford and Brad Pitt on the set of *Spy Game* (Universal Pictures, 2001).

Tony Scott and his producers opted not to delay the release of *Spy Game*. The same went for Ridley's military docudrama, *Black Hawk Down*, which was released on schedule in December and went on to gross over $100 million domestically. The early screenings for *Spy Game* were generally positive, and the presence of Hollywood royalty in Robert Redford and new superstar in Brad Pitt seemed like the only marketing tool they needed to sell the film.

Spy Game opened strong on the weekend of November 22 to $21.7 million, understandably behind two massive hits in *Harry Potter and the Sorcerer's Stone* and Pixar's animated fantasy *Monsters, Inc.* in slots one and two, respectively. The second weekend, however, the bottom dropped out. The film saw an almost 50 percent decline in ticket sales, and fell off precipitously over the next six weeks, bowing at the box office with a meager $62.3 million domestically. The $80 million international take helped turn a profit for the film, which had a sizeable $115 million budget because of the grand scale and complicated sets.[2]

The failure of *Spy Game* is maybe the most curious case of poor ticket sales in Tony Scott's career. The tragic events of 9/11 may have hindered the film—a cynical and paranoid look at the inner workings of the CIA—but those events also bolstered Ridley's *Black Hawk Down*—in contrast, a jingoistic tale of heroism and survival for American soldiers. There was a rallying point for audiences in *Black Hawk Down*, but there was no such pull working for *Spy Game*.

On top of these external forces, the fact that the film fell off the cliff in its second weekend is indicative of poor word of mouth. *Spy Game* is a complex, convoluted, wordy plot, loaded with dense expository scenes in boardrooms that stifle momentum at times. No matter how Scott tried to punch up these scenes, they simply did not connect with audiences. That, and the fact the romance between Pitt and Catherine McCormack was trimmed down significantly to mere window dressing, left very little for audiences to latch onto, so they moved on to other movies at the multiplex.

Scott was, as always, undeterred. The lack of consistent success may have been troubling for Scott somewhere deep down—especially since his brother, Ridley, had recently won an Academy Award for *Gladiator*. Scott knew he would never be invited into that club, but he had plenty of exciting plans to keep him busy, and keep his mind off the competition he always fostered with Ridley. One of those plans involved collaborating with BMW.

In the early 2000s, Internet video and streaming was still in its infancy. There was no YouTube yet, but savvy, forward-thinking companies saw the value in marketing their products online, on their company websites. BMW took that notion a step or two, or ten, further down the road, and created a series of short films that would showcase their cars in a cinematic setting. The series was called *The Hire*, and a different notable filmmaker would direct each entry. The stories would focus on a character known simply as "The Driver," and would serve as an action essay wherein the BMW could flex its muscles. There would be one constant throughout them all, and that would be the Driver, who was played by a relatively unknown British actor named Clive Owen.

The first film, released in April of 2001, was called *Ambush*. John Frankenheimer, one of the most prolific action filmmakers of his generation whose credits include *Birdman of Alcatraz*, *The Manchurian Candidate*, *French Connection II*, and the underrated spy thriller *Ronin* in 1998, directed *Ambush*. The second film in *The Hire* was called *Chosen*, directed by Ang Lee, fresh off the critical and commercial success of *Crouching Tiger, Hidden Dragon*.

Kar-Wai Wong, one of the greatest filmmakers of the Hong Kong cinematic movement through the late 1980s and into the 1990s, directed the third film in the series, *The Follow*. British crime director Guy Ritchie directed the next film, *Star*—which also featured his wife at the time, Madonna—and Mexican filmmaker Alejandro González Iñárritu directed *Powder Keg*.

The series of films were an early Internet sensation, and they effectively drove consumers to the BMW website. DVDs were created for prospective BMW buyers, and dealerships could not keep enough in stock. Critics even praised the work BMW did, and marveled at their ability to hire the best and brightest talent in Hollywood for what amounted to nothing more than a crafty marketing campaign. Naturally, the car manufacturer came back to the table with plans for a second season of *The Hire*, and they picked up right where they had left off.

Hong Kong legend John Woo came on board to direct a short, as did a young upstart writer and director named Joe Carnahan. Both Woo and Carnahan were working from stories created by director David Fincher, but Fincher's work on his upcoming thriller *Panic Room* had taken priority over his role with BMW and he had to step aside. He was replaced with Ridley and Tony Scott, and Tony subsequently jumped at the chance to direct one of the shorts.

Written by David Carter, Greg Hahn, and Vincent Ngo, *Beat the Devil* was a departure from the other films in the series. The other shorts had featured fantastical stories, but all had been grounded in some sort of reality. A diamond dealer, a spoiled celebrity, a movie mogul, and an immigrant Asian child were the subjects of the first season of films. They were heightened action, but tethered to the ground. Not *Beat the Devil*, which would feature R & B legend James Brown on a quest to reclaim his soul from Satan himself.

In the story, Brown had sold his soul for fame and fortune, but as age began creeping in, the pop star wanted to renegotiate the terms of the deal. This leads Owen's Driver character to a drag race against Satan's assistant. The plot was wild and the visuals surreal and something entirely different from the other entries, and Tony Scott had an incredible amount of creative space for such an abbreviated picture.

He brought in Gary Oldman to play the devil. To play Bob, Scott hired Mexican genre actor Danny Trejo, and James Brown would play himself. Goth/metal rocker Marilyn Manson appeared in a brief cameo at the end, as Satan's neighbor who was fed up with the noise because it was disturbing his bible study. *Beat the Devil* feels like a precursor to the type of exaggerated, vibrant action storytelling Scott would employ for the rest of his career, and most consider it the best entry in *The Hire*. As he did with all of his commercials, Scott was testing his creativity and some new technology on a smaller scale before employing them in his films.

After a decade of Bruckheimer films, an epic misfire in *The Fan*, and what amounted to a middling thriller with *Spy Game*, Tony Scott was once again ready to return to his dark roots. He was a powder keg, and *Beat the Devil* was merely a warning shot to the rest of Hollywood.

Scott was ready to pour his soul out on the big screen.

PART V

The Denzel Years

17

Mexico City Bloodletting

In the years following *Spy Game*, Tony Scott turned his focus to producing, directing the short film for BMW, and enjoying life as a new dad. He was nearing his sixties, but he still had the drive and the motivation to tweak his filmmaking, to try new things and command the set. Perhaps it was the second wind that came with being a new father, or perhaps it was a lifetime of adventure, and misfires, and ups and downs, and demons all boiling to the surface; whatever was driving Tony Scott in the early years of the 21st century, it all spilled out onto the screen in 2004, when he painted his masterpiece.

* * *

Philip Nicholson was born in England in June of 1940, in the middle of an air raid in the ongoing war with Nazi Germany, and upon graduating school he dove headfirst into building a career. He became a textiles trader and moved to Hong Kong, and that was when he helped save a man's life.

On a flight to from Tokyo back into Hong Kong, an Italian man suffered a heart attack. Before the crew of the flight called for an ambulance, Nicholson stepped in and suggested a different hospital, where he had close friends and where the man would receive immediate, excellent care. The decision may have saved the Italian man's life, and it also steered Nicholson into a life-changing trajectory.

Nicholson always knew he wanted to be a writer, but his textiles career had been serving him well. The desire never stopped burning, however, and soon after the incident on the flight, Nicholson began reading reports of Italy's current events, and became caught up in the media reports of high-profile kidnappings across the country. Mafioso were using kidnapping as leverage and extortion against politicians and wealthy bureaucrats, and it had reached epidemic levels in the late 1970s. Eager for authenticity, Nicholson reached out to his Italian friend from the flight, who was more than willing to give insight into the current mood in the country.[1]

Nicholson published *Man on Fire* in 1980 under the pseudonym A.J. Quinnell—a decision Nicholson made to retain his anonymity—and the book was a sensation almost immediately. The story is about a former military operative, John Creasy, burnt to the very end of his rope, tasked with protecting a young girl from kindappers in Italy. The job is a lifeline for Creasy, set up by his partner and friend, Guido. The haunted man and precocious young girl bond over time, and when the girl is kidnapped, Creasy's fury is let loose in a flurry of bloodshed. It was ripe for a film adaptation, and in 1987 producers Arnon Milchan and Robert Benmussa did that very thing.

The 1987 version of *Man on Fire*, set in Italy, starred Scott Glenn as John Creasy, Joe Pesci as his friend and partner, David, and Jade Malle as the young girl, Samantha. It was a bomb, opening in 178 theaters one weekend in October of 1987 and earning a paltry $519,000. Video sales did not fare better, and the film disappeared into the ether of shapeless late-80s action thrillers that filled rows upon rows of video rental stores.

Tony Scott was a fan of Quinnell's book, and as early as 1983 he tried to get a budget for an adaptation. But in 1983, Tony Scott was still a commercial director for his big brother's company, so he could not secure funding. Once *The Hunger* happened, Scott tucked the idea back into the recesses of his mind and moved on to *Top Gun*.

One night, a restless Arnon Milchan was channel surfing and came across his 1987 version of the story. The next morning, he called Tony and asked if he was still interested in the project, and that there was more potential than what showed in the first adaptation. Tony was more than ready to tackle Quinnell's material.[2]

Tony wanted this *Man on Fire* to be epic, big and bold and raw and personal. He was energized, maybe more than he'd been in years, and he was ready to show audiences all the tools in his belt. First things first, he needed to find a screenwriter, and he knew exactly who he wanted.

Back up to 1989, to Manhattan Beach, California, and a young screenwriter named Brian Helgeland scanning titles in Video Archive, his local rental spot where he would often visit and ask for recommendations. Helgeland had his own movies on those shelves in 1989—the horror films *A Nightmare on Elm Street 4: The Dream Master* and *976-EVIL* were both solid horror hits in 1988—and the clerks treated him like a friend.

On this day in 1989, one clerk, a young aspiring screenwriter named Quentin Tarantino, recommended *Man on Fire* to Helgeland.

For the next several years, Helgeland penned schlocky horror films, like a sequel to *976-EVIL*—appropriately named *976-EVIL II*—and *Highway to Hell*. He wrote the screenplay for the Sylvester Stallone/Antonio Banderas action thriller *Assassins* in 1995. Two years later, Helgeland came out of nowhere and won an Academy Award for his adapted screenplay of James

Ellroy's Los Angeles crime drama *L.A. Confidential*. From there, Helgeland became more prolific; his films were more noticeable too, from *Conspiracy Theory*, to *The Postman*, to the cleverly anachronistic medieval jousting adventure *A Knight's Tale* starring a young burgeoning star named Heath Ledger. In 2003, he adapted Dennis Lehane's dark drama *Mystic River* for Clint Eastwood, and earned a second Oscar nomination.

Tony Scott was a fan of *Mystic River*, and he knew Brian Helgeland would be a perfect fit for *Man on Fire*. Helgeland never imagined the B-grade action flick Quentin Tarantino handed him back in 1989 would come back around, but he was more than willing to write the sort of robust action thriller Tony Scott wanted.[3]

And Denzel Washington was bored.

On March 24, 2002, Washington won Best Actor for his portrayal of the dastardly, corrupt detective Alonzo Harris in Antoine Fuqua's hit cop thriller *Training Day*. In Alonzo, Washington was able to release the sort of furious energy he had become so skilled at repressing in films like *Malcolm* X and *The Hurricane*, only now he was free of any historical restrictions and was able to dive fully into the genre trappings of such an outlandish character. Denzel was let loose, and the result was a groundbreaking crime drama. The win for *Training Day* was his first leading actor statue, and a much-deserved win for such a towering, wicked personality.

But after *Training Day*, Washington starred in *John Q.*, the strange healthcare thriller where he plays a father who holds hospital staff hostage

Tony Scott (left) and Denzel Washington discuss a scene for *Man on Fire* (20th Century–Fox, 2004).

until his son gets the operation he needs. It was a moderate success, bolstered by the star power of Washington, but *John Q.* will never be confused with his more memorable works. The same can be said for *Antwone Fisher*, Washington's directorial debut in which he also starred. The motivational navy drama made money–$21 million against an estimated $12.5 million budget—but it was another collective shrug for most audiences.

Out of Time, his next film, was a financial flop and a mediocre potboiler where, arguably, Denzel Washington begins showing the aforementioned boredom in his performance. He needed to be motivated to act again because nothing was holding his attention. It did not take long for the infectious energy of Tony Scott to rub off on Washington, who saw potential in the John Creasy role. It would be the second time Scott and Washington worked together, but it would be far from the last.

For Pita, the plucky young victim and the other half of this unconventional love story, Scott and the producers had one name, and one name only, in mind: Dakota Fanning. Since she was six years old, the older Fanning sister (her younger sibling, Elle, is also an actress) had appeared in front of the camera, and was a natural performer from the beginning. From small parts on television series like *ER*, *Ally McBeal*, and *CSI*, Fanning eventually made her way to features in 2001, where she starred alongside Sean Penn in *I am Sam*; Fanning played the daughter to Penn's mentally-handicapped Sam in the family drama, and almost immediately she became a star.

She appeared in both film and television over the next few years, playing young versions of both Ellen DeGeneres and Reese Witherspoon in *The Ellen Show* and *Sweet Home Alabama*, respectively, and starring as Sally in the 2003 big-screen adaptation of *The Cat in the Hat*. *Man on Fire* would be a substantial step forward for Fanning, a leap into serious drama that would serve her well for a few years afterward. She read first with Tony Scott, then with Tony and Denzel Washington; the decision to cast Fanning as Lupita was arguably the easiest of the whole process.

Bonnie Timmerman worked with Scott on the rest of the cast. Timmerman had been the casting director for Scott on *Beverly Hills Cop II*, and in the meantime had assembled terrific casts in films like *Bull Durham*, *Awakenings*, *Glengarry Glen Ross*, *Carlito's Way*, *Heat*, *The Insider*, and most recently in Ridley Scott's *Black Hawk Down*, which has since become an impressive collection of rising young talent. By 2003, Timmerman had cemented her legacy in Hollywood, and was known for uncovering such talent as Liam Neeson, Scarlett Johansson, George Clooney, and Meryl Streep. She was also known for suggesting surprising and bizarre choices for supporting roles, as she did for *Man on Fire*, suggesting pop singer Marc Anthony for the role of Lupita's cornered, doomed father, Samuel Ramos.

Anthony, an accomplished musical superstar by 2003, had only appeared in a handful of small acting parts over the last decade, none of which suggested he had the pathos to handle a complicated and dark role like Ramos, a man who basically sells out his daughter to kidnappers in hopes of getting her back while also fixing his financial troubles. His most recent substantial film role was in Martin Scorsese's dark New York journey through hell, 1999's *Bringing Out the Dead*, where he played a drug-addled homeless man named Noel; nothing in the character hinted at Ramos. But Timmerman saw something in Anthony, and he eventually won Scott over during the auditions. Rhada Mitchell—an Australian actress who had been consistently busy in TV and movies since 1989 when she starred as a 16-year-old named Pixie in the Australian family drama *Sugar and Spice*—won Scott and Timmerman over for the role of Lisa, Lupita's mother and Samuel's trophy wife from Houston.

For two supporting roles outside Creasy and the family, Scott and Timmerman recruited two fascinating actors. Christopher Walken, who had worked with Scott a decade earlier on *True Romance*, agreed to play Creasy's closest friend and partner in numerous misdeeds over the years, now named Paul Rayburn rather than Guido from the novel. For Jordan Kalfus, the Ramos family attorney and eventually one of the men implicated in Lupita's kidnapping, Scott and Timmerman brought Mickey Rourke "back to life."

The 1980s was a star-making decade for Mickey Rourke that would rival any such decade for any actor in Hollywood. The shy, simmering, rugged leading man, who left his solid career as a boxer on the Golden Gloves circuit to become an actor, first caught audience's attention in Barry Levinson's coming-of-age drama, *Diner*. The next year, he played The Motorcycle Boy in Francis Ford Coppola's black-and-white street drama *Rumble Fish*, and he was off and running. From there, he became a leading man in *The Pope of Greenwich Village*, Michael Cimino's *The Year of the Dragon*, Adrian Lyne's sexually-charged *9 1/2 Weeks* opposite Kim Basinger, and as private investigator Harry Angel in Alan Parker's *Angel Heart*. These films were all in succession, and all hits for Rourke, either at the box office or in critical circles—often times both.

Then, his choices began to waver right around the time he began rejecting the matinee idol moniker he had been given over the last handful of years. Rourke continued to make movies—dreadfully reviewed financial flops like *Wild Orchid*, Michael Cimino's remake of *Desperate Hours*, and the ill-conceived futuristic action-thriller *Harley Davidson & the Marlboro Man* starring alongside Don Johnson—but he also returned to the boxing ring. For a few years, he tried to ascend to fight for the title in his weight division, but was unsuccessful.

What did happen during Rourke's brief return to boxing was he suffered several facial injuries, which required reconstructive surgeries. It permanently altered his formerly boyish good looks, which had always juxtaposed his sultry delivery to perfection; now, Rourke would be relegated to supporting roles as creeps and weirdos in a handful of forgettable movies until his presence virtually faded from the collective memory. In the early 2000s, he was starring in obscure thrillers and direct-to-video schlock like *They Crawl* and *Spun* for the most part, right about the time he got the Kalfus role in *Man on Fire*. Having Rourke in the role would signal immediately that this lawyer was somehow involved in shady dealings, and it would kick start a comeback for the actor that would culminate in an Oscar nomination four years later for playing a has-been professional wrestler in Darren Aronofsky's drama *The Wrestler*.

There was a slight issue with Brian Helgeland's screenplay, one he likely did not even consider during the writing process. If the story were still going to be set in Italy, as it was in the early drafts, *Man on Fire* would have to become a period piece set in the late 1970s. In 2003, the entire country of Italy had 0.2 kidnappings per 100,000 people. This averages out to roughly 114 kidnappings for the country in 2003, which is far from the epidemic it was in the late 1970s.[4] It would make no sense to have such pomp and circumstance surrounding an epidemic in a country that no longer suffered from said epidemic.

Mexico City, on the other hand, had tragically become the kidnapping center of the world over the last several years. By 2003, Kidnappings often surpassed 1,000 per year in the country, with wealthy businessmen and politicians understandably suffering the majority of the attacks. Scott knew Mexico—he admired it from the time he spent there back in the late 1980s filming *Revenge*—and he knew Mexico City was the perfect setting for *Man on Fire*, even if it was a little dangerous for everyone involved.

Scott took Helgeland down to Mexico City to get a feel for the local flavor, and inject said flavor into the screenplay. One aspect Scott wanted to add was the practice of Santeria, a cult-like offshoot of Catholicism, which was prevalent among the criminal element in the country. Scott wanted to lean into the mystical symbolism of the tangential religion to paint a more colorful portrait of his villains, modeling their intense methods after infamous cartels and criminal syndicates which were covered extensively in the country's media.

The aforementioned criminal element was prevalent in and around the set, as it was across the city. Armed security guards hired by Fox 2000, an offshoot of 20th Century–Fox who was distributing the picture along with Scott Free, kept an eye on the cast and crew. Often times, security were undercover bodyguards monitoring the set and the actors who, in a region in the world known for extortive kidnapping, had become serious liabilities.

According to Scott's commentary, one night around 11 p.m., Scott and four other members of the crew decided to pay a visit to Neza-Chalco-Itza, a slum in the Northeastern corner of the city and one of the most dangerous areas in an already dangerous region, to do some location scouting. It did not take long for this crew of middle-aged white men, all wearing expensive watches and sporting cameras and technical equipment, to draw the attention of a handful of street kids, who quietly began to surround them. Nearby, a group of older Teamsters, similar to Scott and his team in age, also took an interest in the crew's accessories. The bodyguard drew his gun, which in turn was met by a handful of the younger kids and the older Teamsters brandishing their own firearms.

As tensions began to flare, a third element invaded the standoff in the form of a lone police officer, who sped up to the scene and demanded the bodyguard relinquish his weapon. The situation reached a boiling point, a standoff straight out of a Tony Scott picture, and in a flash both the bodyguard and police officer were attacked by the two different mobs. Scott and his crew managed to escape the middle of the fray and find their way to a walkway running along the slum and away from the violence.

However, the assailants had the bodyguard, beaten and bloody by this point, and threatened to kill him if someone on Scott's party did not come down to retrieve him. In the commentary, Scott said he cannot fully remember the resolution to the incident, but everything was ratcheted down and the bodyguard was eventually released; after surgery to reconstruct his nose and install a new set of front teeth, which had been knocked out in the fight, the bodyguard was back on his feet and back at work.

The studio heads at Fox were not pleased with the developments in the Neza slum. They were ready to pull the plug on the film and relocate it to a safer area. But Scott, who had been down this road with executives and assuaging their fears on set before, worked out a deal with the studio: they would not visit Neza or the area in and around the slum the rest of the time.

The shoot began to take on the personality of its fearless, adventurous leader—a trait almost all Tony Scott films have in common. His energy was infectous, and it shows itself on camera. Scott and Denzel Washington found they were terrific collaborators, even stronger than they had been a decade earlier on *Crimson Tide*, and the star had palpable chemistry with Dakota Fanning. The film continued, shooting almost entirely in sequence, and without another serious brush with criminals in Mexico City.

It did, however, have to pause for a volcanic eruption.

The final scene of the film involves Creasy meeting up with "The Voice," the puppet master behind the kidnapping, and exchanging his own life in exchange for Lupita. The climactic reunion between Washington and Fanning was shot on a bridge outside Puebla, a city roughly 30 miles southeast of Mexico City. On June 21, 2003, the day they were to shoot this final scene—

and Tony Scott's fifty-ninth birthday—Popocatépetl, the volcano in Puebla, erupted. Black smoke billowed into the sky, the vibration shook the camera and lighting equipment and, more importantly for Scott and his crew, it delayed the shoot until the volcano died down. Luckily, that wound up being less than a day, and Scott and his crew were able to capture those final moments of the film with a majestic outline of Popocatépetl surrounded by thick, heavy clouds. It was a small, but symbolic hiccup in the process, quite literally wrapping production with a bang.

Christian Wagner had worked with Tony Scott previously on *True Romance*, *The Fan*, and *Spy Game*, so he knew what to expect when Scott turned over reels upon reels of his *Man on Fire* footage. While Wagner served as the film's central editor, shaping the expanse of celluloid into a workable print, the always thinking and perpetually experimental Tony Scott wanted to try something new with the edits. Wagner would run the show, but Skip Chaisson and Robert Duffy were brought in to edit key moments throughout the film where the emotion of the characters is charged in one way or another.

During the shoot, Scott had employed hand-crank cameras and cameras with reversal stock, all with the intention of heightening the action sequences through frantic edits and frayed aesthetics. Chaisson cut together the kidnapping scene during the opening credits and Lupita's kidnapping, and Duffy handled Creasy's attempted suicide and several of the driving sequences. Scott's intention was to have the editors inject specific techniques into the moments they cut, giving these scenes a different energy depending on the situation.

Skip Chaisson was also responsible for creating the unconventional use of subtitles in *Man on Fire*. Borrowing from classic Kung-Fu films, Chaisson created the moving, inconsistent subtitle that eventually became a calling card for the film, and an often-duplicated technique in the years that followed. Scott used the subtitles when necessary, but also sometimes not where they were needed. He felt the scrolling and fading words could serve to keep the audience at bay during the film's intensely violent moments. For example, the scene between Creasy and Daniel Sanchez, played by Robert Sosa, where Creasy systematically severs Sanchez's fingers one by one in a hot car, is virtually all in English. But Scott, who recognized the intensity of the situation and the claustrophobic nature of the set, wanted the subtitles in the scene to allow audiences to keep their distance psychologically. It created an easy aesthetic diversion, a break from the suffocating setting and the blood soaked front seat of this car.

Shooting *Man on Fire* was an adventure in the mold of its fearless leader, whose intrepid personality lit up the film with a new, focused energy that had been missing from many of Scott's films throughout the 1990s.

Man on Fire opened April 21, 2004, in the first wave of summer movies, an approach that has all but disappeared from the modern business model in Hollywood. This sort of adult action film with a moderate budget could very likely find a home on Netflix, or it might be shoved into a late August or early September release slot. But, in 2004, *Man on Fire* was the major release and it opened the weekend at number one with a robust $22.8 million box office.

The next weekend it fell to number two behind the surprise comedy hit *Mean Girls*, but still managed over $15 million. It finished its theatrical run with $77.9 million domestically, and another $52 million overseas. Against a $70 million budget, *Man on Fire* was not some landmark success; it was still a hit, however modest, and an indicator that Tony Scott had managed to channel all of his dark desires into decent box-office returns. Critics were particularly unkind to *Man on Fire* at the time, however, and were disapproving of all the moments—the frenetic editing and violence, specifically—that make the film a true masterpiece today.

18

Tony Scott's Signature Masterpiece

Man on Fire was not Tony Scott's first masterpiece.

Top Gun is arguably a masterpiece, though that definition is frontloaded with certain implications. It may be less a masterpiece of cinema than it is a masterwork of American jingoism personified in the wry smile of Tom Cruise, a signal beacon from the middle of the hedonistic, patriotic decade of the 1980s. It is a marketing masterpiece, above all else.

The frantic whirlwind of talent and star power (and ego) at the heart of *The Last Boy Scout*—easily Scott's most tormented shoot—has merit as a sort of unwieldy masterpiece of elevated B-movie crime-drama tropes. In certain circles, ones whose lifeblood owes itself to the sharp genre filmmaking of the '80s and '90s, *The Last Boy Scout* belongs in the discussion alongside *Lethal Weapon* and *Point Break* as one of the very best action films of the era. But it is still somewhat imperfect, a little slipshod and messy; it's part of the film's charm, but also partly what keeps it from being a masterpiece.

The clear tour de force of Scott's early career is *True Romance*. It is a youthful, propulsive film loaded with heart, humor, violence, and every other emotional beat an audience responds to in their entertainment. It is the total package, and Scott's management of the monumental egos and youthful energy on set, and his crucial injection of empathy for Clarence and Alabama in the final moments of the film all help to save the nihilism of Quentin Tarantino's screenplay. Had Tarantino directed such an expansive film right off the bat, with a big canvas and a substantial cast, the story would not have functioned on the same emotional level as it does in the hands of Tony Scott.

But *True Romance* still belongs, at least in part, to Tarantino. Scott's paintbrush made the film, and his empathy rescued it from a bleak finale, but Tarantino's screenplay supplies all the colors; it is a masterpiece, but creative credit must be split between the two filmmakers, as Tarantino's voice is undeniable. *Man on Fire*, somewhere along the way, became the primal scream of its director, an exposed, open wound of a film, full of heavy ideas about life and death that were clearly in Scott's head more than he let on. It is a Tony Scott film, through and though, and for that reason it is his signature film. *His* masterpiece.

Tony Scott did not write *Man on Fire*; credit to Helgeland and Nicholson are absolutely warranted. But Helgeland's screenplay—unlike the idiosynchratic rhythms of a Quentin Tarantino script—had malleability. Scott was able to mold the existing script and preceding novel into his own creation; with *True Romance*, the road met in the middle. This time, the story unfolds exclusively in Scott's blood-soaked coliseum, where his visceral aesthetics work equally as hard as the dialogue to rip open his characters' souls and expose raw emotion.

Critics took issue with Scott's frantic editing techniques, the gruesome violence, and the hefty 146-minute runtime of *Man on Fire*. Roger Ebert said the film "needs more depth to justify the length."[1] Lisa Schwarzbaum of *Entertainment Weekly* called it "a coldly violent revenge drama that tarts up scenes of wanton sadism with lush art direction."[2] There is little merit in rebutting dozens of negative reviews, or praising positive reviews; the very nature of film criticism is reactionary. Often times, it takes some films several years to age gracefully in the collective pop-culture consciousness, and eventually they are re-evaluated in a new light; *Man on Fire* belongs squarely in this camp.

In 2004, Scott's distorted, rapid-fire sequences were fresh, and the newness was off putting for some; the shaky-cam aesthetics of Paul Greengrass and his *Bourne* sequels were just about to become the modus operandi for a decade of action films later that summer. Scott's film was three months before *The Bourne Supremacy*, and fifteen years later the criticisms against his frantic style are antiquated. Once again, as he had been his entire career, Tony Scott was a step ahead of the trends, so much so that his contribution is overlooked.

The kidnapping scene from *Man on Fire* (20th Century–Fox, 2004).

That being said, the editing in *Man on Fire* that critics took issue with is not particularly frantic for a majority of the film. It moves quickly, even for a movie clocking in at nearly two-and-a-half hours, and there are fewer cuts in the quieter scenes. The frayed, hand-crank camera and reversal stock are only employed to convey severe emotion, at specific times of stress or chaos. When the story intensifies, or the action kicks in, the film is suddenly distressed and hysterical, thus adding a layer of bedlam to an already chaotic set piece. Often times, these hyper-stylized edits are used to show Creasy's inner turmoil. They keep the audience off balance, struggling to hang on to the moment just as Creasy is fighting to survive. The edits are done with intention, and they have only enhanced the rhythms and emotion of the film over time. The look of these sequences, however, was so jarring in the early 2000s, that they apparently overwhelmed the rest of the story for critics.

The quiet moments, of which there are many in the film's first half, are still shot with a manageable attention to performance and dialogue; the edits are calmer, more subdued, and they allow enough room for the actors to pull us into their world and invest in their journeys on an emotional level. *Man on Fire* has a solid hour of character development before unleashing hell on John Creasy, therein causing Creasy to return the favor. It's an element of the picture that is often overlooked in the shorthand analyses.

Giving the audience so much time with Creasy and Lupita only enriches their relationship, due in large part to the incredible chemistry between Washington and Fanning. Since the film was shot mostly in sequence, it allowed a genuine camaraderie to organically manifest itself between the two actors, and Washington's method approach added authenticity to their friendship.

In the early scenes, when Creasy is still in the throes of his alcohol addiction and regretting taking a job as bodyguard to a nine-year-old, Washington kept his distance from Fanning on set, avoiding any small talk. Then, as Creasy began to warm to Lupita in the film, Washington did the same behind the scenes. The approach helped create one of the more convincing, unconventional father/daughter relationships in modern cinema. Washington and Fanning volley marvelously off one another, and their improvisations during the shoot sell the paternal love story. Both Washington and Fanning are selling every little exchange, every small conversation with such warmth and heart it's easy to buy into their relationship.

When the violence is unleashed in the second half, it has been earned. Though it is often gruesome and cruel, the hour of backstory and buildup validates most of John Creasy's extreme methods of interrogation and revenge. Creasy visits three men responsible for Lupita's kidnapping (and what he believes to be her murder for the majority of the second half), and each interrogation and subsequent murder is in a new setting, with a new tone, and each sequence expands Creasy's growing mythical aura of invincibility.

The first interrogation takes place inside a car, and is cramped and sweaty and desperate. The second is in a nightclub, which doubles as a holding cell for kidnapped children. Here, Creasy is vengeance personified, and his fire and fury razes the club to the ground. In the third confrontation, where the information he receives from Victor Fuentes leads him back to Lupita's father, John Creasy has shed all semblance of covert investigation. He is now, officially, a Man on Fire, and has no more fear holding him back. The attack is conducted in broad daylight, on a busy city street, and the death of Fuentes under the bridge, courtesy of an explosive Creasy put inside his body, is bold and loud and a clear indication that our hero has but one fate in the story.

We have witnessed the poking of the great bear, the awakening of a once-great man who has been lost inside his own head for years, waiting for someone to stir him from his slumber. The arch is not new in Scott's films. Kevin Costner's Cochran in *Revenge* underwent a similar transformation, albeit a less convincing, less emotionally-engaging way; Joe Hallenbeck and Jimmy Dix are stirred from their slumber to become the hero in *The Last Boy Scout*; in *The Fan*, it's Gil Renard's insanity is the fire that is stoked by certain plot developments. The downtrodden hero (or villain, in the case of *The Fan*) was Tony Scott's go-to for most of his better, more personal films. Here, it was the ultimate version of that archetype.

Man on Fire is crafted succinctly in the image of its director, full of darkness and violence and romance and action. The fact that it is a sprawling, sometimes messy 146 minutes only enhances the experience, and further signifies it as the summit of Scott's career as a filmmaker. Every brilliant bit of technique and storytelling from Scott is spilled out onto the screen here, and he gets all of his actors to meet him in the middle. Washington delivers one of his very best performances in *Man on Fire*, a mixture of the focus and realism he brought to films like *Malcolm X* and *The Hurricane*, and the ferocity he delivered in *Training Day*. Much like Scott, this is where Washington could show all the tools in his bag, and the result is masterful.

All the performances in the film are raw, open wounds of regret and anger and isolation, wounds that may have touched Scott at an even deeper level than anyone could have imagined back in 2004.

19

The Model and the Bounty Hunter

Sometimes, the truth is indeed crazier than fiction.

Zvi Mosheh Skikne was born in Britain in 1928, the youngest of three brothers. In 1934, his family moved to South Africa; he joined the allies in World War II, where he was assigned to managing entertainment for the troops. Inspired by his work in the military, Skikne returned to South Africa with stars in his eyes, determined to become an actor. After attending London's Royal Academy of Dramatic Arts, he adapted a necessary stage name: Laurence Harvey.

His first film role was the lead in the 1948 horror picture *House of Darkness*, where he played Francis, a young man visiting a house haunted by the ghost of a man who was murdered there. For the next two decades, Harvey remained a consistent actor, appearing as the lead in a number of minor works before playing Romeo in Renato Castellani's adaptation of William Shakespeare's *Romeo and Juliet*. He portrayed William Travis in *The Alamo*, John Wayne's directorial debut; in 1962, he was Raymond Shaw, the brainwash victim at the heart of John Frankenheimer's paranoia-fueled thriller *The Manchurian Candidate*.

And, in August of 1969, Harvey's extramarital affair with model Paulene Stone produced a young daughter they named Domino.

From the time she could walk, Domino Harvey exhibited a marked aggressiveness. She beheaded her dolls, cut their hair, and she wanted to play in the mud with the boy's action figures. This disposition did not blend well when Harvey was sent to English boarding school once her mother married Peter Morton, the Hard Rock Café proprietor, and moved to the United States.

Harvey was antagonistic in school, moving four times before finally finding inspiration at the unconventional Dartington Hall in Devon, England. The curriculum was more physically demanding, and Harvey learned survival skills and Martial Arts while at Dartington. Then she graduated, and was set adrift in Great Britain.

For a while, Harvey tried her hand at being a DJ, she made shirts, and she dabbled in modeling. But the modeling world was too demanding, too manipulative for Harvey's disposition, so she abandoned the world in which she had grown up virtually alone; in 1989, she moved to San Diego, California, to be closer to her mother. In San Diego, she tried to work as a ranch hand. While ultimately unsuccessful as a career, the ranch is where Harvey began to handle firearms and learn her way around guns. From there, she became a firefighter for a few years, but in 1993 her trajectory forever changed when she got a job at Celes King Bail Bonds in Los Angeles, under the tutelage of a fellow bounty hunter named Ed Martinez, and his partner called Choco.

Harvey took to being a bounty hunter almost immediately, in spite of her lean, slight frame and striking beauty, an anachronism for the modern-day bounty hunter profession. She would fearlessly stride into slums and ghettos to apprehend bail jumpers, all the while living with her mother nearby in a Los Angeles mansion. In one of her more dangerous situations, Harvey became embroiled in a standoff with a bail jumper in Texas that devolved into a gun battle. Domino embraced the adventurous lifestyle of being a bounty hunter, and before long she became known as one of the best in the business.[1]

Not everything was perfect, however. Harvey and Martinez fell into serious drug and alcohol abuse during their years of successful bounty hunting. The drugs were often around when they apprehended their target and Domino and Martinez, unbridled by the standard rules of law enforcement, would regularly swipe the narcotics and use them. The cocaine and heroin abuse eventually spurred a trip to rehab for Domino in 1997. She never had many friends, and bounced from one romance to another, regardless of the gender of said romantic interest. It was a life rich with cinematic possibilities, almost too fantastic to be true, and not long after her career as a bounty hunter began to gain traction in the London media, Domino found a kindred spirit in Tony Scott.[2]

In 1993 Neville Shulman, Tony Scott's business manager, sent the director an article from an English tabloid newspaper profiling the wild life of Domino Harvey. Scott was immediately smitten with Domino's adventurous spirit and risk taking. He sought her out, and that same year the two met at her mother's home in Beverly Hills where she had to stay in the pool house—the assault rifles and various weaponry required for her profession were not welcome in Paulene's house.

Despite Scott's warnings that her line of work would prove fatal, Domino Harvey continued kicking in doors and sticking shotguns in criminals' faces. Scott wanted to adapt her life for the screen, so in 1995 he purchased the rights to her story for more than $300,000. Then, nothing happened. Screenplays came and went, and Scott moved on to other projects while Harvey continued to struggle with drug abuse. By the time Scott was ready to shoot Domino's story the bounty hunter had been into rehab, back into the real world again, and by 2003 she had once again relapsed and was arrested in possession of crystal methamphetamine.

A handful of screenwriters attempted to adapt the story of Domino for Scott, but none of them were able to capture the sort of frenetic energy for which Scott was searching. Everything was a straightforward narrative, unoriginal and uninspiring for the director, who had fully embraced the avant-garde action filmmaking techniques he had perfected with *Man on Fire*. Scott had officially crossed over into a style of filmmaking he fully wanted to embrace in his later years, a style where emotion was external, visible not only in the performance but in the look of the picture. He wanted the script to have the same sort of buzzing, fractured energy he intended to bring to it on a visual level, and he eventually found the right partner in Richard Kelly.

Kelly, a Newport News, Virginia, native, had burst onto the scene in 2001 with his directorial debut, *Donnie Darko*, based on a screenplay he had written. The film, a bizarrely nightmarish, time-shifting thriller, had made a star out of young Jake Gyllenhaal, and it made Richard Kelly a hot commodity. Scott had seen and loved *Donnie Darko* and he wanted Kelly to infuse his off-kilter darkness and black humor into the Domino story—much in the same way he had seen Brian Helgeland's work on *Mystic River* and sought him out for *Man on Fire*.

From the beginning, Kelly wanted to be transparent with the real Domino Harvey. He spoke to her several times during his writing process, and relayed to her the truth that this film version would veer away from fact more often than not. It would be a narrative cobbled together from various stories throughout her manic life, and several moments throughout the picture would be pure fabrication. Domino was on board, and seemed excited about the prospect of her life story gracing the big screen.

Still, the Domino Harvey movie was not going anywhere yet. Despite Scott's success with *Man on Fire* and the wildly cinematic allure to Domino Harvey's personal life, studios were hesitant to bankroll Scott's vision of the bounty hunter. The project was on its last legs, even as Scott continued to shop it around as he was piecing together *Man on Fire* in the editing room, when producer Samuel Hadida swooped in and agreed to fund the project with New Line Cinema. Hadida was one of the producers who worked with Scott on *True Romance*, and he was no stranger to controversial, edgy material. He produced the cult thriller *Freeway* starring Kiefer Sutherland and a young Reese Witherspoon, Milla Jovovich's apocalyptic zombie franchise *Resident Evil*, and dozens of other genre films before betting on *Domino* in 2004.

With funding and a studio securing production, Tony Scott tackled the

19. The Model and the Bounty Hunter

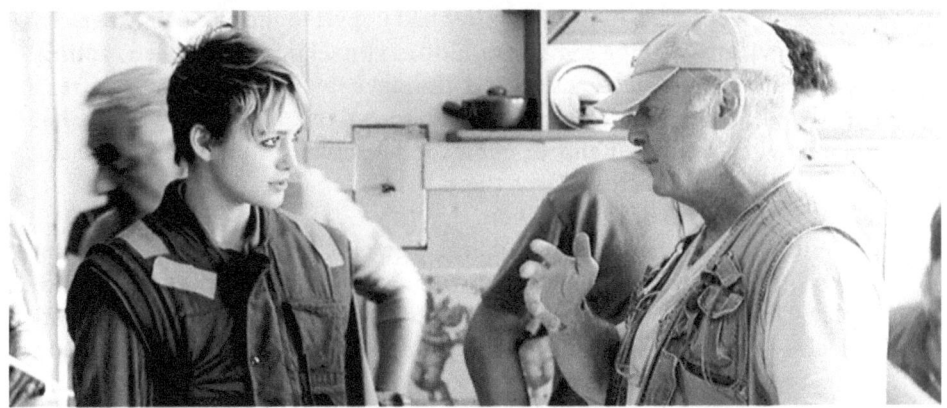

Keira Knightley and Tony Scott on the set of *Domino* (New Line Cinema, 2005).

most difficult task of the production: finding Domino Harvey. His friend Jerry Bruckheimer had just recently produced *Pirates of the Caribbean: The Curse of the Black Pearl* for Disney. The 2003 adventure, directed by Gore Verbinski, had surpassed all box-office prediction metrics and wound up as the third highest-grossing film of 2003, behind only the third entry into the *Lord of The Rings* trilogy and Pixar's animated ocean adventure *Finding Nemo*. The film earned Johnny Depp an Oscar nomination, and it made stars out of both Orlando Bloom and his romantic interest, a plucky young English actress named Keira Knightley.

Knightley had been working as an actress since she was eight, appearing in British television shows and TV movies before landing a bit part in *Star Wars: The Phantom Menace*. From there, she began to transition into feature films, eventually breaking out in the surprisingly successful independent soccer drama *Bend It Like Beckham*. The following year she appeared in Verbinski's first of a handful of *Pirates* films, and she became a star overnight.

The petite young British actress did not have the same sort of hard-edged attitude of Domino Harvey; she did, however, have the prim and proper mannerisms down pat, and the background of English sensibilities that defined Domino in the early years. Scott knew he could coax the edge out of Knightley once the cameras started rolling.

To play her bounty-hunting partners, Ed Moseby and Choco—the latter of which would partly serve as a romantic interest—Scott sought out an old acquaintance and a rising young star. For Moseby, Scott had his longtime friend and recent *Man on Fire* collaborator Mickey Rourke in mind from day one. For Choco, Scott and his casting director, Denise Chamian, found a kindred spirit and, physically, a Latin-American equal for Mickey Rourke in an actor named Edgar Ramírez.

Born in Venezuala in 1977, Ramírez had not yet found a role in American film or television when he came in to audition for Choco; he had been acting, however, in Venezualan television and film since 1990. Scott saw, in Ramírez's rugged handsomeness, the right actor to balance Rourke's patriarchal dynamic with Domino. Ramírez cut a similar look as Rourke, but their age (Rourke was 52, Ramirez 27) fit the dysfunctional family dynamic Scott wanted with his trio of thrill seekers.

With his typical unending well of energy, and his roguish British charm, Tony Scott put together a deep supporting cast of stars, both young and old. To play Claremont Williams, the proprietor of the bail bonds agency, Scott felt Delroy Lindo's mixture of charm, style, and wit was a perfect injection of street-level class. Lindo, a hardworking character actor, had gained more mainstream notoriety over the last decade with strong turns in popular film like the ensemble comedy *Get Shorty*, Ron Howard's kidnapping thriller *Ransom*, Danny Boyle's *A Life Less Ordinary*, and *Gone in Sixty Seconds*, a Jerry Bruckheimer production starring Nicolas Cage and Angelina Jolie.

To play Domino's Beverly Hills mother, Sophie Wynn (not Paulene Stone), Scott brought legendary British actress Jacqueline Bisset into the sandbox. Bisset had been a star since the 1960s, when she starred in *Cul-De-Sac*, a 1966 thriller from a young Polish filmmaker named Roman Polanski. She appeared in classics like *Bullitt*, François Truffaut's *Day for Night*, and Sidney Lumet's 1974 adaptation of *Murder on The Orient Express*. Unlike many of her female contemporaries, however, Jacqueline Bisset did not fade from Hollywood after a solid run of success in the '60s and '70s. She continued to work, and work often, in a slew of feature films, TV movies, and TV series like *Ally McBeal* and *Law & Order: Special Victims Unit*.

Dabney Coleman, who, for decades, had been a go-to for slimy boss characters after the success he had found in the 1980 comedy hit *9 to 5*, was cast as a tyrannical manager at the Department of Motor Vehicles; actress Mo'Nique was cast as his employee, who is involved with a subplot involving fake identification cards. Musician Macy Gray and *American Beauty* breakout star Mena Suvari filled supporting roles, and Christopher Walken happily went straight from *Man on Fire* to the *Domino* set to play Mark Heiss, a maniacal production executive for the WB Network. Scott even brought in Tom Waits, a musician, a prolific soundtrack presence, and a part time actor, to play a wily, unhinged religious zealot who confronts Domino and her crew one day in the desert.

And then there was Ian Ziering and Brian Austin Green playing themselves as the stars of the hit '90s prime-time teen soap *Beverly Hills 90210*, who would become pawns in the larger plot that would eventually send the film to a fiery climax atop the Stratosphere Hotel in Las Vegas.

From the beginning, Tony Scott was attacking the shoot with reckless abandon. He was also risking his own life, once again, to research the characters and scout locations. Scott went on a ride along with a real bounty hunter named Zeke Unger, a ride along that put him in some of the toughest neighborhoods in Southern California. More than once, guns were pulled, and a few times shots were fired, and eventually Scott began to realize this may have been one extreme research project too many. He survived, as did Unger, and eventually Scott convinced himself that risking his life was just a part of capturing the right amount of authenticity in his films.

The gloves were off, and according to his commentary Scott was ready to "exorcize his rock and roll demons." Still, early in the shoot, Scott's empathy kicked in; in the opening scene, the script had a dog being shot to death by a shotgun blast. Tony did not want to kill the dog—in fact, he had cut a similar scene from the final version of *True Romance* where a dog is shotgun blasted—so he changed the setup where the shotgun blows a hole in the floor right in front of the dog and the dog escapes the crossfire.[3]

Throughout his feature filmmaking career, Scott continued to direct commercials because he recognized the freedom for experimentation in thirty-second clips. He directed commercials for Marlboro cigarettes, which could only air in the U.K. as the United States had banned television advertisements for tobacco, and he shot a short film for a small but burgeoning internet company named Amazon.com. In these commercials, Scott tested different cameras and techniques, ones he wanted to test in measured amounts for *Man on Fire* and fully exploit in *Domino*.

The industry standard for film frames per second, where people and objects move normally, is 24 frames per second (FPS). Scott would shoot as low as one frame per second, making the image speed up considerably; from there, he would print at six frames per second, and the five-frame difference created a rapid blurring effect. Scott featured the technique dozens of times during this shoot.

He also brought back his hand-crank camera, which repeatedly over and under exposed the footage, giving it a pulsing, flashing effect. He once again employed cross processing to distort the film, the same way he did in *Man on Fire*; however, he employed the technique at a much higher frequency this time around. The same can be said for his use of reversal stock on *Domino*, which he leaned into much more often; excess was clearly Scott's motivation with this film.

The climactic showdown between Domino's crew, the cops, and the crooks, was shot at the Stratosphere Hotel in Las Vegas, the tower that resembles the space needle in Seattle—only with a rollercoaster on top. This being 2004, only three years removed from the terror attacks of September 11, the sight of a helicopter furiously circling the Stratosphere, which was itself lit up with mock gunfire and flash bangs was enough, according to Scott's commentary, to generate more than 900 calls to Las Vegas Police and 9-1-1.

To add a nice signature to the film, Tony Scott brought in the real Domino Harvey for the final shot; she stood outside the Stratosphere, smoking a cigarette as a fiery ball of debris landed on the ground behind her.

The shoot wrapped a few days before Christmas in 2004, and Scott and his editors William Goldenberg and long-time collaborator Christian Wagner were tasked with piecing together Scott's normal excess of footage. During post-production, rumors were floated out that Domino Harvey no longer supported the fictionalized story of her life, and wanted nothing to do with Scott's film. There were also rumblings that Harvey was unhappy that Scott, Kelly, and the team of producers opted to ignore her bisexuality; any of these rumors cannot be nailed down to a specific source, and most tend to come from second or third hand accounts. What became more concerning during this process, and in the midst of these surprising criticisms, was Harvey's increasingly erratic behavior in general.

Despite countless stints in rehab clinics, Domino was having difficulty shaking her drug habit. The addiction was at least partly responsible for her manic mood swings, which could have been mostly to blame for her sudden disdain for a fictionalized film about her life, directed by one of her close friends and surrogate fathers.

Tony Scott (right) directs Edgar Ramirez through a scene on the set of *Domino* (New Line Cinema, 2005).

On June 27, 2005, Domino Harvey's life of excess and danger took its final, ultimate toll. She was discovered drowned in her bathtub. Toxicology reports showed the cause of death as an overdose of fentanyl, a dangerous opioid that has, in the years since Domino's death, been responsible for a drug crisis in the United States and the cause of death for pop culture icons like Michael Jackson, Prince, Tom Petty, and Cranberries lead singer Delores O'Riordan.[4]

Domino's death was just over three months before the film's release, and was not the sort of noteworthy death that would generate a morbid bit of buzz for Tony Scott's upcoming film. In fact, nothing worked to salvage the film upon its release.

Met with dismal reviews in October 14, 2005—most of which expressed frustration with Scott's supercharged, erratic style—*Domino* opened in seventh place to $4.6 million. Ann Hornaday, critic for the *Washington Post*, said the film is "like a ferret on crystal meth that belatedly discovers ecstasy."[5] Many considered it a tiring endurance test, gradually wearing down the audience under its manic style.

The next weekend, *Domino* fell over 50 percent, out of the top ten, and in four weeks it was out of theaters with a paltry $10.1 million haul. International ticket sales only brought the total up to just over $22 million, still less than half the $50 million budget. It would wind up as the second worst box-office total for Scott, one step above *The Hunger*'s $6 million total.

But Tony Scott was still a man driven by a desire to entertain, to try again, and to keep moving for fear of stagnation. He said time and time again he never wanted to repeat himself, to get stale, and perhaps that repetitiveness was *Domino*'s ultimate downfall. He had taken everything that worked in *Man on Fire* and elevated it to unmanageable levels, and the sensual assault does become too much to process in the end. The idea makes sense; as Domino's life and career spirals out of control, the intensity of the camera techniques accelerates to mirror Harvey's instability. Nevertheless, it does not quite land the same way it did in *Man on Fire*, where the techniques are used more economically.

In a way, *Domino* works as a parody of everything Scott had worked to so carefully craft in *Man on Fire*. He was ripping off his own work, but not being clear enough to create honest satire. The result is a film somewhere in the middle, in limbo, set adrift like the story's tragic antihero.

Keep moving. On to the next project. Tony Scott knew no other way. He would waste no time in grabbing another project, and he needed his secret weapon back on board.

He needed Denzel, and he would get him, but this time around the pairing would be no match for the fury of Mother Nature.

20

A Film Built Around Tragedies

Terry Rossio had been a screenwriter in Hollywood since 1988, when he sold his first screenplay for a family fantasy movie called *Little Monsters*. The film, starring child star Fred Savage and comedian Howie Mandel, was barely released in theaters but it found a cult following on home video. Three years later, however, Rossio would pen the screenplay for Disney's *Aladdin*, which would be the highest-grossing movie of 1992, besting the sequels *Home Alone 2: Lost in New York* and Tim Burton's *Batman Returns*.

Rossio would continue to produce screenplays through the 1990s with a mixture of success and failure before, in 2001, earning a surprising Academy Award nomination for his screenplay for *Shrek*, the animated fairy-tale farce from Dreamworks Studios that wound up as the third highest grossing film of that year. Despite his success, Rossio would remain curious, and would continually search for collaborative voices. He would often float around America Online (AOL) chat rooms filled with aspiring writers and movie buffs, bouncing ideas off one another and talking what worked and what didn't in the current Hollywood system. That's where he met Bill Masilii early in 2001.

At the time, Masilii was working for Merrill Lynch in Manhattan's financial district, 3,000 miles away from Rossio. Nevertheless, the two men began discussing films, film history, writing and, ultimately, an idea Rossio had for a new time-traveling murder mystery/romance film. The story would begin with a tragic event—a terrorist bombing—and unfold from there, incorporating time travel into the plot. The idea sparked a creative flame in Masilii, who began working feverishly on a screenplay. He would compare notes with Rossio, who would write passages himself, and the two would share their work over email; Masilii was practically half way through the script when September 11, 2001, put a halt to everything.

The terror attacks in Lower Manhattan brought Masilii's world—and his dreams of being a screenwriter—to a sudden halt. While he struggled to make sense of this new global anxiety that had a stranglehold on the world, the idea of a screenplay revolving around a terrorist bombing was not necessarily on top of his to-do list. He put the screenplay away, and moved on with his life; Rossio did the same, teaming up with Jerry Bruckheimer in 2003 to write the screenplay for *Pirates of the Caribbean: The Curse of the Black Pearl.*

Around the time the first *Pirates* movie was hitting theaters and becoming an overwhelming success, Masilii found a new spark of creativity, and decided to pull the screenplay out of the drawer. He arranged a meeting in Los Angeles with Rossio, and for a week the two finally got together in the same room and began putting the pieces of *Déjà Vu* together.

After weeks of email and AOL meetings and discussions, Rossio and Marsilii had a completed first draft. Rossio also knew his *Pirates* producing partner, Jerry Bruckheimer, was looking for a new, original action story; he brought the screenplay to Bruckheimer, who was immediately taken aback by the ingenuity in this time-traveling action thriller, and he knew just who to bring on board to direct.

Tony Scott was in the middle of *Domino* post-production when Jerry Bruckheimer approached him with the *Déjà Vu* script. The title of the film itself, being brought to Scott by one of his oldest and closest collaborators, felt fitting. Rossio and Marsilii's story was set in Long Island, New York. Scott jumped into *Déjà Vu* with both feet, but first he wanted the location to change. He wanted something more textural, more romantic than Long Island. He wanted a place like New Orleans, Louisiana, so he and a scout visited the area; within hours, Scott was in love with the energy of the city, and both men were convinced this was the right place for the film.

Denzel Washington and Tony Scott first worked together more than a decade before *Déjà Vu*, on *Crimson Tide*, but on the set of *Man on Fire* the two clearly found a new level of synchronization. Since *Man on Fire*, Washington had worked with Jonathan Demme on a remake of *The Manchurian Candidate*, and Spike Lee in the labyrinthine bank-robbery thriller *Inside Man*, which was one of the biggest hits of Lee's career.

Washington clearly had an ability to get the best out of Tony Scott. As the director was getting older, and thoughts of mortality began creeping into his mind, he was eager to take more risks and throw caution to the wind with his films. Both *Man on Fire* and *Domino* were pulled from the same avenue of emotional unrest in Scott's head, but where *Domino* spiraled out of control, the mere presence of Washington seemed to help keep *Man on Fire*'s whirring energy grounded. More than once, Washington convinced Scott to change his mind on the direction of certain scenes; more importantly, the director listened. The two men worked in concert with one another, and now, on top of it all, they were becoming friends. It did not take much for Scott to convince Washington to play Doug Carlin, an ATF agent and the hero of *Déjà Vu*.

Beyond Washington's casting, there were three central characters Scott needed to cast, and a plethora of agents and supporting characters that had to have memorable faces. First up was Claire Kuchever, the victim of the terrorist plot whom audiences see die in the first scene in the film before agent Carlin retroactively figures out how to save her life. It was a strong female role—even if there was a great deal of time spent with the character being beaten and held hostage by the villain—and it drew the attention of a number of marquee actresses who read for the part.

One of the hopefuls was a young unknown actress named Paula Patton. The Los Angeles native had just recently got a taste of Hollywood with small roles in the 2005 Will Smith comedy, *Hitch*, and the microscopic independent drama *London*, co- starring Chris Evans, Jessica Biel, and Jason Statham. In 2006, she was third-billed in the musical drama *Idlewild*, a showcase for its two stars André Benjamin and Big Boi, also known as the rap duo Outkast.

Idlewild did not make any waves in Hollywood, falling short of its $15 million budget. Patton's résumé paled in comparison to her competitors when she auditioned for *Déjà Vu*, but Tony Scott liked what he saw in her reading. Patton beat the field, and was hired as the co-lead in a Scott/Bruckheimer/Washington vehicle, a far cry from independent features.

Agent Pryzwarra is the character in the film in charge of the shadowy government operation utilizing time travel and complex surveillance techniques to try to catch the terrorist; to fill this role, Scott turned to an old friend who he knew could deliver the dialogue with some energy and creativity, and someone who was more than wiling to work with him again: Val Kilmer.

The journey of Val Kilmer from the top of the Hollywood mountain, to the depths of B-grade schlock, is a road littered with stories of what seemed like the actor's willingness to be difficult on set. After his breakout role as Iceman nearly twenty years before *Déjà Vu*, Kilmer followed suit with strong turns in successful films like Ron Howard's fantasy adventure *Willow* and Oliver Stone's Jim Morrison biopic *The Doors*, where he spent six months researching the troubled lead singer to the point where Kilmer and the late Morrison seemed to be one in the same.

Following *The Doors*, Kilmer weathered the poor receptions of his Native American reservation murder mystery *Thunderheart* and the caper film *The Real McCoy*, and bounced back with a stirring, award-worthy turn as the doomed Doc Holliday in George P. Cosmatos' Wyatt Earp Western, *Tombstone*, two years after portraying Elvis for Tony Scott in *True Romance*. Kilmer's take on the Doc Holliday character all but erased a strong performance from Dennis Quaid as Holliday in Kevin Costner's *Wyatt Earp*, also released in 1994. Then, in 1995, Kilmer decided to don the cape and cowl for *Batman Forever*, and things began to fall apart.

Kilmer took over the role of Bruce Wayne/Batman from Michael Keaton, who had appeared as the Caped Crusader in both Tim Burton films but had no interest in returning a third time once Burton dropped out. Director Joel Schumacher stepped in as the new director, and he brought with him new ideas that would steer the franchise into camp sensibilities reminiscent of the late 1960s television show. Before long, Schumacher and Kilmer were warring on the set.

Schumacher has stated time and time again that Kilmer was difficult during the *Batman Forever* shoot, to the point where the two were rumored to not be speaking to one another on set. While Kilmer's reputation for being a tough collaborator had preceded *Batman Forever*, this was the first time the rumors reached such a wide swath of mainstream media. Schumacher has since backtracked on his claims that Kilmer was "the most psychologically troubled human being" the director had ever had to deal with, but at the time the rumors were enough.[1]

Despite the tumultuous relationship between director and star, *Batman Forever* was failure proof, racking up $184 million domestically and finishing in second place in 1995 behind Pixar's *Toy Story*. The success was not enough to convince Kilmer to come back, however, lending credence to the idea he and Schumacher may not have gotten along. At the end of 1995, Kilmer appeared in Michael Mann's epic crime classic *Heat*, but in 1996 he cemented his status as a "difficult" actor in one of the most calamitous productions in the history of Hollywood.

The Island of Dr. Moreau was set to be a big-budget adaptation of the H.G. Wells novel, directed by a fresh young horror filmmaker named Richard Stanley and starring Kilmer and Marlon Brando, the poster boy for difficult actors. From there, everything fell apart in epic fashion. Stanley was fired, unable to match wits with Marlon Brando, whose intentional sabotage of the film had spiraled out of control following the suicide of his daughter during pre-production. Hurricanes delayed the shoot, makeup and special-effects problems persisted, and Val Kilmer was sulking throughout the entire process, making unreasonable demands and insisting his part in the film be cut by more than half.

John Frankenheimer was brought in to replace Stanley and try to make heads or tails of the film, but he found the task no more promising. He and Kilmer butted heads even more, and the film slogged through its doomed shoot to stumble across the finish line and swiftly disappear in late August 1996. The film was a disaster top to bottom, and Kilmer's reputation was permanently tainted.[2]

The next decade was a muddled mess of low-rent thrillers, genre misfires and forgettable dramas for Val Kilmer. From the decent Stephen Hopkins action thriller *The Ghost and the Darkness*, to the flaccid adaptation of *The Saint*, to the romantic drama *At First Sight*, to the science-fiction bomb *Red Planet*, it was clear Kilmer's star power had faded, replaced with a bad reputation and diminishing returns at the box office as he stumbled from one lackluster effort to the next.

Nevertheless, Kilmer continued to work, but the projects were of increasingly poor quality. In 2004 he resurfaced in Oliver Stone's *Alexander*, a sweeping period epic about the great conqueror, played by Colin Farrell. It was intended to be a blockbuster and an Oscar player, and a return to form for its maligned director, but it wound up nothing more than an embarrassingly bad film by any metric. By the time Tony Scott gave his friend a call to appear in *Déjà Vu*, Kilmer had been humbled. He was a different person from the petulant diva who had helped sabotage *The Island of Dr. Moreau* a decade earlier, and he was grateful to get another chance in a big-budget thriller.[3]

To play Carroll Oerstadt, the terrorist responsible for the bombing of the ferry and the kidnapping of Claire, Scott approached Jim Caviezel, fresh off playing Jesus in Mel Gibson's 2004 controversial global blockbuster *The Passion of the Christ* which, despite its unflinching brutality and hard R rating, became the third-highest-grossing movie of the year. Scott told Caviezel that Timothy McVeigh, the American terrorist who bombed the federal building in Oklahoma City in 1995, was the motivation for Oerstadt, so Caviezel took the idea and expanded on it by researching McVeigh, the Unabomber Ted Kaczynski, and a collection of domestic terrorists and serial killers to try to tap into the emotional state of his character.

The rest of the *Déjà Vu* cast was populated with recognizable character actors, whose familiarity helped keep the moving parts of the dense plot visually distinguishable. Adam Golberg, who had appeared in modern classics like Richard Linklater's *Dazed and Confused* and Steven Spielberg's World War II epic *Saving Private Ryan*, was brought in to play Denny, the I.T. expert who lays out the time-travel aspects of the plot to Washington's Doug Carlin. Elden Henson joined as another tech geek, Bruce Greenwood was cast as Kilmer's superior, Jack McCready, and Matt Craven was added to play Denzel Washington's partner, Larry Minuti, who becomes a key element to the time-traveling investigation.

With the cast in place, it was time for Scott, Bruckheimer, and his crew to scout locations in and around New Orleans. It was the summer of 2005, however, and in August of that year Hurricane Katrina made landfall in Louisiana and disrupted not only Scott's film, but the lives of everyone in the Big Easy.

Katrina hit New Orleans August 29, breaching levees and destroying much of the low-income areas outside the city, especially the vulnerable 9th Ward. More than 1,000 people were killed, and the weeks that followed Katrina's destruction were that of displacement, death, and danger for thousands of New Orleans natives. Many were eventually relocated to Houston, Texas. Relief efforts involved anyone and everyone, including Jim Caviezel, who traveled to the region a day after Katrina's landfall with the 82nd Airborne to help recover bodies from flooded homes.[4]

Meanwhile, Bruckheimer and Scott's film was put on hold indefinitely. Neither producer nor director wanted to start over in a new location—Scott was adamant that the picture resume in New Orleans as soon as possible—but they also could not move on the project without their star, Denzel Washington, whose busy schedule might pull him away. In the end, this was a moment bigger than future projects and film schedules, and the trio all agreed to wait until New Orleans was at least functional enough to accommodate their needs, which already included a complicated ferry explosion on the Mississippi River and an even more involving car chase across the city. The decision would ultimately stimulate the city's understandably fragile economy with $30 million in revenue and jobs.[5]

In February of 2006, Scott, Bruckheimer, Washington, and Paula Patton held a press conference announcing they would return to New Orleans and begin shooting *Déjà Vu*; it would be the first film to shoot in the city since Hurricane Katrina, and the screenplay had been tweaked to add the morass of the storm's destruction into scenes near the end of the film.

Shooting in February also gave Scott the chance to film the opening against the backdrop of Mardis Gras; the celebration would be a perfect representation of New Orleans, and the unflappable spirit of the region in the face of disaster. This picture belonged to New Orleans as much as it belonged to anyone involved.

Scott returned to his *Enemy of the State* days to recreate the high-tech surveillance footage in *Déjà Vu*, only this time he had the advantage of high definition cameras to capture the intricacies of the technology. And again, he used his hand-crank cameras and exposure techniques he had employed—to varying degrees of success—in his previous two films. Here, however, Scott knew a more subdued approach to his hyperkinetic aesthetics would better suit such an intricate plot.

Resources were understandably thin in the city when it came to police, firemen, and paramedics, but Scott and his team tried their best to steer clear of the recovery efforts. The city embraced Scott and his team, looking for any signs of progress and positivity to help New Orleans return from the abyss.

Regardless of the limited assistance from the city, Scott managed to pull off the film's major set piece, a ferry explosion, with relative ease. The Algiers ferry was blown up just off the shore from its Canal Street port in a controlled detonation, and the casualties were then added in postproduction.

Tony Scott (left) and Denzel Washington study the scenery on the set of *Déjà Vu* (Touchstone Pictures, 2006).

Déjà Vu hit theaters November 22, 2006, marketed as the sort of mid-budget thriller aimed at adults that have all but disappeared from the multiplex in the age of Netflix and the obsession with content over quality. The film had no major aspirations other than a fun time at the cinema, but the reviews were generally positive so it landed at number three over the holiday weekend with a strong $20.5 million take, behind the animated penguin film *Happy Feet* and the reboot of the James Bond franchise, *Casino Royale*. It held the third spot for a second weekend before it began to dip into the teens by Christmas. The final domestic take was a meager $64 million, but *Déjà Vu* saw one of the better international box-office successes of Scott's career, bringing in $116.5 million overseas. The $180.5 million take, against a $75 million budget, made it a bona-fide success.[6]

Tony Scott grappled with *Déjà Vu* from the outset. It was his first foray into science fiction, and the fine line that genre brought with it made Scott anxious. Too much emphasis on the fantastical, and Scott feared he could lose sight of the real-world stakes and the trueness and humanity of his characters he so desperately clung to in all of his films.

He hadn't lost sight of anything.

21

Going Underground

In the summer of 2008, Tony Scott embraced his adventurous spirit somewhere other than behind the camera. He took his wife, Donna, and their twin sons, eight years old at the time, to Cortina, in the Italian Alps, for a mountain-climbing expedition with his longtime climbing partner, Enrico Maioni. Scott had been on several climbs with Maioni, and Scott attacked the Five Towers on the outskirts of the Italian villa with the verve and vigor of a man half his age.[1] If anything stoked a fire in his soul more than film-making, it was scaling rock walls, and pushing his body past the limit.

After summiting the Five Towers, Tony Scott descended back to earth and returned to the director's chair. Then, he decided to go underground.

* * *

Morton Freedgood was born in Brooklyn, New York, in 1913; by the time he reached his twenties, he had already become a prolific writer, publishing short stories and essays in a myriad of magazines from *Cosmopolitan* to *Esquire*. When he was thirty-four he published both *Yankee Trader*, a historical fiction novel he co-wrote with his brother, Stanley, and *The Gun and Mr. Smith*, a crime novel he wrote on his own.

From there, Freedgood became a productive crime novelist, publishing nine novels over the next twenty-five years—the crime fiction would be published under the pen name of John Godey, and the historical works under his real name. In 1973, Hollywood took notice of Freedgood's work when he published *The Taking of Pelham One Two Three*.

The novel takes place in heart of the New York City subway transit system, where four heavily armed men hijack a train car and, with 17 hostages on board, retreat into the bowels of one of the subway tunnels where they begin negotiating with police and transit authorities. While the four villains were well defined, and a number of the authorities trying to negotiate were given characteristics, Freedgood (under Godey), used upwards of 30 different character points of view to paint a broad picture of the city as a melting pot of different cultures and backgrounds. The dizzying array of personalities to navigate through may have been a tough idea to see materialize on a movie screen, but producer Edgar Scherick saw potential in the material.

If Edgar Scherick believed in a project in the early 1970s, it had solid odds of being made. Scherick was the mastermind behind ABC's *Wide World of Sports*, the earliest amalgamation of a TV series focused solely on sports news and competition, which he had sold to the network for $500,000 in 1960. Later in the decade, Scherick began producing feature films, beginning with the 1968 Sidney Poitier romantic drama *For Love of Ivy*. He produced William Friedkin's first serious feature, the thriller *The Birthday Party*; in 1969, he executive produced Woody Allen's first film, *Take the Money and Run*.[2] One of his biggest early hits was the 1972 Elaine May romantic comedy *The Heartbreak Kid*, starring Charles Grodin and a rising young star named Cybill Shepherd. Whatever caught Scherick's eye in the *The Taking of Pelham One Two Three* novel motivated the producer and his partner, Gabriel Katzka, to purchase the rights and option it for production immediately.

Prolific action director Joseph Sargent was hired to direct; the hangdog everyman Walter Matthau was cast as the affable hero, Garber, and the guarded, grizzled veteran actor Robert Shaw was brought in to play Bernard Ryder, the leader of the quartet of hijackers. Focusing on the hero/villain dynamic between the two unconventional stars allowed Sargent and screenwriter Peter Stone narrow the focus of the novel while retaining its eclectic cast of characters.

Once again, Edgar Scherick was spot on with his predilection. Critical reception was generally positive in October of 1974, when *The Taking of Pelham One Two Three* hit theaters. Many critics praised the film as a movie that captures the unique kaleidoscope of culture that is New York City, and Walter Matthau's genial humor was the perfect antidote to the intense plot developments. The box office followed suit, more than tripling the $5 million budget, and today *Pelham One Two Three* still finds a spot on any "Best Of" lists concerning New York movies, alongside films like *Manhattan*, *Taxi Driver*, and *Do the Right Thing*.

The film was remade for television in 1998, and starred Vincent D'Onofrio as the leader of the band of hijackers. Edward James Olmos played Piscotti, and the rest of the cast was full of venerable TV actors like Richard Schiff, Donnie Wahlberg, and Lisa Vidal. The reviews of ABC's *Pelham* were uninspiring, and the film drifted away from everyone's consciousness in short order.

A decade later, Hollywood was finding fewer and fewer spaces on the release schedule for original, mid-budgeted movies. Superhero films like *Iron Man* and *The Dark Knight*, both in 2008, launched the modern era of superhero filmmaking and "Shared Universe" franchise storytelling that would become commonplace over the next decade. In the meantime, the unstoppable franchises of Michael Bay's *Transformers* at Paramount and Jerry Bruckheimer's *Pirates of the Caribbean* at Disney continued to churn out sequels which, despite diminishing returns of quality, proved to be critic proof blockbusters. Hollywood in the late 2000s was split between studio excess and grandiosity, and independent films fighting for scraps at film festivals; the "middle class" of moderately priced, character driven genre thrillers and dramas that had dominated theaters for decades was being squeezed out.

But remakes were still hot commodities.

Remaking old dramas in this space still made sense to studios, mostly because it reduced the legwork that would be required to sell an entirely new intellectual property. By 2006, with remakes of *The Omen*, *The Wicker Man*, *The Hills Have Eyes*, and *When a Stranger Calls* crammed into multiplexes, the horror genre was seeing a genuine epidemic of recycled material. There was also the remake of *The Poseidon Adventure*, under the new title *Poseidon*, and a new take on John Carpenter's *Assault on Precinct 13* a year earlier. These new versions of old films from the 1970s were not dominating the box office, but they could be made relatively cheap and the familiarity would draw eyes.

The Taking of Pelham One Two Three fit right into this narrow window of New Hollywood era remakes, at least it did to the producing trio of Steve Tisch, Todd Black and Jason Blumenthal. The three were equal partners in Escape Artists, a new production company who had produced only a handful of films since 2001 when they released the Heath Ledger period adventure *A Knight's Tale*. Since then, Escape Artists had been a place for mid-budget dramas and genre pictures—like Nicolas Cage's dark comedy *The Weather Man* and Will Smith's *The Pursuit of Happyness*—to secure funding. Once they secured rights to *Pelham One Two Three*, the Escape Artists trio brought in the prolific and rock steady screenwriter David Koepp to write an adaptation.

For nearly two decades, David Koepp had been a consistent, reliable screenwriter whose impressive credits ranged from the Robert Zemeckis comedy *Death Becomes Her*, to Ron Howard's superior newspaper drama *The Paper*, to Brian De Palma's *Carlito's Way* and *Mission: Impossible*. He penned the adaptation for Steven Spielberg's *Jurassic Park*, and went on to work with the icon on the sequel, *The Lost World*, as well as *War of the Worlds* in 2006 and, most recently, *Indiana Jones and the Kingdom of the Crystal Skull* in 2008.

Koepp went through multiple drafts of a *Pelham* screenplay, trying to incorporate the technological advancements and surveillance techniques operating in modern-era New York City into the story. Tony Scott took an interest during post-production on *Déjà Vu*, and began scouting areas of the Big Apple to shoot; like all of his projects, Scott wanted authenticity in location. Whatever could be accomplished in the New York transit system would be, and very little would be relegated to a sound stage.

Scott's vision never gelled with Koepp's in the early days of scouting and research, so the producers at Escape Artists brought in Brian Helgeland, Scott's screenwriter on *Man on Fire* (which was the last script he had penned when he was brought in for this) to mold the story into Scott's vision. That delayed things a bit, while Helgeland re-wrote the adaptation from the ground up.

Even though his *Pelham 123* adaptation was on the back burner for a few months, Tony Scott kept moving. He knew no other way.

The same year as *Déjà Vu*, Scott served as executive producer on *Orpheus*, a TV movie for CBS from *Driving Miss Daisy* director Bruce Beresford, as well as the little-seen James Franco medieval romance remake of *Tristan + Isolde*. In 2007, Scott produced the prestigious Cold War drama for TNT, *The Company*, starring Chris O'Donnell, Alfred Molina, and Michael Keaton. Two months later, Tony was one of 13 executive producers attached to the release of Andrew Dominik's meditative western, *The Assassination of Jesse James by the Coward Robert Ford*, starring the Scott brothers' friend and frequent collaborator, Brad Pitt.

The rest of 2007 and 2008 was a mishmash of TV movies, including an independent film from Greece called *Tell Tale*, and a mini-series adaptation of Michael Crichton's *The Andromeda Strain* for the A&E network, which accumulated seven Prime Time Emmy nominations. Scott's producing nomination was the third of his career, having won the award in 2002 for his involvement with HBO's Winston Churchill biopic *The Gathering Storm*.

In 2005, Tony Scott and Scott Free debuted a new dramatic series for CBS called *Numb3rs*. Scott was on board as executive producer for the series, which starred Rob Morrow as a special agent for the FBI whose brother, a brilliant mathematician (David Krumholtz), helps the agency solve perplexing crimes. *Numb3rs* had been a steady hit for CBS, lingering in the top 40 with an average eleven million viewers.

Scott had remained executive producer through the entire run of *Num3rs*, and only once did he decide to step behind the camera. In 2007, Scott was in between film projects and decided to direct the first episode of season four, "Trust Metric." Once again, Scott brought Val Kilmer to his set; Kilmer played a character named Mason Lancer. The episode aired on September 28, 2007, and was one of the better-rated episodes of the entire series. But the steadiness of television was not enough to seduce Scott away from the silver screen.

Scott also kept testing his tools in commercials, creating a hard-charged Dodge commercial in 2008, complete with Dodge pickup trucks plowing through wooden structures and outrunning fireballs; a true Tony Scott production.

Finally, Helgeland's *Pelham* screenplay made sense to Scott, and the project was up and running once again. This new version of the story was a major departure from both the book and the original film in terms of perspectives and character development. In the book, and to an extent in the film, there were dozens of points of view to tell the story; Helgeland's story dispatches with most of the peripheral stories in the original version(s), narrowing the focus almost entirely to a battle of wills between Ryder and a pudgy, embattled dispatcher named Walter Garber. There is also a darker, more cynical spirit to Helgeland's screenplay—especially in his take on the Ryder character, calm and measured in the original but ferocious and unpredictably violent here— which was undoubtedly one of the reasons Scott was satisfied this time around. Helgeland knew trying to mimic the cold detachment of Robert Shaw's Ryder would be a mistake, which is why he went in the other direction. And Scott was always searching for the dark angle to his stories, for a chance to increase the intensity of the action.[3]

He did not need to search far and wide to find his film's hero, Walter Garber; Denzel Washington was all too ready to work with Scott again, as the two had developed a shorthand and a deep understanding of one another's skills and how best to use them througout the years. Finding Garber was easy, and for Ryder, the film's central villain, Scott ventured outside his close-knit Hollywood circle and decided to bring in John Travolta.

Of all the marquee idols from bygone eras, John Travolta had seen the most dramatic ebbs and flows in a four-decade career of any of his contemporaries. From early breakout roles in the dance/musical pairing of *Grease* and *Saturday Night Fever*, Travolta's star fizzled throughout the 1980s. He found minor success in the family comedy *Look Who's Talking*, but was thrust back into the mainstream as a heavier, more character-focused star in Quentin Tarantino's *Pulp Fiction*.

The role revived Travolta's career, and he capitalized on his new fame with big roles in *Get Shorty*, *Broken Arrow*, *Phenomenon*, and the classic John Woo action thriller *Face/Off* opposite Nicolas Cage. Eventually, however, Travolta began saturating the market, much like he did in the 1980s. His film choices began to wane until 2000 when he produced and starred in his passion project, *Battlefield Earth*, based on a novel from Scientology founder L. Ron Hubbard, a religion of which Travolta is deeply associated. The film was a disaster; it became the new shorthand for complete and total Hollywood failures for the foreseeable future, and it crushed John Travolta's star power in one fell swoop.

In the 2000s Travolta starred in the absurd Dominic Sena action picture *Swordfish*, the forgotten *Stepfather*-style remake *Domestic Disturbance*, John McTiernan's messy military thriller Basic, and a handful of increasingly mediocre films like the failed *Get Shorty* sequel *Be Cool* and the middle-aged biker comedy *Wild Hogs*. In spite of the recent run of misfires, John Travolta still had that intangible charisma when he found the right role. As he was aging, and leaning towards the thriller genre more regularly, Travolta appeared more energized and engaging when he could "chew" the scenery, and Scott felt the Ryder character would be the perfect place for such an elevated performance. Shortly after Scott and Denzel Washington announced their intentions to remake *Pelham One Two Three* (now changed to *The Taking of Pelham 123*), Travolta signed on.

For a cast made up mostly of New York citizens and city workers, Tony Scott pushed for authenticity. He wanted as many Bronx natives and New York actors as possible to lend certain credence to the situations. Lower East Side native Luis Guzman was cast as Phil Ramos, a disgruntled former employee of the transit authority who is now serving as Ryder's right-hand man; Brooklyn mainstay and expert character actor John Turturro was brought in to play Camonetti, a lieutenant who butts heads with Washington's Garber during negotiations; Scott's friend and previous collaborator James Gandolfini who, in 2009, had just ended his run as Tony Soprano on HBO's game-changing series, was brought in to play the mayor.

Tony Scott's desire for authenticity even led him to a collection of mug shots.

Tony Scott (left) directs a villainous John Travolta on the set of *The Taking of Pelham 123* (Columbia Pictures, 2009).

21. Going Underground

For Ryder's criminal henchmen, Scott wanted as much truth in their performance as he wanted across the entire picture. He asked Don Ferrarone, a former DEA agent who had also assisted Scott as either technical advisor or associate producer (sometimes both) on *Enemy of The State*, *Spy Game*, *Man on Fire*, and *Déjà Vu*, to help him find the right criminal to serve as a technical advisor to the actors who would eventually fill the roles. That's when Ferrarone handed him a mug shot of Victor Gojcaj.

Detroit native Gojcaj was twenty-four at the time, but had already made a name for himself in the criminal underworld. He was a known captain of a "crew" of low-level gangsters, and Tony Scott was so charmed by the mere thought of such a young man being so well respected in the underworld that he wanted Victor Gojcaj to play the role of Bashkin, Ryder's most dangerous henchman. The producers initially rejected such an absurd idea, bringing a known criminal on board, but Scott persisted in his desire to cast Gojcaj. He wanted the sort of realism only Gojcaj could deliver; eventually, the producers acquiesced.[4]

Tony Scott and his team of producers brought in the Metropolitan Transportation Authority (MTA) as consultants for the film, much in the way Scott and Jerry Bruckheimer did bringing in the navy for *Top Gun* and NASCAR for *Days of Thunder*. As much as Scott wanted to use real-world locations, even he knew he would not be able to film a captured subway train in a tunnel in Manhattan's operating rail system; instead, with the help of the MTA and the New York City Transit Authority, Scott and his production team and set designers built a section of tunnel rails for the hostage scenes and a full-scale, detailed replica of the rail command center for Washington's scenes.

Alberteen Anderson, the director of film and special events for the MTA, had overseen other subway pictures like the Woody Harrelson/Kiefer Sutherland comedy *The Cowboy Way*, and the Woody Harrelson/Wesley Snipes action picture *Money Train*. He saw this new version of *Pelham 123* as an opportunity for the New York subway system to flex its muscles. The original *Pelham* did not have the same sort of technical prowess as a Tony Scott production, and Anderson had been burned by previous iterations of the transit system in the aforementioned films, both box-office failures, so she worked hand in hand with the director to make the inner working of the subways look as authentic as possible.

Meanwhile, Scott filled in the film surrounding these two major sets— the primary focus of the picture—with real-world shots of subway trains and platforms full of local extras; all of the scenes taking place at street level were shot on location.[5]

Aside from the authenticity in the sets, every last person involved with the film who may have to walk around the live subway rails had to take an eight-hour safety course, which was held in an abandoned schoolhouse on

Coney Island. The course was half classroom education, half simulated railway navigation in an empty tunnel setup beneath the school. Tony Scott had to leave the airport after taking a red-eye flight across the country and go straight to the classroom to take the final written exam, which he initially failed, probably because this was Scott's first time ever being in a subway.[6]

Principal photography on *The Taking of Pelham 123* wrapped in the back half of 2008, with the film set to debut the following summer, June 12, 2009. This meant the editing room for Tony Scott and his frequent collaborator, Chris Lebenzon, and it meant the cast would move on to either decompress, or move on to the next role. John Travolta jumped straight to an action comedy called *From Paris with Love*; once that finished Travolta, his wife Kelly Preston, and their children Jett and Ella, went to the Bahamas to bring in the New Year. That is when tragedy struck.

Their 16-year-old son, Jett, had been diagnosed with Kawasaki disease as a child, a rare condition that cause the arteries in young children to become inflamed. He also suffered from asthma and occasional seizures. It was a seizure on January 2, 2009, that caused Jett to fall and his head on the bathtub while in the Bahamas. He was declared dead later that day at Rand Memorial Hospital.[7]

Jett Travolta's death obviously devastated John and his family, and it sent shockwaves through Hollywood. The inconceivable tragedy brought Travolta's

Tony Scott running the show on the set of *The Taking of Pelham 123* (Columbia Pictures, 2009).

public life to a complete halt, and understandably so. He retreated with his family, away from red carpets and press tours, and that meant he would not be doing the promotional circuit for *The Taking of Pelham 123* in May and June. Everyone involved with the picture, from Tony Scott down, fully supported Travolta's decision.

Denzel Washington took over spokesperson duties for Travolta, speaking on his behalf whenever questions would arise. Washington's wife, Pauletta, had been a friend to Travolta and Kelly Preston for longer than Denzel, but during the *Pelham* shoot Denzel and John grew close. After Jett's passing, Washington would sometimes listen to Travolta on the phone for hours at a time to try to help him cope with such an unimaginable situation.

Two thousand nine was a strange year for the movies. After 2008, where Marvel Studios stumbled into the idea for their shared cinematic universe and Christopher Nolan's *The Dark Knight* redefined superhero drama, 2009 was a down year across the board. Zack Snyder's *Watchmen* tried to capitalize on *The Dark Knight*'s success, but the material proved to be too esoteric to reach a wide audience.

The summer movie season got off to a rocky start as well, with three major tent pole films—the new *X-Men* offshoot from Fox, *X-Men Origins: Wolverine*, a fourth *Terminator* film called *Terminator: Salvation*, and a sequel to the Dan Brown/Ron Howard/Tom Hanks global sensation *The Da Vinci Code*, *Angels & Demons*—all failing to meet expectations. An early surprise hit was the Las Vegas comedy *The Hangover*, and J.J. Abrams' *Star Trek* reboot with an all-new cast was dominating the May box office; beyond that, the release schedule was surprisingly thin compared to the previous season.

Buzz for *The Taking of Pelham 123* was tepid before it was released on June 12. Reviews were middling at best, with some critics lamenting the action injection and the mean streak of the film. Most critics simply shrugged. Roger Ebert said, "There's not much wrong with [Pelham 123], except that there's not much really right about it."[8] At *The Atlantic*, critic Ed Koch said, "The original film was far superior … the current remake will soon be forgotten."[9]

Pelham 123 opened third that weekend behind the aforementioned *The Hangover*, in its second week at number one, and Pixar's animated film *Up*, with a respectable $23.3 million in ticket sales. Like so many Tony Scott films over the years, however, there was very little staying power.

The film dropped almost 50 percent the next weekend, landing at number five as two more new releases—the Ryan Reynolds, Sandra Bullock romantic comedy *The Proposal* and the caveman comedy *Year One*—pushed it back. From there, it dwindled precipitously before bowing in August with a final domestic tally of $65.5 million. That number fell well below the $100 million budget, but the international boost of $84.7 million helped the film turn a profit, however meager it may have been in the end.

Nevertheless, *The Taking of Pelham 123* failed to capture any major headlines in 2009. It may have been the first indication that these sort of films were dying out; the demographic that had once championed mid-budget action movies began gravitating towards superheroes and franchises, leaving little to no room for a low-key thriller. The R rating was also proving to be a tough sell in the summer months.

Still, *The Taking of Pelham 123* was a simple remake, nothing more and nothing less; it proved to be a minor blip in Tony Scott's oeuvre. That didn't deter the filmmaker, at least outwardly. In fact, Scott had fallen in love with the intricate working and heavy machinery of trains and railway systems, just as he had done with military aviation during *Top Gun* or submarines during *Crimson Tide*. This new obsession with trains also steered him towards his next project, which he began researching before production on *Pelham 123* even wrapped.

22

Unstoppable

Moving locomotive freight cars was part of everyday life on the Stanley Rail Yard in Walbridge, Ohio, except one morning on May 15, 2001, when a mundane task became a national emergency.

The engineer at Stanley had been tasked with moving 47 freight cars, weighing in at almost 3,000 tons, from one set of tracks to another. That required him to drive the locomotive attached to the front of these freight cars—a seasoned old engine sporting the number 8888—across the sets of tracks. At the last minute he spotted a rail switch ahead of him that had malfunctioned, which would prohibit the transfer; he hopped off the train to get ahead of it and adjust the track manually, hitting the airbrakes as he left.

The problem was, in rail yards, locomotive air brakes are typically disconnected for easy maneuvering; such was the case for #8888. The engineer realized the problem, but the failsafe brake in the cab had also been disabled, and any attempt he made to correct the issue was met with a dead end. Meanwhile, #8888 continued to roll. Out of answers, the engineer applied all the throttle power to the traction motor, which is meant to slow down trains with the help of natural friction. Again, however, the absence of the air brakes was a problem; instead of the throttle causing the train to slow down, it simply accelerated.

Now, #8888 was picking up steam and heading out of the yard, unmanned, for a trek across rural Ohio. The engineer tried to jump aboard the train as it collected speed but was unsuccessful, instead coming away with minor cuts and bruises after being dragged alongside the outside of the train for a few yards. To add insult to injury, two of the freight cars attached to #8888 were carrying molten phenol, a dangerously toxic cocktail of chemicals used as an ingredient in aspirins and various pharmaceutical drugs that could cause serious problems in the case of a derailment.[1]

As the locomotive began to accelerate, reaching speeds in excess of forty miles per hour, Ohio State Police tried to derail the train in a remote section of the railway with a portable derailing device that attached to the tracks and pushed one side of the locomotive into the air in the hopes it would topple the cars. It was moving too fast, however, and the device stood no chance. There was very little to do to stop #8888 as it thundered through one small Ohio town after another, a ground-level missile loaded with toxic chemicals that could potentially derail in a crowded area, causing all manner of chaos, injury, and likely death.

Another problem was on the horizon in the form of locomotive #8392, a train carrying freight cars northbound on the same track as #8888. Veteran railway engineer Jess Knowlton and his rookie conductor, Terry L. Forson, were operating the northbound train, and they made it to a section of track siding where they could park their freight and get out of harm's way. Here, Knowlton and Forson devised the plan that they would pursue the runaway train from behind, catch up to it, and use their own dynamic braking system to slow #8888.

Knowlton and Forson caught up with the train as it neared Kenton, Ohio, topping fifty miles per hour. They coupled to the rear car of #8888 and began pumping the dynamic brakes to slow it, all the while being careful enough to keep the couplings together. As they traveled through Kenton, the men eventually got the locomotive slowed to eleven miles per hour allowing fellow engineer Jon Hosfeld, who had met up with the two men and the runaway train at the right spot, to jump on board and cut the throttle.

For two hours, #8888 covered 66 miles of Ohio railroad unmanned, carrying dangerous chemicals across unsuspecting populations. It was a story of true heroism, ripe for a cinematic treatment, and screenwriter Mark Bomback knew the story of #8888 would be thrilling on the silver screen.

Bomback, the New York native, had been in Hollywood since the mid–1990s and had only one writing credit to his name by 2001, a low-rent riff on the Clint Eastwood thriller *Play Misty for Me* called *The Night Caller*. In 2003, he sold his script for *Godsend*, which became a middling supernatural thriller starring Robert De Niro, Rebecca Romijn, and Greg Kinnear. Bomback's time in Hollywood was challenging as he struggled to make his way up the ladder of the studio system and pitch screenplays. Eventually, a wife and two children reorganized the priorities of his life, and he moved with his new family back to Westchester, New York in 2004.[2]

He arrived in Westchester having recently read the account of the CSX 8888 incident, and began churning through his first draft of *Unstoppable*. While he toiled away, trying to work through the arduous technical detail required to tell the story, Bomback also managed to sell his screenplay for 2007's *Live Free or Die Hard*—the fourth *Die Hard* film in the long-running Bruce Willis franchise—to 20th Century–Fox, and doors began to open for him back in Hollywood, from where he had just left with his family. *Live Free or Die Hard* would go on to make over $380 million globally.

The success of *Live Free or Die Hard* generated a bit more interest for *Unstoppable*. Producer Julie Yorn and Fox were eager to get this train on the tracks, and they knew whom they wanted behind the camera: Martin Campbell.

In 2006, Martin Campbell had resurrected James Bond—one of the longest-standing cinematic franchises in the history of Hollywood—in *Casino Royale*, introducing the world to a new, more rugged version of 007 in Daniel Craig (he had done the same thing, albeit in a different way and in a different era, in 1995 when he directed Pierce Brosnan's first foray as Bond in *Goldeneye*). *Casino Royale* was an international hit, and Martin Campbell was a hot commodity when he agreed to direct *Unstoppable*.

But the road a film is required to travel from conception to existence is paved with the pitfalls of scheduling conflicts, budgetary shortcomings, disagreements, and just plain bad luck. Much of Hollywood could not avoid the economic recession that hit the United States in 2008. Unless a brand icon like Steven Spielberg or James Cameron was involved in a project, the belt loops had been considerably tightened across the industry. The new emphasis on the bottom line also meant the window for the $30 million movie star salary was closing. The very concept of movie stars, as Hollywood had known it for decades, was beginning to disappear.

Budget concerns in regards to casting were what initially delayed *Unstoppable*, and it is what forced Martin Campbell to leave the film; he would move on to direct Mel Gibson in an adaptation of his British mini-series, *Edge of Darkness*. Meanwhile, *Unstoppable* was stuck on the shelf at Fox, a project twisting in the winds of the new (albeit temporarily) lean economic landscape.

Directors would flirt with the film occasionally, but nobody could manage to lock down the right approach. Early in 2009, during postproduction on *The Taking of Pelham 123*, Bomback's screenplay found its way to Tony Scott's hands. Scott, a new fan of the railway life, salivated at the thought of filming these locomotives in a race against time; he signed on to direct and, as always, he demanded as much authenticity as humanly possible.[3]

Scott's demands for practical action sequences, for real operable trains, and for use of large sections of functional railway did not sit well with 20th Century–Fox and their new approach. Even when Scott convinced his muse, Denzel Washington, to move right over from the command center of *Pelham 123* into the cab of the train to play the veteran rail man Frank in *Unstoppable*, Fox did not feel the pairing had enough clout to carry a film that was definitely headed for a $100 million budget. The casting of the young rookie, Will, eased Fox's concerns, albeit for a short while.

Los Angeles native Chris Pine had been climbing his way up the acting ranks since the early 2000s, appearing in one-off roles on TV shows like *ER* and *CSI: Miami*, and amassing a collection of independent, low-budget films along the way. Two thousand six was a busy year for Pine, who starred a pair of forgotten romantic comedies—*Just My Luck* alongside Lindsay Lohan and the obscure movie *Blind Dating*—before finally showing off his physicality and roguish charm in a small role in Joe Carnahan's hyper-violent casino action extravaganza, *Smokin' Aces.*

In 2009, however, Pine's future as an actor changed permanently when he was cast as the new James T. Kirk in J.J. Abrams' *Star Trek* reboot. Pine was again able to showcase his physicality—not to mention even more of the aforementioned charm—playing Kirk. *Star Trek* was one of the biggest hit films of 2009, and it allowed Pine the opportunity to take on virtually any role he wanted; the role he wanted was Will in *Unstoppable.*

And yet, even with the trio of Scott, Washington, and Pine ready to begin filming *Unstoppable*—which had been set for a fall 2009 shoot and a summer 2010 release—Fox was still gun shy. Scott's films, however wildly they may have varied in budget or overall quality, were not sure bets at the box office. Washington could still carry pictures, and Pine was a rising star, but the studio remained hesitant.[4] They wanted both Scott and Washington to shave a substantial amount from their salaries—$3 million for Scott, who was commanding $6 million by this point in his career, and $4 million for Washington, who was one of the highest-paid actors in Hollywood. Scott agreed, but Washington and his agent balked at the proposal.

The budget gridlock went on for three months until, in July, Denzel Washington finally exited the film to pursue other projects. It proved to be a wake-up call for Fox, who was still eager to get the film done. Meanwhile, the budget drama and Washington's impatience had not deterred Tony Scott from beginning his research and working with Mark Bomback to find the perfect draft of the action-heavy script.

Scott initially envisioned Bomback's story taking place in the arid deserts of the American West; the open plains and foreboding rock structures of the region, Scott knew, would be a striking backdrop for the action. Except the stakes would not feel as high, with a train out of control in the middle of nowhere. Visually, it would sing, but the story would suffer. If the train crashed in the middle of the desert, so what? Eventually, Scott and Bomback settled on the northern cusp of the rust belt, in Pittsburgh and its surrounding small towns, where tight railways and precarious situations involving pedestrians and cars on the track would further intensify the experience. The grey landscape and intimate texture of the small towns also reminded Scott of his hometown North Shields in the United Kingdom, an industrial city almost always covered by clouds. It also meant the sort of shoot Scott wanted, with helicopters filming the action and real trains operating on real rail systems, would be a logistical nightmare.

That worry was for another day. First, Scott wanted to get the story right. He urged Bomback to develop the script further, to learn more about the characters in these rail yards and to find the human element in a story revolving around a nameless, faceless antagonist. At the same time, Scott wanted the first act tightened; he wanted Bomback to give these characters an effective backstory, but get them on the train and in pursuit as quickly as possible without short-changing the emotions. Scott wanted him to thread the needle. Eventually, after a number of drafts, Bomback threaded that needle and Scott was satisfied.

Washington's hiatus from *Unstoppable* lasted only nine days. Before the calendar changed to August, he was back on board, having won his salary dispute with Fox. *Unstoppable* was given the green light, and everyone headed to Pittsburgh to begin filming.

The cast of *Unstoppable* was structured similarly to *The Taking of Pelham 123*: two main stars, flanked on all sides by strong character actors. Rosario Dawson, who had been steadily working in films of all shapes and sizes since her 1995 debut in Larry Clark's disturbing docudrama *Kids*, was cast as Connie, the railway manager stuck in a control room trying everything she can to help Frank and Will chase down the runaway locomotive. As for the pair of bumbling conductors who accidentally set the train loose, Scott and casting director Denise Chamian chose Ethan Suplee, a regular in Kevin Smith films, and T.J. Miller, a young stand-up comedian turned busy character actor.

A trio of character-acting Kevin's was brought in to fill out various bureaucratic and train expert roles. Kevin Dunn, who may have appeared in more movies than not in the early days of the 21st century, was cast to basically do his thing, and play an obstructionist executive worried about the bottom line more than innocent lives in the path of the locomotive; Kevin Corrigan, who appeared briefly as a henchman in Scott's *True Romance*, and in small roles in Martin Scorsese's *Goodfellas* and *The Departed*, was brought in to play a bookish train expert who just so happened to be in the railway command center when the incident occurred; lesser known Kevin Chapman, often hired to play heavies and henchmen himself, was hired to play a fellow engineer named Bunny.

Principal photography on *Unstoppable* began August 29, 2009. The schedule had been pushed back a bit, and the film was now set for a November 2010 release date in place of the initial summer release. The readjustment did nothing to ease the tension of a tight schedule, however, not to mention Scott and his crew was faced with an incredibly complex logistical task. Such is the case on set of a Tony Scott film, where tactile authenticity always outweighed quick fixes in postproduction.

First and foremost, Scott had to secure trains and sections of railway to use. This was a tough task, as the railways were used daily and would need to be re-routed for a month during filming. The Nittany Bald Eagle Railroad, a seventy-mile stretch of track in rural Pennsylvania, agreed to lend a portion of their system for the film; Scott also commissioned a few of their employees to serve as technical advisors. Now, Scott needed the stars of the show, the locomotives.

The Canadian Pacific Railway leased four trains to the production, and Scott was allowed to paint them according to his plan. He painted the runaway red, and the heroes' vessel blue and yellow—a task the art department was still working on the night before shooting. One of the hero trains was retrofitted with a 360-degree camera dolly system that Scott could use to film the dialogue exchanges between Washington and Pine's characters.

The trains were on the tracks, but only half the battle was won. Now came the arduous, and extremely dangerous, task of shooting these trains hurtling across Pennsylvania. Expert stunt pilots were brought in to operate two helicopters: one would be a "story ship," the News chopper in the narrative, and the other would be a "camera ship" filming the action. The cameras aboard the helicopter were fit with 42:1 zoom lenses; these zooms would push in close enough to see Washington and Pine performing a great deal of their own stunts on the outside of these trains, while creating a frenetic, rapid-moving background to help give the trains the illusion of moving much faster than were in reality. On the ground level, four-wheel-drive trucks were retrofitted with high-arching crane camera systems, which could extend up beyond what the trucks could capture as they sped down the gravel road running parallel to the tracks. Ground cameras were also set up mere feet from the tracks to capture high-angle glimpses of the trains as they blew through one small town after another.

The trains were not always flying down the tracks, however. In some of the more dangerous sequences in the small towns, the trains were going roughly ten miles per hour. Scott and his camera technicians then sped up the film stock in postproduction to give it the illusion that the trains were hurtling through town.

The largest set piece in the middle of the film involved a different train derailment and subsequent explosion. Tony Scott pushed for a real derailment, and he got his way. The scene was shot with a careful, controlled derailment system using the same type of tool the characters in *Unstoppable* try to use on their runaway train. They had only one opportunity to get this right, and Scott's crew coordinated every moving part down to the last inch; the crash was perfect, and Scott's vast collection of rolling cameras captured any possible angle.

Animal sounds were added in the sound mixing to give the runaway locomotive and even more threatening presence on the screen. One scene required the train to barrel through a horse trailer, but a train going at these

22. Unstoppable

Chris Pine (left) and Denzel Washington in *Unstoppable* (20th Century–Fox, 2010).

speeds hitting a trailer would almost entirely obliterate it. Scott wanted a portion of the trailer left to give the event more of a visual punch, so the entire shell of the horse trailer had to be retrofitted with a reinforced steel endoskeleton to help soften the scope of destruction.

Scott also had to race the weather. When they began the shoot in the last days of August, the foliage in rural Pennsylvania was lush and green, but as the filming moved into October the leaves began to change and fall from the trees. To try to combat this, Scott shot the action set pieces and chase sequences in some semblance of continuity, and saved the majority of the control room scenes with Rosario Dawson and Kevin Corrigan until the end of the shoot.[5]

Critics responded to the early screenings of *Unstoppable* with overwhelming positivity; it was Tony Scott's best-rated film since *Crimson Tide*, and several reviews cited the action singularity and the pureness of the story as benefits to Scott's aesthetic. In a sense, this is Tony Scott stripped down to his most rudimentary talents, shooting unrelenting action and telling harrowing stories about complicated men, at a crossroads in their lives, stuck in impossible situations. It was exactly the type of story in which Scott shined.

Unstoppable opened November 12, 2010, in second place behind the animated film *Megamind*, with a respectable $22.7 million. While it dipped almost 43 percent in its second week, *Unstoppable* rebounded the third week and lasted a month in the top ten before bowing out of theaters in early March with an $81.5 million haul. Somehow, despite the popularity and the decent box office run, the film could not recuperate its $100 million budget without the international sales, which boosted the film's overall take to $167.8 million. It was Scott's sixth-highest grossing domestic feature, a crowd pleaser, and a well-received action spectacle, but it still had to scratch and claw to reach the black, financially.

PART VI
Into the Wind

23

A Full Slate

Tony Scott's never ending quest to direct his next action thriller or suspense film may have been bordering on an addiction as the calendar changed over to a new decade, his fourth as a director. He chased the adrenaline he got on set, and in those brief moments where he was not working, the thrill seeking outdoorsman was likely getting his fix hanging on the side of a cliff or shooting down Southern California freeways in one of his prized Porches. Before *Unstoppable* had even been completely put together in the editing room, Scott was moving on to his next project, then his next, and his next, feverishly filling his time it seems.

By the summer of 2010, the Marvel Studios cinematic universe was picking up significant steam with the release of *Iron Man 2*. There was a plan in place, the plan was growing but also becoming more defined, and at one point the plan involved satellite films like an adaptation of writer Mark Millar and artist Steve McNiven's graphic novel, *Nemesis*.

Mark Millar had recently evolved from revered comic-book writer to one of the creative geniuses responsible for the new comic movie renaissance. His 2004 graphic novel *Wanted* was turned into a 2008 action film starring Angelina Jolie, Morgan Freeman, and James McAvoy; another publication from 2004, *Kick-Ass*, was adapted into a sort of underground, gritty 2010 action comedy starring Nicolas Cage and a teenage Aaron Taylor-Johnson. His storylines in the *X-Men* comics of the early 21st century also contributed heavily to the new film franchise, and he would eventually team up with director Matthew Vaughn (who also directed *Kick-Ass* and *X-Men: First Class*) to write the screenplay for *Kingsman: The Secret Service* and its 2017 sequel, subtitled *The Golden Circle*.

In 2006, Millar would work with Steven McNiven on Marvel's ambitious storyline, *Civil War*. Under the Icon Comics imprint—owned by Marvel—Millar and McNiven created *Nemesis*, a fascinating photo negative to DC's Batman. The protagonist of *Nemesis* is Matt Anderson, a billionaire with a backstory not unlike Bruce Wayne. Like Batman's alter ego, the death of

Anderson's parents are what drive him; except Matt Anderson's parents were villains, and Nemesis is one of the most prolific terrorists and one of the most evil super villains on the market.

Nemesis—decked out head to toe in a bright, intrusively white costume—spends his life taking out high-ranking police officers while also managing kill thousands at the Pentagon with a poisonous gas attack, hijack Air Force One and crash it into a crowd of hundreds in Washington, D.C., hold the president hostage, and wipe out almost a hundred men in a prison escape. It may have been a fantasy anti-hero fable splashed across the pages of a graphic novel, but it could not have been more fit for the eye of Tony Scott. The entire *Nemesis* run, from May to October of 2010, was stuffed with action set pieces and plenty of opportunities for Scott to indulge in his more rock and roll sensibilities.

In August, in the middle of the comics' run at Icon, 20th Century-Fox acquired the rights to Millar and McNiven's nihilistic creation. At the time, Scott was juggling three possible projects ahead of *Nemesis*. One was *The Associate*, a John Grisham novel adaptation starring Shia La Beouf; another possibility was *Hell's Angels*, a crime drama to which Shia LaBouf's name was also attached, this time alongside Mickey Rourke. The third film was *Potzdamer Platz*, a New Jersey organized crime thriller, also starring Rourke, who had once again become a hot commodity following his 2008 Best Actor nomination for his role and Randy "The Ram" Robinson in Darren Aronofsky's *The Wrestler*.[1]

When Scott caught wind of *Nemesis* at Fox, he pushed the three overlapping projects down the road and decided to direct his first comic book adaptation. The marriage made more sense when the nature of the Nemesis character was taken into consideration. He was excited about taking a new step in his career, leaping into the burgeoning subgenre of superhero and comic book adaptations, but it was still not enough to fill his tank. He had something bigger in store.[2]

For years, the whispers of a *Top Gun* sequel had been nothing more than that, faint rumors floating around Hollywood, eventually drifting off with a thousand more just like it. The three central figures in the mythos of *Top Gun*—Scott, Tom Cruise, and Jerry Bruckheimer—had all transformed into some of the biggest influencers of the entire industry, so scheduling and timing were perpetually holding the idea of *Top Gun 2* at bay. That did not stop Scott from searching for the right screenplay to bring the story into the new millennium; he found the inspiration on a flight back from Las Vegas.

Scott had flown out to the nearby Red Rock National Park to do some rock climbing, and on the way back he chatted up a young Air Force officer who had been hitting the casinos hard and was fighting through a hangover. The young officer mentioned his work on an aircraft carrier, and the way most military maneuvers involve drone warfare—the officers fly these drones like they are playing a video game, only they have the capacity to kill hundreds of people with the push of a button.[3]

The story was enough to pique Scott's interest, so he began researching this new world of drone warfare. He had no screenplay, nor did he have word from Jerry Bruckheimer or Tom Cruise that they would be available, although Bruckheimer had entertained the idea more than once in the recent past. Confirmation or no, that didn't matter for Scott, who often willed these sorts of projects into existence through his unwavering determination.

In the middle of editing *Unstoppable*, and developing *Nemesis* for the big screen, Scott and Bruckheimer officially agreed to team up for *Top Gun 2*; Tom Cruise, himself in need of a decent hit following the pair of duds that were the ill-conceived Nazi thriller *Valkyrie* and the swing-and-miss action comedy *Knight and Day*, was willing to come back and play Maverick in a smaller part. The capacity of Maverick's role in the film would be in the hands (at least initially) of *Usual Suspects* scribe Christopher McQuarrie, who had also just worked with Cruise as the *Valkyrie* screenwriter.[4]

That didn't necessarily mean *Top Gun 2* was taking off right away. There were still logistical issues, schedules had to be coordinated, and a proper screenplay was required in order to reach any semblance of true pre-production. Cruise wanted his reduced role to be more than a fan-pandering cameo, and Scott wanted the story and the film to feel almost entirely new. It would take some time, a concept to which Tony Scott does not adjust well. He continued to research *Top Gun 2*, *Nemesis*, and the press junket for *Unstoppable* had just begun, with the release date just under a month away.

After *Unstoppable* came and went, Scott and his Scott Free production company funded a pair of small TV movies and a documentary called *Life in a Day*, a time capsule chronicling the lives of everyday people around the globe on June 24, 2010. Scott also produced *The Grey*, an existentialist survival story starring Liam Neeson and directed by Joe Carnahan. Meanwhile, *Top Gun 2* remained in limbo as Tom Cruise signed on to star in *Rock of Ages*, a musical comedy/drama mash up that proved to be another strike against Cruise's now-fading star power.

Just as Tony Scott did not wait to begin researching *Top Gun 2*, he did not sit on his hands waiting to get the green light for the sequel. He continued searching for potential projects, and perhaps started to spread himself too thin; certainly, one or more of Scott's potential projects would have to be delayed, reassigned to another director, or scrapped altogether.

Writer David Guggenheim had just sold his spec script for an action thriller named *Safe House*, which was now a film starring Denzel Washington and Ryan Reynolds, and was set for a February 10, 2012, release. Guggenheim was already shopping another action spec script called *Narco Sub*, a story about the low-rent submarines South American drug cartels would use to try to smuggle drugs into the United States. It was a combination of some of Scott's previous films—*Crimson Tide* with a dash of *Domino* and a hint of *Man on Fire*—and producer Simon Kinberg knew it would be a perfect vehicle for the director. He agreed in November 2011 to shoot *Narco Sub*; or at least he put it on his expanding schedule. Scott was not finished adding projects.[5]

Three months after agreeing to direct *Narco Sub*, while *Top Gun 2* toiled away in its infant stages and *Nemesis* was beginning to fade from everyone's memory, Scott found yet another potential movie. This one was called *Lucky Strike*, and it told the story of DEA agents working with a smuggler to upend a drug cartel in Central America. Vince Vaughn, who had never truly dipped his toes in the waters of "Action Star," was one of the actors attached.[6]

Then, there were the remakes.

As far back as 2005, Tony Scott had expressed at least a passing interest in *The Warriors*. The 1979 film was directed by Walter Hill, who would go on to direct genre classics like *48 Hrs.* and *Streets of Fire*, and told the story of warring New York City street gangs sometime in the near future. The film arrived on the cusp of a sea change in The Big Apple, where the punk rock movement was pushing back against the platforms and disco club scenes of the 1970s; it fit right in with the shifting times, and over the next three decades *The Warriors* would only appreciate in popularity and cultural significance. This meant Hollywood, never shy of cashing in on the cyclical nature of pop culture, was floating around the idea of a remake.

Tony Scott was, for a while at least, committed to the remake. He had the idea of moving the setting from New York to Los Angeles, because he had a plan to make these rival street gangs not hundreds, but thousands of people. He also wanted to paint a picture of West Coast gang culture to juxtapose the grime and grit of Hill's graffiti-stained metropolis. By 2009, after *Pelham 123*, things seemed to be taking shape, until a runaway train came and stole Tony Scott's attention.

The Warriors was nothing more than a thread of Scott's potential career moves in 2011, somewhere in line behind *Nemesis*, *Top Gun 2*, *Narco Sub*, and *Lucky Strike*. *Hell's Angels*, one of the three possible films he passed on, was also back in the fray, and now Scott wanted Jeff Bridges to fill the role originally intended for Mickey Rourke. The trade papers in Hollywood could barely keep track of what Tony Scott was doing, and when he was doing them; it did not slow Scott, however, who once again pushed all of his projects back a notch to try to get a remake of a classic off the ground.

It would not take anyone long to see the similarities between Tony Scott and Sam Peckinpah. Peckinpah, a hard-living California filmmaker, had built a tremendous career on violence, bloodshed, and dark genre masterworks like the Dustin Hoffman home invasion thriller *Straw Dogs*, Steve McQueen and Ali MacGraw in *The Getaway*, *Bring Me the Head of Alfredo Garcia*, and the classic, blood-spattered Western *The Wild Bunch*.

Released in 1969, at the precipice of the New Hollywood movement, *The Wild Bunch* starred some of the greatest studio legends—William Holden, Ernest Borgnine, and Robert Ryan—in a nihilistic glimpse of the outlaw west as it faded into the history books. *The Wild Bunch*, like all of his films, reflected Sam Peckinpah's own troubled life as a man haunted by alcoholism. He turned his own pain into cinematic beauty time and time again, but arguably no more successfully than in *The Wild Bunch*. Tony Scott may not have battled the same demons as Peckinpah, but he did carry that same adventurous and tactile approach to filmmaking.

Both men were merchants of cinematic violence, and if anyone should remake *The Wild Bunch*—a debate in and of itself—Tony Scott made the most sense. Of all the options at his feet, Scott was leaning towards *The Wild Bunch* before any others. He had never made a true Western—*Revenge* was his closest foray into the genre. He brought in Brian Helgeland to work on a first draft. That same day Tony's brother, Ridley, announced he would be returning to the world of his 1982 science-fiction noir, *Blade Runner*.

The Wild Bunch was now officially next in line for Tony, ahead of at least eight other potential film projects. That being said, if the Powers That Be could manage to line up schedules and produce a working script for *Top Gun 2*, *The Wild Bunch* would join *The Warriors*, *Nemesis*, *Narco Sub*, as one of a growing collection of projects the 67-year-old filmmaker would willingly put on the backburner.

24

August 2012

On Friday, August 17, 2012, Tony Scott and Tom Cruise were meeting up at a naval air station in Nevada, researching *Top Gun 2*. That previous May, everything for the sequel began to fall into place. Jerry Bruckheimer was drumming up interest and inching closer and closer to official pre-production, and *The Town* screenwriter Peter Craig was hired to replace Christopher McQuarrie, who could never quite get a draft ironed out.

Tom Cruise had also officially agreed to come on board, and was excited to return as Maverick. As different as the two men may have been from the early days of *Top Gun* throughout their succeeding careers, Tony Scott and Tom Cruise still came together and bonded over their love for speed and adrenaline. The prospect of a new *Top Gun* had both men's blood pumping. They left the naval station in Nevada that Friday with plans to get *Top Gun 2* on Paramount's schedule.

Los Angeles was bright, clear, and hot on Sunday, August 19, 2012. A heat wave was creeping across Southern California as the calendar pushed through the dog days of summer and temperatures tipped 90 degrees. At around 12:30, while the heat intensified, Anthony David Leighton Scott parked his black Toyota Prius at the crest of the Vincent Thomas Bridge—an iconic structure captured in dozens of films and television shows, connecting San Pedro with Los Angeles across the Los Angeles Harbor—climbed over the railing, leapt over the side, and plummeted some 184 feet to his death.

In the blink of an eye, and mere feet in front of a tour boat that had been passing under the Vincent Thomas Bridge, Tony Scott was gone. He was 68.

The jump was in the middle of a busy Sunday afternoon on the Vincent Thomas Bridge, and a busy tourist weekend (as was the case just about every day in Los Angeles during the summer), so there were witnesses on both ends of the tragedy who watched Scott's final seconds on earth. One witness, Dan Silva, told the *Los Angeles Times* that he watched Scott as he climbed over the railing and jumped, claiming that Scott "looked nervous." The port

The Vincent Thomas Bridge in Los Angeles, where Tony Scott committed suicide (Wiki Commons).

police, who captured footage of Scott's jump, had a different take on the event, and said the director took the plunge "without hesitation."[1]

At approximately 4:30 in the afternoon, officials who were using sonar technology retrieved Tony Scott's body from the Los Angeles Harbor. Later that evening, Scott was identified at the coroner's office, and a note was found inside his Prius with names and contact numbers. Another note was found at his office, an alleged suicide note that has never been made public.

By the time the Monday news cycle began the following morning, word of Tony Scott's death had spread across the globe. The outpouring of emotion and support from dozens of Scott collaborators and peers—from Ron Howard, to Joe Carnahan, to *Domino* co-star Edgar Ramirez, to Denzel Washington and Tom Cruise—was vast and heartfelt.

Scott's death shook the industry, and affected everyone who had ever crossed his path, no matter how briefly. Bruce McGill, who only worked with Scott for a few scenes on *The Last Boy Scout* 22 years prior, still thinks of the director whenever he is in San Pedro. "I look at that bridge," McGill said, "and it's never the same. It's just not the same bridge. I've been on a cruise ship going under the bridge, and I still look up and go 'why?' Now, for me, it's the Tony Scott Memorial Bridge.... I'm sure that nobody will ever really know [the reason why], including Ridley, but I know that it was very devastating for anybody that ever knew the guy."

Dariusz Wolski did not work with Tony after the back-to-back shoots of *Crimson Tide* and *The Fan*, but he would soon become a prolific collaborator with Ridley, and remained close to both men throughout Tony's life. The weekend Tony died, Wolski was on set with Ridley in London shooting *The Counselor*.

"It was Friday," Wolski said. "We were shooting a scene inside Michael Fassbender's apartment ... we had windows, with curtains, and we're setting up the scene and Ridley says 'Just open up the windows.'" Wolski tried to talk Ridley out of opening the windows because outside was London, not the Midwestern United States where The Counselor is set. Ridley persisted, and wanted to put fans behind the curtains with the windows open.

"The curtains are blowing," Wolski said, "and [Ridley] looks at me and says 'you know, my brother is an expert in blowing curtains.' I'll never forget that. It was literally Friday, there was a long weekend, and Sunday he committed suicide."

The "why" quickly became the genesis of wild speculation in the hours, days, and weeks following Scott's shocking death. Almost immediately, a rumor sprang up that Scott had inoperable brain cancer, first reported by ABC News per a source close to Scott's family.[2] However, nobody in Scott's immediate circle had heard anything about brain cancer. Donna Wilson Scott, his widow, told TMZ that Scott did not have any terminal illness that would have influenced his decision.[3] The autopsy, which was performed Monday the 20th, would hopefully shed some light on Scott's health.

Almost immediately, a collection of opportunistic barnacles on the hull of society tried hocking their cell phone videos of Scott's final moments atop the Vincent Thomas Bridge. TMZ viewed the footage but, wisely, did not purchase and release it to the public.[4]

While the family awaited the results of the autopsy, there was the business of figuring out what to do with the hefty collection of projects Tony Scott had committed to prior to his death. First and foremost was *Top Gun 2*, which he and Tom Cruise were mapping out mere days before Scott's death. It was the closest project to principal photography. As Scott, Cruise, and Jerry Bruckheimer began prepping for the long-rumored sequel back in April, Bruckheimer and Paramount saw an opportunity to cash in on new home theater technology: 3-D.

The 3-D craze had hit theater chains by the late 2000s, with the number of 3-D screenings of blockbuster movies regularly outnumbering standard, 2-D screenings. Not only were new films being shown in 3-D, classics were beginning to get the 3-D conversion treatment. The head of this new spear was James Cameron, the most technologically forward-thinking filmmaker in the history of cinema. Cameron released his Best Picture winner, *Titanic*, in theaters with a 3-D conversion, and it almost effortlessly picked up another

$342 million for the picture, and for Paramount. The conversion to 3-D cost only $18 million, and studios had stumbled upon a get rich quick (and cheap) scheme. This would be a flash in the pan, and Paramount knew they needed to get more of their big legacy tent poles converted to 3-D and released in theaters. The first film on that list, no matter who put it together behind the scenes, was absolutely *Top Gun*.

With Tony Scott and Tom Cruise already gearing up for the sequel and scouting locations, Paramount now had an even greater marketing base to re-release *Top Gun* with the 3-D conversion. Then Scott's death put everything on hold, and on Monday, October 22, autopsy reports revealed that Tony Scott's death was indeed a suicide, and Scott had "therapeutic levels of the anti-depressant Remeron and the sleep aid Lunesta in his system."[5] None of the dosage would immediately lend credence to any theory that Scott was under the influence of drugs when he jumped. As for the mysterious cancer diagnosis, there was no evidence of cancer at the time of death. The autopsy cleared up little to nothing regarding Scott's motivation. Everyone was stumped.

Not long after the autopsy results, it appeared that *Top Gun 2* would be put on hold indefinitely. As for the 3-D release of *Top Gun*, there was a matter of taste. Mystery still enshrouded Scott's death, and the Scott family had understandably retreated from interviews and public appearances. Releasing *Top Gun 3-D* might appear like a cynical cash in on Scott's death, though it was never intended as such.

Paramount decided to double down on the release, pairing the *Top Gun 3-D* theatrical release on February 8, 2013, with the February 19 release of a new special edition Blu-ray, which would come in both 2-D and 3-D formats as well. It was marketed properly, tastefully, and it felt more like a celebration of Scott's most iconic film—a man at the beginning of a storied career—than a soulless cash grab.

There were two projects Tony Scott had produced at the time of his death, but had yet to his theaters. The first was *Stoker*, a macabre thriller directed by Chan-wook Park and starring Nicole Kidman, Mia Wasikoswa, and Matthew Goode; it opened in limited release in March 2013, and found moderate praise and success among genre fans. The second film was *Out of the Furnace*, a bigger picture from *Crazy Heart* director Scott Cooper and starring Christian Bale, Woody Harrelson, Casey Affleck, Willem Dafoe, and Zoe Saldana. It fizzled in November of 2013 with a paltry $11 million box-office haul.

As for the films Tony Scott had on the ledger to direct, they gradually dissolved into the landscape of the Hollywood business scene, collateral damage of a tragedy that knocked the entire industry off its axis. *Nemesis*, the comic book adaptation Scott had begun working on in the middle of *Unstoppable* postproduction, was handed over to director Joe Carnahan, whose previous film, *The Grey*, was produced by Tony Scott and Scott Free. After a series of false starts under Carnahan, the project went dormant until 2018 when it was announced *Nemesis* would begin production once again, though the particulars of the project remained a mystery.[6]

Narco Sub went to director Doug Liman for a few months, then Antoine Fuqua took over in 2014 before ultimately moving on to direct Denzel Washington in an adaptation of *The Equalizer* and shoot the Jake Gyllenhaal boxing drama, *Southpaw*, in 2015. From there, *Narco Sub* flittered away. Both *The Warriors* remake and *Lucky Strike*, the drama Scott was circling with Vince Vaughn in mind, dissipated and transformed into other projects for everyone rumored to be involved.

On the day of Tony Scott's death, Brian Helgeland was on page 46 of the *Wild Bunch* screenplay he had been working on with Scott. In a 2015 interview with the website *Mandatory*, Helgeland detailed the modern spin on their version. This was not a western, in fact, but a modern story about corrupt police officers trying to avoid prison and traveling to Mexico to rob a bank. Helgeland never wrote another word of the screenplay after August 21, 2012.[7]

Top Gun 2 finally found new life in the summer of 2017, when Paramount slotted it for a July 12, 2019, release date, and a new title: *Top Gun: Maverick*. Tom Cruise was still ready to reprise his Maverick role, and the story still revolved around Cruise's aging pilot being phased out in a world of drone warfare. Replacing Tony Scott would be Joseph Kosinski, who had previously directed Cruise in *Oblivion*, a peculiar science fiction actioner that was nothing more than a footnote in 2013.[8] In June of 2018, Val Kilmer told *Entertainment Weekly* he would be joining *Top Gun: Maverick*, reprising his role as Iceman. A few weeks later, actor Miles Teller was cast as the son of Anthony Edwards' Goose, and would be the star of the sequel.

Some of Tony Scott's projects pushed through, most fell apart, and one stopped cold on a computer screen—like the clocks aboard the *Titanic*—that fateful August day in 2012. It would stay on page 46 forever, just as Tony Scott would be 68 for eternity.

25

The Rock and Roll Alchemist

Since he was a young boy, Tony Scott wanted to be a painter. Eventually, he satisfied that dream, though he never imagined scope of the canvas, and the power of the paintbrushes he would be using.

And it was never easy for Tony Scott, perpetually in his older brother's shadow, furiously locked in loving competition until the end. He had to fight his way to a feature, he had to scratch and claw and learn things the hard way, but he never stopped trying. While his brother, and his peers from RSA, were directing their first films and finding immediate legitimacy in the profession with Oscar nominations and box-office domination, Tony toiled away, his head down and his appetite growing by the minute, tinkering with his craft and sharpening his tools. The oversight is what drove him in those early years, and it even burned deep inside him after decades of success. It's most fitting that Scott's primary hobby in his down time, however little down time that may have been, was scaling rock facings, suspended in midair with only himself and his instincts keeping him in one piece. It was an apt metaphor for the way Tony Scott lived his entire life, and it makes his sudden fatal decision all the more confounding.

The Hunger may have been nothing more than a feature-length commercial for lustful, sad vampires, but what a stylish feature-length advertisement it is. Soaked in the night and bleached with billowy curtains—a Scott signature—*The Hunger* at least marked the introduction of a new style. Ridley, Tony and, to an extent, Adrian Lyne, all shot with the same backlit, high-contrast approach, but Tony accelerated the look in his gothic soap opera. The problem may have been he was trying to mirror the patient approach Ridley had taken in *The Duellists*, *Alien*, and especially *Blade Runner*. That wasn't Tony's strong suit, the patience and deliberate pacing; he needed a little more rock and roll, and it didn't take him long to realize it.

Once Jerry Bruckheimer and Don Simpson's vision for *Top Gun* finally

Tony Scott with his wife, Donna Wilson Scott, and their sons, Frank and Max, at the premiere of *Unstoppable* (20th Century-Fox, 2010).

clicked for Tony, his trajectory branched off in a different direction. The producing powerhouses wanted high-flying macho posturing, adventure, romance; they wanted soundtrack sales and butts in seats. Scott had found a place in his career where he could be as adventurous and daring as he had been in his personal life, and he tackled the complicated task of blockbuster filmmaking with an infectious zeal that would appear to be with him the rest of his life.

Top Gun was Scott's skeleton key to Hollywood, and it opened doors for just about anyone involved. *Beverly Hills Cop II*, then, was something of a favor, and probably a little insurance policy that would secure him for the foreseeable future. *Cop II* is not a good movie; it is a paltry sequel with half the humor of the original—an '80s classic—and very little in the way of compelling storytelling. That didn't matter, though, because it was Eddie Murphy back as Axel Foley. The film was immune from critical backlash, and it was a staggering success from day one. Looking back, it's a shrewd move from Scott, a great way to get a passion project green lit, no questions asked. Who would deny funding to the man who just directed the biggest hit of 1986 and the third-biggest hit of 1987? He proved himself twice, probably because he felt he had to.

Revenge had the potential to be a brilliant modern Western, and the first evidence that Tony Scott had another card up his sleeve. The beginning of the film begins, quite literally, with Scott bidding adieu to the world of the fighter pilot, as Kevin Costner's Cochran retires from the Air Force under the opening credits. Scott was letting us know he had moved on, and he was ready to spill a little bit of his own inner turmoil out onto the screen.

The affair with Brigitte Nielsen was an unfortunate mistake for the former Mrs. Sylvester Stallone and Tony Scott, and no doubt Scott's own struggle with that time in his life was informing *Revenge*. It should have been another step in Scott's evolution, proof that he was a serious filmmaker under all the fireworks. The shortsightedness of producer Ray Stark, who was never the right match for the material, may have corrupted Scott's vision for the film. While the director's cut corrects some of what ails *Revenge*, the damage at the time had been done.

And so Tony Scott's rollercoaster ride began. He returned to the warm confines of Simpson and Bruckheimer for *Days of Thunder*, but even that wound up a flawed, borderline success at best. He followed it up by performing a miracle.

It's tough to imagine another director who could have held *The Last Boy Scout* together the way Tony Scott did. Under siege by unchecked egos and shot under a perpetual cloud of tension and bickering, another filmmaker may have buckled. Everything about the production of *The Last Boy Scout* could have doomed it to the same fate as *Ishtar*, or *Waterworld* a few years later, had it not been for the dogged determination of Tony Scott. One reason Scott stayed busy is he was reliable, and he was in charge, and he delivered his work on time, no matter what obstacles may arise.

If *The Last Boy Scout* is a masterpiece of steadfastness in the face of adversity, *True Romance* is a sublime marriage of style and sound. Scott and Tarantino's collaboration is serendipitous, though it was not recognized as such at the time; that was the way Scott's career would go.

He hit it big once again with Simpson and Bruckheimer on *Crimson Tide*. It's the most controlled work of his career; more importantly, it was Scott's introduction to Denzel Washington. Then, there was *The Fan*, Scott's most interesting failure. Up with *Enemy of the State*, down with *Spy Game*, Scott spent more than a decade on the rollercoaster, until he let got every ounce of darkness and doubt, of frustration and anger and passion, out on the screen in 2004.

Man on Fire is Scott's crowning achievement, a film that has only improved with age; the kinetic flourishes Scott unleashed as a visual cue into the turmoil of John Creasy have softened over the years. It no longer feels as manic and unfocused as it did in 2004, quite the opposite in fact. Over the next decade, shaky-cam technique and frantic action filmmaking reached a fevered pitch thanks to the work of Paul Greengrass and Michael Bay, retroactively taming the energy of a film like *Man on Fire* in the best way possible.

This is Tony Scott at his absolute peak, spinning inside a cauldron of violence and self-doubt to paint a true masterpiece. This is, above all other films in his oeuvre, the one whose searing imagery belongs on the wall of a pop culture museum.

Scott may have been overzealous during *Domino*. Fresh off the certain reinvigoration from *Man on Fire*, Scott wanted to push the envelope a little further, to scale a higher rock facing without a net. The result is an explosion of chaos and madness that too quickly becomes an endurance test. It's the excessive id of its creator run amok, and it might also be why Scott sought out Denzel Washington once again.

Sometimes, actors and directors find a perpetual groove. Martin Scorsese and Robert De Niro (and later, Scorsese and Leonardo DiCaprio), John Ford and John Wayne, Tim Burton and Johnny Depp; Scott and Denzel Washington fit right into this list. They're films were generally successful, save for *The Taking of Pelham 123*, but Washington had a clear ability to get the best out of Tony Scott. They were both strong set presences, and Washington was one of the few friends he made over the years who could sway his opinion.

Tony Scott made friends everywhere, on just about every set he commanded. He earned respect, and he offered praise and friendship, and he often gravitated to actors and people on the fringes of regular society. That's why it's easy to see how Scott could become close with Timothy Leary, or Domino Harvey, people who operate with a different set of rules and worry about consequences later. He found a kindred, antiestablishment spirit in these people, and the cigar-chomping adventurer personality he exuded never got in the way of his empathy.

Filmmaking is alchemy, a process of transformation, wherein dozens upon dozens of factors are formed into one distinct vision. Tony Scott was one of the best at getting all the pieces in place; so many times, and over the span of an entire era of Hollywood, Scott was one of the very best at fusing the core elements into precious metal. All the while, in his workman-like perfectionism, he would forever fight for his rock and roll visions.

In 2006, Scott performed another miracle, a miracle of perseverance in getting *Déjà Vu* to the screen after the devastation of Hurricane Katrina. He showed steadfastness and determination in the face of adversity, once again. It was the only way he knew how to be. Perhaps, over the years, he had built a thick skin.

Tony Scott's life was also littered with tragedy, beyond the tragedies of his own making. His brother Frank in 1980, stunt pilot Art Scholl on the set of *Top Gun*, Timothy Leary, Don Simpson, Domino Harvey, all gone at different points in his career. There is no way to know what sort of effect these tragic ends did or didn't have on Scott, but there is no reason to even speculate they may have played a part in his own decision.

Projecting theories onto Tony Scott's death is reckless, and pointless, and even as a mental exercise it creates more questions than answers. There was no cancer, at least not at the time, and there was no indication that Scott had grown weary of his life; too often, the darkest of demons haunting our soul never make their way to the surface. Scott had two young sons, a beautiful wife, and he was brimming with life and drive and desire, or so it seemed. With a list of potential projects stretching a mile long, it looked like business as usual. Until it wasn't.

Beyond the crushing tragedy Scott's suicide had on his family and loved ones, an entire cross-section of action cinema seemingly died along with him. For the last two decades, nobody has been able to balance thrilling action spectacles with manageable budgets and schedules and a demographic that skews older than someone like Michael Bay. Even Paul Greengrass' films have fallen out of favor after an ill-conceived fourth *Bourne* film failed to connect with audiences in 2016. Scott's films were for adults, and they rarely ran into budgetary complications. Except, that is, for *Unstoppable*, which may have been an indication that the types of films Scott wanted to make were no longer feasible. When he died, he left behind a gaping hole in the industry.

Since his death, the Tony Scott size and scope has been marginalized and pushed primarily to streaming services. Franchises matter in the modern Hollywood system, not movie stars or audiences over twenty-five years old. If any filmmaker is doing their best to carry the mantel of what Tony Scott perfected, it would be Antoine Fuqua, who still manages to find a space for his action films. He has hits and misses, police thrillers like *Training Day* and *Brooklyn's Finest*, genre pictures like *The Magnificent Seven* and *King Arthur*, and four Denzel Washington collaborations (*Training Day, Magnificent Seven*, and two *Equalizer* films) to boot. Fuqua's pictures tend to stretch longer, and the flourishes are traditionally more muted than Scott, but his collection of solid mid-level action movies, and his career of ups and downs mirror that of the late auteur.

There will never be another Tony Scott. It's a thought very few people had while Scott was directing. He was dismissed, defined as a workmanlike filmmaker who couldn't control his impulses and let his bad instincts get the better of him. But, like so many famous painters, Tony Scott's work has found new appreciation among film fans and historians. His work was, more often than not, much more than simple popcorn pyrotechnics. That style belongs to Michael Bay, a definite result of Tony Scott's success, but a result who took Scott's action beats and ramped them up to absurdist levels, added another $100 million to the budget, and surgically removed all empathy from the storytelling. It worked for quite some time, but the shine appears to be wearing off Michael Bay's approach to blockbuster filmmaking.

Tony Scott never felt stale.

Scott's films had a heart somewhere inside them, often a deep and dark heart, but a heart nonetheless. He created a vast, complete world of wonderful supporting performances, typically from hand picked actors who would go on to become stars. His casting abilities, from *Top Gun* to *True Romance* to *Crimson Tide* and *Enemy of the State,* are the most underappreciated tool in his belt. He paid attention to the environment of his scenes, and he had a vision beyond the surface; finally, that vision is finding recognition.

There may never be another Tony Scott, but thankfully, we are beginning to celebrate the fact there once was.

Filmography

The Hunger (1983), MGM Pictures
Top Gun (1986), Paramount Pictures
Beverly Hills Cop II (1987), Paramount Pictures
Revenge (1990), Rastar Pictures
Days of Thunder (1990), Paramount Pictures
The Last Boy Scout (1991), Warner Bros.
True Romance (1993), Warner Bros.
Crimson Tide (1995), Hollywood Pictures
The Fan (1996), TriStar Pictures
Enemy of the State (1998), Touchstone Pictures
Spy Game (2001), Universal Pictures
Man on Fire (2004), Fox 2000 Pictures
Domino (2005), New Line Cinema
Déjà Vu (2006), Touchstone Pictures
The Taking of Pelham 123 (2009), Columbia Pictures/MGM Pictures
Unstoppable (2010), 20th Century—Fox

Chapter Notes

Chapter 1

1. "Fish knabber" is a British regional nickname associated with people from North Shields, a reference to the primary occupation for men in the bay town.
2. Delaney, Sam, "Jets, Jeans, and Hovis," *The Guardian*, 23 Aug. 2007, web.

Chapter 2

1. Leader, Michael, "Looking Back at Tony Scott's The Hunger," *Den of Geek*, 29 May 2013, web.
2. Vineyard, Jennifer, "Susan Sarandon Revisits Her 1983 Film *The Hunger*," *Vulture*, 5 Nov. 2014, web.
3. Tony Scott, "Audio Commentary," *The Hunger*, DVD (Burbank: Warner Bros. Home Entertainment, 2004).
4. Kehr, Dave, "The Hunger," *Chicago Reader*, 1983, web.
5. Ebert, Roger, "'The Hunger' Review," *Chicago Sun-Times*, 3 May, 1983, web.

Chapter 3

1. "American Gigolo," boxofficemojo.com
2. Thomson, David, "I'm Don Simpson; and You're Not," *Independent*, 6 Apr. 1996, web.
3. "Beverly Hills Cop," boxofficemojo.com.
4. "Danger Zone: The Making of Top Gun," *Top Gun*, DVD (Hollywood: Paramount Home Entertainment, 2011).
5. Galloway, Stephen, "Galloway on Film: As 'Top Gun' Turns 30, Jerry Bruckheimer Reveals Secrets of the Film's (and His Own) Success," *The Hollywood Reporter*, 20 June 2016, web.
6. O'Toole, Lesley, "Val Kilmer: No More Mr. Bad Guy," *Independent*, 15 Dec. 2006, web.
7. *Behind the Movie: Top Gun*, VH-1, 1999.

Chapter 4

1. Evje, Mark, "'Top Gun' Boosting Service Sign-ups," *Los Angeles Times*, 5 July 1986.
2. Falk, Ben, "Top Gun: Is There Really a Gay Subtext? We Asked the Writer," *Yahoo! Movies*, 19 May 2016, web.

Chapter 5

1. Gruson, Lindsey, "Exit Stallone, Enter Eddie Murphy," *New York Times*, 16 Dec. 1984, p. 29.
2. "Making of *Beverly Hills Cop II*," *Beverly Hills Cop II*, DVD (Hollywood: Paramount Pictures, 2008).
3. "Beverly Hills Cop II," boxofficemojo.com.

Chapter 6

1. Mansnerus, Laura, "Timothy Leary, Pied Piper of Psychedelic 60's, Dies at 75," *New York Times*, 1 June 1996.

Chapter 7

1. Tony Scott, "Director's Commentary," *Revenge*, DVD (Culver City, CA: Sony Pictures Home Entertainment, 2007).
2. "Revenge," boxofficemojo.com.

Chapter 8

1. Newman's performance would earn him the only Best Actor Oscar statue of his illustrious career.
2. Smith, Adam, "Tony Scott on Tony Scott," *Empire Online*, 20 Aug. 2012, web.
3. Ressner, Jeffrey, "On 'Thunder' Road with Tom Cruise," *Rolling Stone*, 12 July 1990, web.
4. "Days of Thunder," boxofficemojo.com.

Chapter 9

1. Black, Shane, "The Last Boy Scout," dailyscript.com.
2. Dougherty, Marion, and Robert Roussel, *My Casting Couch Was Too Short*, Xlibris, 2015, pp. 335–36.
3. Williams, Owen, "Who Killed the Last Boy Scout? Bruce Willis, Shane Black and the Making of an Action Masterpiece," *The Telegraph*, 31 May 2016, web.

Chapter 10

1. Johnson, Megan, "Here's One Tinseltown Estate Worthy of an 'E! True Hollywood Story,'" *Trulia*, 11 Nov. 2015, web.
2. Spitz, Marc, "True Romance: 15 Years Later," *Maxim*, 25 Apr. 2008, web.
3. "Charlie Sexton," billboard.com.
4. Tony Scott, "Movie Commentary," *True Romance*, DVD (Warner Bros. Entertainment UK, 2017).
5. Ebert, Roger, "'True Romance' Review," *Chicago Sun-Times*, 10 Sept. 1993, web.
6. *The Fugitive* would end its run with $183.9 million, becoming the third highest grossing film of 1993 behind *Jurassic Park* and *Mrs. Doubtfire*.
7. This $13 million is nothing more than an estimate based on rumors.

Chapter 11

1. Wakeman, Gregory, "Why the First Screening of Reservoir Dogs at Sundance Was a Disaster," *Cinema Blend*, 30 Apr. 2017, web.
2. The Academy Awards for 1994 films were held on March 27, 1995.

Chapter 12

1. McCurrie, Tom, "Forget It Bob, It's Hollywood: 'Chinatown's' Oscar-Winning Scribe, Robert Towne," *Writer's Super Center*, 31 May 2005, web.
2. Mell, Eila, *Casting Might-Have-Beens: A Film-by-Film Directory*," McFarland, 2013, p. 62.
3. Manuel-Logan, Ruth, "Denzel Washington Says He Squashed 7-Year Feud with Quentin Tarantino," *News One*, 13 Dec. 2012.
4. Vincent, Mal, "Navy Refused to Cooperate with the Making of Sub Movie 'Crimson Tide,'" *Deseret News*, 23 May 1995, p. 3.
5. "The Making of *Crimson Tide*," *Crimson Tide*, DVD (Burbank: Hollywood Pictures Home Entertainment, 2008).
6. Gleiberman, Owen, "Movie Review: 'Crimson Tide,'" *Entertainment Weekly*, 12 May 1995, web.
7. "Crimson Tide," boxofficemojo.com.

Chapter 13

1. King, Thomas R., and John Lippman, "Fatal Attraction: How Sex and Drugs Brutally Ripped Apart Hot Hollywood Team," *Wall Street Journal*, 26 Jan. 1996, web.
2. Thomson, David, "I'm Don Simpson; and You're Not," *Independent*, 7 Apr. 1996, web.

Chapter 14

1. Ripken famously holds the record for most consecutive games played in Major League Baseball with 2,632.
2. Rosenbloom, Steve, "Glove Story," *Chicago Tribune*, 15 Aug. 1996, web.
3. Levy, Shawn, *De Niro*, Random House, 2014, p. 442.
4. "The Fan," boxofficemojo.com.

Chapter 15

1. "The Making of *Enemy of the State*," *Enemy of the State*, DVD (Burbank: Touchtone Pictures, 1998).
2. Black played a technician in the background of *The Fan*, and his part as a theater manager in *True Romance* was cut from the final print.
3. "Enemy of The State," boxofficemojo.com.

Chapter 16

1. Tony Scott, "Feature Commentary," *Spy Game*, DVD (Universal City, CA: Universal Studios Home Entertainment, 2011).
2. "Spy Game," boxofficemojo.com.

Chapter 17

1. Staff, "A.J. Quinnell: Pseudonyms Author of 'Man on Fire,'" *Independent*, 16 July 2005, web.
2. Tony Scott, "Audio Commentary," *Man on Fire*, DVD (Beverly Hills: 20th Century–Fox Home Entertainment, 2004).
3. Dalton, Dan, "This Is Why 'Man on Fire' Is a Goddamn Masterpiece," *Buzzfeed*, 19 Aug. 2015, web.
4. "Italy—Kidnapping Rate," *Knoema*, 2015, web.

Chapter 18

1. Ebert, Roger, "'Man on Fire' Review," *Chicago Sun-Times*, 23 Apr. 2004, web.
2. Schwarzbaum, Lisa, "Man on Fire," *Entertainment Weekly*, 21 Apr. 2004, web.

Chapter 19

1. Weiner, Allison Hope, "A Lust for Life and Danger," *New York Times*, 9 Oct. 2005, web.
2. Lee, Chris, "The Fall of a Thrill Hunter," *Los Angeles Times*, 22 July 2005, web.
3. Tony Scott, "Director's Commentary," *Domino*, DVD (Beverly Hills: New Line Home Entertainment, 2006).
4. Edemariam, Aida, "She Loved Bringing in the Sleazebags," *The Guardian*, 30 June 2005, web.
5. Hornaday, Ann, "'Domino': As Bad as She Wants to Be," *Washington Post*, 14 Oct. 2005, web.

Chapter 20

1. Jackson, Matthew, "Joel Schumacher Defends Val Kilmer as the Best Batman Ever," *SyFy*, 15 Dec. 2012, web.
2. Collin, Robbie, "Brando's Madness, Val Kilmer's Ego, and the Madness of Dr. Moreau," *The Telegraph*, 4 Aug. 2015, web.
3. O'Toole, Lesley, "Val Kilmer: No More Mr. Bad Guy," *Independent*, 15 Dec. 2006, web.

4. Staff, "Déjà Vu, Val Kilmer," *LondonNet*, web.
5. Breznican, Anthony, "'Déjà Vu' Starts Production in New Orleans," *USA Today*, 2 Feb. 2006.
6. "Déjà Vu," boxofficemojo.com.

Chapter 21

1. Maioni, Enrico, "An Adventure with Tony Scott," guidedolomiti.com, 2012, web.
2. Scherick is listed as an uncredited producer on the film's IMDb page.
3. Ordoña, Michael, "'Taking of Pelham 123' Stars Travolta, Denzel," *SFGate*, 7 June 2009, web.
4. "Victor Gojcaj," imdb.com.
5. Dominguez, Robert, "Behind the Scenes of 'The Taking of Pelham 123,'" *New York Daily News*, 6 June 2009, web.
6. Kennedy, Randy, "Manhattan Transfer: Remaking 'Pelham,'" *New York Times*, 1 May 2009, web.
7. Staff, "John Travolta's 16-Year-Old Son Dies," *People*, 2 Jan. 2009, web.
8. Ebert, Roger, "'The Taking of Pelham 123' Review," *Chicago Sun-Times*, 10 June 2009, web.
9. Koch, Ed, "The Taking of Pelham 123: Not as Good as the Original," *The Atlantic*, 15 June 2009, web.

Chapter 22

1. "Subject: CSX 8888 Runaway Investigation," Kohlin.com
2. Kramer, Peter D., "A Writer's Life: Mark Bomback, Hollywood Telecommuter," *lohud*, 3 Feb. 2016, web.
3. Fleming, Mike, "Tony Scott Boards 'Unstoppable,'" *Variety*, 27 Mar. 2009, web.
4. Fleming, Mike, "Fox Dealing with 'Unstoppable' Budget," *Variety*, 29 June 2009, web.
5. Tony Scott, "Audio Commentary," *Unstoppable*, DVD (Beverly Hills: 20th Century–Fox Home Entertainment, 2010).

Chapter 23

1. Fleming, Mike, Jr., "Tony Scott Has to Choose Among Pic Trio," *Deadline*, 4 Aug. 2010, web.
2. Fleming, Mike, Jr., "Fox and Tony Scott Plot Movie Version of Millar & McNiven's 'Nemesis,'" *Deadline*, 6 Aug. 2010, web.
3. Ellwood, Gregory, "Exclusive: Tony Scott Doesn't Want a Remake or Reinvention for 'Top Gun 2,'" *Uproxx*, 24 Oct. 2010, web.
4. Brodesser-Akner, Claude, "'Top Gun 2' Is Heading to the Runway," *Vulture*, 13 Oct. 2010, web.
5. Staff, "Fox Powers Up David Guggenheim and Tony Scott on 'Narco Sub,'" *Deadline*, 28 Nov. 2011, web.
6. Fleming, Mike, Jr., "Is 'Lucky Strike' Up Next for Tony Scott, with Vince Vaughn?" *Deadline*, 15 Feb. 2012.

Chapter 24

1. Winton, Richard, and Andrew Blankstein, "Tony Scott Death: Director 'Looked Nervous' Before Jumping Off Bridge," *Los Angeles Times*, 20 Aug. 2012, web.
2. Staff, "Tony Scott Brain Cancer Report Appears in Doubt," *ABC News*, 20 Aug. 2012, web.
3. Staff, "Tony Scott Suicide: No Brain Cancer," *TMZ*, 20 Aug. 2012, web.
4. Staff, "Tony Scott Death Video Being Shopped," *TMZ*, 21 Aug. 2012, web.
5. Staff, "Tony Scott Had Taken Anti-Depressants and Sleeping Pills Before He Jumped Off Bridge to His Death as Autopsy Confirms Director Wasn't Suffering from Cancer," *Daily Mail*, 22 Oct. 2012, web.
6. Kit, Borys, "Former Warner Bros. Executive Sue Kroll Launches New Banner, Will Produce 'Six Billion Dollar Man,'" *The Hollywood Reporter*, 4 Apr. 2018, web.
7. Bibbiani, William, TIFF 2015 Interview: Brian Helgeland on 'Legend' and 'The Wild Bunch,'" *Mandatory*, 16 Sept. 2015, web.
8. Fleming, Mike, Jr., "Paramount Sets 'Top Gun 2' for July 2019; Joseph Kosinski Firmed for Tom Cruise Pic," *Deadline*, 30 June 2017, web.

Bibliography

Allen, Nick, "Ridley Scott Breaks Silence on Brother Tony Scott's Death," *The Telegraph*, 28 November 2014, web.
AP Staff, "Ripkens Input Used in Movie, 'The Fan,'" *Seattle Times*, 16 August 1996, web.
AP Staff, "The Summer That Nascar Received Its Close-Up," *New York Times*, 26 June 2010, web.
Behind the Movie: Top Gun, VH-1, 1999.
Berger, Warren, "The Creativity Interview: Tony Scott," *AdAge*, 1 December 2001, web.
Bevan, Joseph, "Man on Fire: Tony Scott," *BFI*, 7 October 2015, web.
Beyl, Cameron, "Tony Scott: The Ultimate Guide to His Films & Career," *Indie Film Hustle*, 29 September 2017.
Bibbiani, William, "TIFF 2015 Interview: Brian Helgeland on 'Legend' and 'The Wild Bunch,'" *Mandatory*, 16 September 2015, web.
Billboard.com.
Black, Shane, "The Last Boy Scout," dailyscript.com.
Blair, Iain, "Tony Scott—Déjà Vu: The First Film Shot in New Orleans Post Katrina," *BNET Business Network*, November 2006, web.
Boxofficemojo.com.
Breznican, Anthony, "'Déjà Vu' Starts Production in New Orleans," *USA Today*, 2 February 2006.
Brodesser-Akner, Claude, "'Top Gun 2' Is Heading to the Runway," *Vulture*, 13 October 2010, web.
Collin, Robbie, "Brando's Madness, Val Kilmer's Ego, and the Madness of Dr. Moreau," *The Telegraph*, 4 August 2015, web.
Dalton, Dan, "This Is Why 'Man on Fire' Is a Goddamn Masterpiece," *Buzzfeed*, 19 August 2015, web.
"Danger Zone: The Making of Top Gun," *Top Gun*, DVD (Hollywood: Paramount Home Entertainment, 2011.
Delaney, Sam, "Jets, Jeans and Hovis," *The Guardian*, 23 August 2007, web.
DiLullo, Tara, "'Deja Vu': Time Tripping to New VFX Heights," *Animation World Network*, 22 November 2006, web.
Ditzian, Eric, "'Taking of Pelham 123' Cheat Sheet: Everything You Need to Know," MTV, 11 June 2009, web.
Dominguez, Robert, "Behind the Scenes of 'The Taking of Pelham 123,'" *New York Daily News*, 6 June 2009, web.
Dougherty, Marion, and Robert Roussel, *My Casting Couch Was Too Short*, Xlibris, 2015, p. 335–36.
Ebert, Roger, "'The Hunger' Review," *Chicago Sun-Times*, 3 May 1983, web.
Ebert, Roger, "'Man on Fire' Review," *Chicago Sun-Times*, 23 April 2004, web.
Ebert, Roger, "'The Taking of Pelham 123' Review," *Chicago Sun-Times*, 10 June 2009, web.

Ebert, Roger, "'True Romance' Review," *Chicago Sun-Times*, 10 September 1993, web.
Edemariam, Aida, "She Loved Bringing in the Sleazebags," *The Guardian*, 30 June 2005, web.
Editor, "Chris Lebenzon—The Taking of Pelham 123," *International Cinematographers Guild Magazine*, 13 July 2009, web.
Ellwood, Gregory, "Exclusive: Tony Scott Doesn't Want a Remake or Reinvention for 'Top Gun 2,'" *Uproxx*, 24 October 2010, web.
Evje, Mark, "'Top Gun' Boosting Service Sign-ups," *Los Angeles Times*, 5 July 1986.
Evry, Max, "5 Things You Should Know About Tony Scott," MTV, 20 August 2012, web.
Falk, Ben, "Top Gun: Is There Really a Gay Subtext? We Asked the Writer," *Yahoo! Movies*, 19 May 2016, web.
Fisher, Bob, "The Taking of Pelham: Then and Now," *MovieMaker*, 10 June 2009, web.
Fleming, Mike, "Denzel Washington Exits 'Unstoppable,'" *Variety*, 13 July 2009, web.
Fleming, Mike, "Fox Dealing with 'Unstoppable' Budget," *Variety*, 29 June 2009, web.
Fleming, Mike, "Tony Scott Boards 'Unstoppable,'" *Variety*, 27 March 2009, web.
Fleming, Mike, "Washington Back on Track with Fox," *Variety*, 22 July 2009, web.
Fleming, Mike, Jr., "Fox and Tony Scott Plot Movie Version of Millar & McNiven's 'Nemesis,'" *Deadline*, 6 August 2010, web.
Fleming, Mike, Jr., "Is 'Lucky Strike' Up Next for Tony Scott, with Vince Vaughn?" *Deadline*, 15 February 2012.
Fleming, Mike, Jr., "Paramount Sets 'Top Gun 2' for July 2019; Joseph Kosinski Firmed for Tom Cruise Pic," *Deadline*, 30 June 2017, web.
Fleming, Mike, Jr., "Tony Scott Boarding 'The Wild Bunch' While Revving 'Hell's Angels' as Next Pic," *Deadline*, 18 August 2011, web.
Fleming, Mike, Jr., "Tony Scott Has to Choose Among Pic Trio," *Deadline*, 4 August 2010, web.
Galloway, Stephen, "Galloway on Film: As 'Top Gun' Turns 30, Jerry Bruckheimer Reveals Secrets of the Film's (and His Own) Success," *The Hollywood Reporter*, 20 June 2016, web.
Galloway, Stephen, "Tony Scott's Unpublished Interview: 'My Family Is Everything to Me,'" *The Hollywood Reporter*, 22 August 2012, web.
Gleiberman, Owen, "Movie Review: 'Crimson Tide,'" *Entertainment Weekly*, 12 May 1995, web.
Goodridge, Mike, "Tony Gilroy on Duplicity's Important Complications," *ScreenDaily*, 12 March 2009, web.
Gruson, Lindsey, "Exit Stallone, Enter Eddie Murphy," *New York Times*, 16 December 1984, p. 29.
Hangmantitan, "Enemy of the State," *Motion State Review*, 28 November 2014, web.
Hanna, Beth, "A Young Tony Scott Stars in Brother Ridley's Short Film, 'Boy and Bicycle,'" *IndieWire*, 24 August 2012, web.
Hornaday, Ann, "'Domino': As Bad as She Wants to Be," *Washington Post*, 14 October 2005, web.
Hough, Andrew, and Nick Allen, "Top Gun Director Tony Scott Dies After Jumping from Los Angeles Bridge," *The Telegraph*, 20 August 2012, web.
"The Hunger," tcm.com.
Hunt, Stacey Wilson, "Jerry Bruckheimer Shares Memories of Making *Top Gun*, *Beverly Hills Cop*, and More," *Vulture*, 1 April 2016, web.
Huver, Scott, "Denzel Washington: John Travolta Struggling Over Son's Death," *People*, 29 May 2009, web.
Imdb.com.
"Italy—Kidnapping Rate," *Knoema*, 2015, web.
Jackson, Matthew, "Joel Schumacher Defends Val Kilmer as the Best Batman Ever," *SyFy*, 15 December 2012, web.
Johnson, Megan, "Here's One Tinseltown Estate Worthy of an 'E! True Hollywood Story,'" *Trulia*, 11 November 2015, web.
Kehr, Dave, "The Hunger," *Chicago Reader*, 1983, web.
Kennedy, Randy, "Manhattan Transfer: Remaking 'Pelham,'" *New York Times*, 1 May 2009, web.
King, Thomas R. and John Lippman, "Fatal Attraction: How Sex and Drugs Brutally Ripped Apart Hot Hollywood Team," *Wall Street Journal*, 26 January 1996, web.

Kit, Borys, "Former Warner Bros. Executive Sue Kroll Launches New Banner, Will Produce 'Six Billion Dollar Man,'" *The Hollywood Reporter*, 4 April 2018, web.
Koch, Ed, "The Taking of Pelham 123: Not as Good as the Original," *The Atlantic*, 15 June 2009, web.
Kohlin.com.
Kramer, Peter D., "A Writer's Life: Mark Bomback, Hollywood Telecommuter," *lohud*, 3 February 2016, web.
Leader, Michael, "Looking Back at Tony Scott's The Hunger," *Den of Geek*, 29 May 2013, web.
Leary, Zach, "IAH—Episode 109—Bruce Margolin," ZachLeary.com, 17 December 2017, web.
Lee, Chris, "The Fall of a Thrill Hunter," *Los Angeles Times*, 22 July 2005, web.
Levy, Emanuel, "Tony Scott on Domino," *Emanuel Levy*, 8 October 2005, web.
Levy, Shawn, *De Niro*, Random House, 2014, p. 442.
Maioni, Enrico, "An Adventure with Tony Scott," guidedolomiti.com, 2012, web.
Makinen, Julie, and Geoff Boucher, "Tony Scott Dies at 68; a Film Career in Retrospective," *Los Angeles Times*, 20 August 2012, web.
"Making of *Beverly Hills Cop II*," *Beverly Hills Cop II*, DVD (Hollywood: Paramount Pictures, 2008).
"The Making of *Crimson Tide*," *Crimson Tide*, DVD (Burbank: Hollywood Pictures Home Entertainment, 2008).
"The Making of *Enemy of the State*," *Enemy of the State*, DVD (Burbank: Touchtone Pictures, 1998).
Mansnerus, Laura, "Timothy Leary, Pied Piper of Psychadelic 60's, Dies at 75," *New York Times*, 1 June 1996.
Manuel-Logan, Ruth, "Denzel Washington Says He Squashed 7-Year Feud with Quentin Tarantino," *News One*, 13 December 2012, web.
Marshall, Rick, "Joel Schumacher on His 'Dark Knight' Movie That Never Happened, and Hollywood's Best Bruce Wayne," IFC.com, 12 October 2011, web.
Masters, Kim, "The Epic Saga of Joel Silver: Money Struggles, Feuds and (Another) Second Chance," *The Hollywood Reporter*, 29 April 2015, web.
McClintock, Pamela, "Tony Scott Spent Final Days Working with Tom Cruise on 'Top Gun 2,'" *The Hollywood Reporter*, 20 August 2012, web.
McCurrie, Tom, "Forget It Bob, It's Hollywood: 'Chinatown's' Oscar-Winning Scribe, Robert Towne," *Writer's Super Center*, 31 May 2005, web.
McLellan, Dennis, "Ned Tannen Dies at 77; Former President of Universal, Paramount," *Los Angeles Times*, 8 January 2009, web.
Mell, Eila, *Casting Might-Have-Beens: A Film-by-Film Directory*," McFarland, 2013, p. 62.
Murray, Rebecca, "Jim Caviezel Tackles the Role of a Bad Guy in the Tony Scott Movie 'Déjà Vu,'" About.com, 2006, web.
"Numb3rs," *ABC MediaNet Archive*, web.
Ordoña, Michael, "'Taking of Pelham 123' Stars Travolta, Denzel," *SFGate*, 7 June 2009, web.
O'Toole, Lesley, "Val Kilmer: No More Mr. Bad Guy," *Independent*, 15 December 2006, web.
"Peter Abrahams Bio," EpicReads.com, web.
Philips, Chuck, and Eric Malnic, "Autopsy Finds Don Simpson Dies of Overdose," *Los Angeles Times*, 27 March 1996, web.
Plaisance, Stacey, "Katrina Debris Part of the Scenery for New Denzel Washington Film," *TMZ*, 2 February 2006, web.
Ressner, Jeffrey, "On 'Thunder' Road with Tom Cruise," *Rolling Stone*, 12 July 1990, web.
Roberts, Sheila, "Bill Marsilii Interview, Screenwriter of Déjà Vu," *Movies Online*, 2006, web.
Romero, Dennis, "Tony Scott Jumps to Death from Vincent Thomas Bridge," *LA Weekly*, 20 August 2012, web.
Rosenbloom, Steve, "Glove Story," *Chicago Tribune*, 15 August 1996, web.
Rugaard, Jason, "Interview: Ward Russell," *Movie Mavs*, 11 November 2010, web.
Sacks, Ethan and Nancy Dillon, "Mystery Surrounds Tony Scott Suicide Leap from Los Angeles Bridge as Reports That the 'Top Gun' and 'Crimson Tide' Director Had Inoperable Brain Cancer Are Shot Down," *New York Daily News*, 20 August 2012, web.
Schwarzbaum, Lisa, "Man on Fire," *Entertainment Weekly*, 21 April 2004, web.

Sheridan, Peter, "Tragis End for British Filmmaker Tony Scott Who Became Hollywood's Top Gun," *Express*, 21 August 2012, web.
Shone, Tom, "Tony Scott's Own Story Was Always Better Than His Movies," *The Guardian*, 26 August 2012, web.
Smith, Adam, "Tony Scott on Tony Scott," *Empire Online*, 20 August 2012, web.
Smith, Emily, "'Top Gun' Director Who Leaped to Death from Bridge Had 'Inoperable Brain Cancer,'" *New York Post*, 20 August 2012, web.
Spitz, Marc, "True Romance: 15 Years Later," *Maxim*, 25 April 2008, web.
Stack, Peter, "Bay Area Back Lot: Big Stars and Big-Budget Films Shooting in Town," *San Francisco Chronicle*, 13 November 1995, web.
Staff, "A.J. Quinnell: Pseudonyms Author of 'Man on Fire,'" *Independent*, 16 July 2005, web.
Staff, "Déjà Vu, Val Kilmer," *LondonNet*, web.
Staff, "Enemy of The State," *Entertainment Weekly*, 21 August 1998, web.
Staff, "Fox Powers Up David Guggenheim and Tony Scott on 'Narco Sub,'" *Deadline*, 28 November 2011, web.
Staff, "From the Archives: Simpson & Bruckheimer Have High Hopes for Jet Pilot Tale," *Film Journal International*, 18 February 2009, web.
Staff, "Inside John Barrymore's Former $29.95 Million Beverly Hills Estate," *Pursuitist*, web.
Staff, "John Travolta's 16-Year-Old Son Dies," *People*, 2 January 2009, web.
Staff, "Paula Patton—Déjà Vu Interview," *Female First*, 4 May 2007, web.
Staff, "R.I.P. Richard Shepherd; Film Producer, Executive & Agent," *Deadline*, 15 January 2014, web.
Staff, "Tony Scott Brain Cancer Report Appears in Doubt," *ABC News*, 20 August 2012, web.
Staff, "Tony Scott Death Video Being Shopped," *TMZ*, 21 August 2012, web.
Staff, "Tony Scott Had Taken Anti-Depressants and Sleeping Pills Before He Jumped Off Bridge to His Death as Autopsy Confirms Director Wasn't Suffering from Cancer," *Daily Mail*, 22 October 2012, web.
Staff, "Tony Scott Suicide: No Brain Cancer," *TMZ*, 20 August 2012, web.
Stein, Ruthe, "'Fan' Strikes Out with Giants: Leagues, Team Ask Changes in De Niro Baseball Thriller," *San Francisco Chronicle*, 25 July 1996, web.
Stern, Marlow, "Tony Scott's Enduring Legacy, from 'Top Gun' to 'True Romance,'" *The Daily Beast*, 20 August 2012, web.
Thompson, Anne, "Quentin Tarantino and Richard Kelly Talk Tony Scott at Double Feature of 'True Romance' and 'Domino,'" *IndieWire*, 27 August 2012.
Thomson, David, "I'm Don Simpson; and You're Not," *Independent*, 7 April 1996, web.
Tony Scott, "Audio Commentary," *Man on Fire*, DVD, 20th (Beverly Hills: Century—Fox Home Entertainment, 2004).
Tony Scott, "Audio Commentary," *The Hunger*, DVD (Burbank: Warner Bros. Home Entertainment, 2004).
Tony Scott, "Audio Commentary," *Unstoppable*, DVD (Beverly Hills: 20th Century—Fox Home Entertainment, 2010).
Tony Scott, "Director's Commentary," *Domino*, DVD (Beverly Hills: New Line Home Entertainment, 2006).
Tony Scott, "Director's Commentary," *Revenge*, DVD (Culver City, CA: Sony Pictures Home Entertainment, 2007).
"Tony Scott," encyclopedia.com.
Tony Scott, "Feature Commentary," *Spy Game*, DVD (Universal City, CA: Universal Studios Home Entertainment, 2011).
Tony Scott, "Movie Commentary," *True Romance*, DVD (Warner Bros. Entertainment UK, 2017).
Vincent, Mal, "Navy Refused to Cooperate With the Making of Sub Movie 'Crimson Tide,'" *Deseret News*, 23 May 1995, p. 3.
Vineyard, Jennifer, "Susan Sarandon on Her Vampire Lesbian Sex Scene with Catherine Deneuve," *Vulture*, 5 December 2014, web.
Vineyard, Jennifer, "Susan Sarandon Revisits Her 1983 Film *The Hunger*," *Vulture*, 5 November 2014, web.

Wakeman, Gregory, "Why the First Screening of Reservoir Dogs at Sundance Was a Disaster," *Cinema Blend*, 30 April 2017, web.
Weiner, Allison Hope, "A Lust for Life and Danger," *New York Times*, 9 October 2005, web.
Williams, Owen, "Who Killed the Last Boy Scout? Bruce Willis, Shane Black and the Making of An Action Masterpiece," *The Telegraph*, 31 May 2016, web.
Willistein, Paul, "High-Caliber Collaboration 'Top Gun' Production Team Reunites for 'Crimson Tide,'" *The Morning Call*, 12 May 1995, web.
Winton, Richard, and Andrew Blankstein, "Tony Scott Death: Director 'Looked Nervous' Before Jumping Off Bridge," *Los Angeles Times*, 20 August 2012, web.
Yonay, Ehud, "Top Guns," *California*, May 1983, web.

Index

Abraham, Marc 118, 119
Abrahams, Peter 103
Alien 16
Alien: Covenant 16
Ammerman, Stephen W. 101
Anderson, Alberteen 161
Anthony, Marc 130, 131
Arquette, Patricia 73, 74, 77–80
Ashton, John 42, 43
The Associate 176
"The Author of Belltrafio" 15

Baird, Stuart 68
Barkin, Ellen 106
Bauhaus 21
Bay, Michael 38, 91, 97, 100, 157, 187–189
Bean, Henry 113
Beat the Devil 124; *see also* BMW; *The Hire*
Beckner, Michael Frost 118
Berlin 35; *see also* "Take My Breath Away"
Beverly Hills Cop 26, 27, 41, 42, 44; *see also* Brest, Martin
Beverly Hills Cop II 42–44, 52, 54, 77, 91, 97, 103, 109, 130, 186
Bierce, Ambrose 13, 14; *see also* One of the Missing
Black, Shane 62–64, 69
Black, Todd 157
Blanks, Billy 66
Blumenthal, Jason 157
BMW 123, 127; *see also Beat the Devil*; *The Hire*
Boldy, Geraldine (Gerry) 14, 16, 17
Bomback, Mark 166, 167, 169
Bonet, Lisa 114
Bowie, David 19, 117
Boy and Bicycle 13
Brest, Martin 41, 42
Brown, James 124
Bruckheimer, Jerry 16, 25–32, 34–38, 40, 41, 43, 45, 52, 55–57, 59, 60, 63, 71, 77, 85, 91–94, 96–98, 100–103, 109, 112–115, 118, 143, 144, 149, 157, 176, 182, 185, 187
Busey, Jake 114, 115

Caan, Scott 114, 115
Cash, Jim 27, 28
Caviezel, Jim 152, 153
Chamian, Denise 143
Chapman, Kevin 170
Chase, Barbara 46–48
Cleveland College of Art & Design 13
Coleman, Dabney 144
Corrigan, Kevin 169, 171
Costner, Kevin 52, 53, 118, 187
Cox, Ronny 42, 43
Craven, Matt 95, 152
Crimson Tide 92, 95–99, 103, 107, 113, 115, 116, 133, 149, 164, 171, 178, 182, 187, 190
Cruise, Tom 28, 29, 32, 34, 37, 38, 40, 55–58, 176, 177, 180, 182–184

"Danger Zone" 35; *see also* Morodor, Giorgio
Darabont, Frank 107
Dawson, Rosario 169, 171
Days of Thunder 56–61, 77, 91, 97, 103, 109, 161, 187
Déjà Vu 149, 150, 152–154, 157, 158, 161, 188
Del Toro, Benicio 107
Deneuve, Catherine 19–21
De Niro, Robert 83, 105–08
DiSarrio, Al, Jr. 97
Disney (Disney Studios) 30, 61, 91, 112, 116, 118, 143, 157
Domino 142, 144, 145, 147, 149, 178, 181, 188
Dougherty, Marion 64–66
Dunn, Kevin 169
Duvall, Robert 57, 59, 92
Dzundza, George 95

Ebert, Roger 22, 81, 137
Edwards, Anthony 31, 32, 184
Eisner, Michael 26, 30
Elwes, Cary 58
Enemy of the State 112, 114, 115, 117, 161, 187, 190
Epps, Jack, Jr. 27, 28, 40
Escape Artists 157

204 Index

Faltermeyer, Harold 34
The Fan 103, 109–11, 112, 114, 116, 124, 134, 139, 182
Fanning, Dakota 130, 133, 138
Ferguson, Larry 42
Ferrarone, Don 161
Field, Chelsea 65
Finerman, Wendy 103–104
Fiskin, Jeff 53
Flashdance 16
Forson, Terry L. 166
Freedgood, Martin 155; *see also* Godey, John

Gandolfini, James 77, 80, 85, 95, 160
Garrow, Peter 28, 29, 32
Gilroy, Tony 113
Godey, John 155; *see also* Freedgood, Martin
Gojcaj, Victor 161
Goldberg, Adam 152
Goldblatt, Mark 68
Goldblatt, Stephen 20, 21
Green, Brian Austin 144
Greenwood, Bruce 152
Guzman, Luis 160

Hackman, Gene 93–96, 98, 99, 112–115
Harris, Danielle 66, 70
Harrison, Jim 51, 53
Harvey, Domino 140–144, 146, 147, 188
Harvey, Laurence 140; *see also* Skikne, Zvi Mosheh
Hefner, Hugh 44
Helfrich, Mark 68
Helgeland, Brian 128, 129, 132, 136, 158, 159
Hell's Angels 176
Hendrick, Richard P. 92
The Hire 123, 124; *see also* Beat the Devil; BMW
Hopper, Dennis 3, 76, 79, 85, 92
Hudson, Hugh 14–16
Hudson Hawk 64, 67
Humphries, Harry 115
The Hunger 18, 19, 21, 22, 29, 32, 112, 117, 128, 147, 185
Hurricane Katrina 152, 153

Jackson, Samuel L. 77, 85

Kael, Pauline 40
Kaiser, Marty 114
Katzenberg, Jeffrey 29, 30
Kelly, Richard 142, 146
Kidman, Nicole 57, 113, 183
Kilmer, Val 31, 32, 75, 76, 78, 79, 94, 150–152, 158, 184
King, Regina 114
Knightley, Keira 143
Knowlton, Jess 166
Koepp, David 157, 158
Kruk, John 107

The Last Boy Scout 63, 64, 67–71, 76, 77, 81, 86, 91, 103, 109, 115, 136, 139, 181, 187
Leary, Timothy 46–48, 188
Leary, Zach 48
Lebenzon, Chris 115, 162
Leguizamo, John 107
Lindo, Delroy 144
Loggins, Kenny 35, 39; *see also* "Danger Zone"; "Playing with the Boys"
Loving Memory 15
Lucky Strike 178
Lyne, Adrian 14, 16, 119, 185

Maioni, Enrico 155
Man on Fire 128–130, 132–139, 142–145, 147, 149, 161, 187
Man on Fire (1987) 128
Marconi, David 112, 113
Masilii, Bill 148
Matthau, Walter 156
McCormick, Catherine 120, 123
McGill, Bruce 66–68
McGillis, Kelly 31, 32, 38, 40, 57
MGM Studios 18
Milchan, Arnon 128
Mitchell, Rhada 131
Mo'Nique 144
Morodor, Giorgio 35; *see also* "Danger Zone"; "Take My Breath Away"
Mortensen, Viggo 95
Murphy, Eddie 26, 27, 41–44, 77, 186

Narco Sub 177–179, 184
Negron, Taylor 66
Nemesis 175–179, 183, 184
Newman, Paul 56
Nezo-Chalco-Itza 132, 133
Nicholson, Philip 127; *see also* Quinnell, A.J.
Nielsen, Brigitte 43, 44
North Shields 11, 12, 168
Numb3rs 158

Oldman, Gary 74, 85, 96, 124
One of the Missing 13, 14; *see also* Bierce, Ambrose

Paramount Pictures (Paramount Studios) 25, 26, 30–32, 43, 51, 61, 100, 157, 182, 183
Parker, Alan 14, 15, 18, 19, 114
Patton, Paula 150, 153
Penn, Chris 77
Pettigrew, Pete "Viper" 27
Phillippe, Ryan 96, 116
Phipps, Kevin 120
Pinchot, Bronson 77, 80
Pine, Chris 167, 168, 170
Pitt, Brad 74, 75, 85, 93, 105, 119–123
"Playing with the Boys" 35, 39–40; *see also* Loggins, Kenny
Preston, Kelly 162, 163

Prochnow, Jürgen 43
Prometheus 16

Quaid, Randy 57
Quinnell, A.J. 128; *see also* Nicholson, Philip

Ramírez, Edgar 143, 144, 181
Rappaport, Michael 77, 80, 85
Rastar Pictures 51
Redford, Robert 83, 118–122
Reilly, John C. 58
Reinhold, Judge 42, 43
Revenge 45, 51, 53–56, 77, 91, 97, 103, 112, 132, 179, 186
Ridley Scott Associates (RSA) 14–16, 21, 22, 96, 185
Ripken, Cal, Jr. 104, 105
Rooker, Michael 58
Ross, Chelcie 69
Rossio, Terry 148, 149
Rourke, Mickey 131, 132, 143, 144, 176
Royal College of Art in London 13, 14, 20
Rubinek, Saul 76, 77
Russell, Ward 69
Ryan, Meg 31

Sanders, Glynis 44
Sarandon, Susan 20, 21
Sargent, Joseph 156
Scherick, Edgar 156
Schiffer, Michael 92
Scholl, Art 34
Scott, Elizabeth 11–13
Scott, Francis Percy (Percy Scott) 11–13
Scott, Frank 11, 12, 17
Scott, Ridley 5, 11–17, 19, 28, 87, 96, 99, 116, 117, 122, 123, 179, 181, 182, 185
Scott Free 116, 117, 132, 158, 184
Sexton, Charlie 78
Shaw, Robert 156
Shepherd, Richard 18–20, 22
Shulman, Neville 141
Silver, Joel 63–65, 67, 68, 76, 77
Simpson, Claire 108
Simpson, Don 16, 25–38, 40, 41, 43, 45, 52, 55–57, 59, 60, 63, 71, 85, 91–94, 96–98, 100–103, 109, 112, 185, 187, 188
Sizemore, Tom 77, 85
Skaaren, Warren 28, 42
Skikne, Zvi Mosheh 140; *see also* Harvey, Laurence
Slater, Christian 72, 73, 76, 82
Smith, Will 38, 91, 98, 114, 115
Snipes, Wesley 105, 107
Sorkin, Aaron 113
Spencer, Norris 120
Spy Game 118–124, 127, 134, 161, 187
Star, Ray 51–54
Stone, Paulene 140, 144
Stone, Peter 156
Stowe, Madeleine 53

Streiber, Whitey 18; *see also The Hunger*
Sutton, Phoef 104, 105, 107, 109, 110
Suvari, Mena 144

"Take My Breath Away" 35; *see also* Morodor, Giorgio
The Taking of Pelham 123 158–164, 167, 169, 188
The Taking of Pelham One Two Three 155–157, 160, 161
Tanen, Ned 30
Tarantino, Quentin 71–74, 76–78, 80–82, 84–87, 92, 94, 95, 119, 128, 129, 136, 159
Teller, Miles 184
Thompson, Fred Dalton 59
Timmerman, Bonnie 130, 131
Tisch, Steve 157
Toback, James 102
Top Gun 27, 28, 30–40, 42, 52, 54, 56–60, 68, 75, 77, 91, 96, 97, 103, 109, 115, 128, 136, 161, 164, 176, 180, 183, 185, 186, 190
Top Gun: Maverick 184; *see also Top Gun 2*
Top Gun 2 176–180, 182–184; *see also Top Gun: Maverick*
Top Guns 27; *see also* Yonay, Ehud
Touchstone Pictures 91, 112
Towne, Robert 57, 59, 92
Travolta, Jett 162, 163
Travolta, John 85, 159, 160, 162, 163
True Romance 71–74, 76–79, 81, 82, 84–87, 91, 92, 95, 103, 109, 112, 114, 115, 131, 134, 136, 137, 145, 150, 170, 187, 190
Turturro, John 160

Uhrig, Steve 114
Unger, Zeke 145
Universal Studios 30, 51
Unstoppable 165–172, 175, 177, 183, 189

Vincent St. Thomas Bridge 180–182
Voight, Jon 114, 115

Wagner, Christian 108, 134, 146
Walken, Christopher 76, 79, 85, 87, 131, 144
Warner Bros. 18, 25, 62, 63, 65, 67
The Warriors 178–179, 184
Washington, Denzel 94–96, 98, 99, 106, 129, 130, 133, 138, 147, 149, 150, 152, 153, 169, 160, 163, 167–170, 188
Wayans, Damon 65, 67
The Wild Bunch 179, 184
Willingham, Noble 66
Willis, Bruce 64–68, 81, 166
Wilson, Donna (Donna Wilson Scott) 51, 72, 117, 155, 182
Wolski, Dariusz 96, 97, 99, 107–09, 182

Yonay, Ehud 27; *see also Top Guns*
Yorn, Julie 167

Zahn, Steve 95
Ziering, Ian 144

www.ingramcontent.com/pod-product-compliance
Lightning Source LLC
Chambersburg PA
CBHW032058300426
44116CB00007B/799